DAVID
LANIGAN

They Gave Me a
HELICOPTER

---

novum ✈ pro

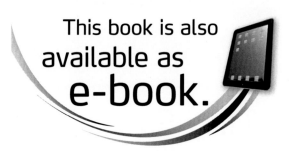

This book is also
available as
e-book.

www.novum-publishing.co.uk

ISBN 978-3-99131-494-3
Editing: Ashleigh Brassfield
Cover photos: David Lanigan
Cover design, layout & typesetting:
novum publishing
Internal illustrations:
p. 18–61, 110–137, 181–280,
290–383 © David Lanigan, p. 92,
146–155, 284 © Ministry of Defence

The images provided by the author
have been printed in the highest
possible quality.

www.novum-publishing.co.uk

Climate neutral
Print product
ClimatePartner.com/16547-2201-1002

Contents

DEDICATION

I doubt I could have had a career in flying without the support of my wife Ann and without my family putting up with me and taking on someone besotted with flying. They say the first 60 years of marriage to a pilot are the most difficult; so all power to your elbow, Ann, still being there in support after all these years.

PREFACE

Now that I am fully retired and still just about in full control of my brain and its associated memories, I have decided to put on record, more or less, the story of my life in aviation, mainly as a helicopter pilot, which started in 1953, aged 12, and lasted some 45 years.

It has spanned vast changes in aviation and has given me a very fulfilled and happy career, for which I am very grateful. Had I put this story on record when I was younger, people would have labelled me as a 'line-shooter,' so bear with me as I give the story in the first person singular and in the present tense as it gently unfolds. Hopefully this will give you a feel of what it was like growing up and becoming involved in aviation in the post-war era, with all its challenges and opportunities.

Chapter 1: Growing Up

1945 – Age 4

My first memories are of walking along Archery Grove in Woolston, Southampton with my older brothers, John and Peter, pausing at the bombed-out houses; piles of bricks, staircases to nowhere, and wires sticking out of walls. It looks to me like an adventure playground. At the end of the road is the corner shop, which is stacked with glass jars full of sweets, tins, blocks of cheese, lard, loaves of bread, and a pair of balancing scales. The walls are covered in posters from the war: Dig for Victory, Waste Not Want Not; also for products: Bistow Gravy, Cadbury's Chocolate, Camp Coffee, and Oxo. To me it is an Aladdin's Cave, full of wonder – all this food, all these sweets, and a big kindly man behind the counter. The doorbell jingles as we leave to return home. I will be coming back, for sure.

Like most families, four boys and one girl, we are struggling to cope with shortages after the war. Food is rationed, including bread and sweets (¼ pound per week). Clothing, too, is rationed. Everything we have is darned to keep it going. Anything that can be knitted, is –scarves, socks, and jumpers, Mum is constantly at it. Balaclavas to keep our heads warm appear in the winter months. Fuel, too, is scarce, and we have one fire in the parlour where we eat at the table and listen to the big radio in the corner with its long wave and medium wave stations. Because it has valves, it takes several seconds to warm up before the programme comes through. One favourite, the BBC Home Service, is the source of all our news and current affairs. For light entertainment, we tune in to shows like ITMA (It's That Man Again) with Tommy Handley and Much Binding in the Marsh. Close by on the dial is Radio Luxembourg, with popular music.

Above the coal fire is the mantlepiece, where candles are stationed with a box of swan matches, ready for the regular evening power-cuts. Dad is often sitting in the big chair near the fire, smoking his Player's Navy Cut – full strength, one after another. His right hand is stained with yellow nicotine right up to his wrist. As a chain smoker, if he thinks he has run out there is shouting, and we children scatter about the house until word comes that he has found another pack. During the war, like many others doing war work on damaged ships in Portland Harbour, he is given tins of 50 cigarettes a day to calm the nerves. I grow up to accept people smoking around me, though fortunately I don't take up the habit, despite trying it out with friends one day, perched up a tree for privacy. We feel sick and throw the half-smoked cigarettes away. That experiment saves my health and a small fortune.

Make do and mend is common. I become aware that Mum saves everything that can be reused. Brown paper parcels tied up with string are carefully unravelled. Food parcels from Uncle Joe in New Zealand come wrapped in metal bands to hold the cardboard boxes together; tins of Spam, tins of meat, tins of stew, and tins of fruit such as Bartlett pears or half peaches in juice. They are welcomed along with the tins that Dad brings home from working at the docks. Some cargo is damaged in transit and are sold off cheaply to get rid of it. The larder from time to time fills with big dented tins with their labels washed off. Sometimes potatoes, sometimes beans, sometimes meat, each one a surprise. Each empty jam jar is washed and stacked at the back of the always cold larder. Milk is delivered to the doorstep by a man in a white coat on his milk float. The metal foil tops are collected along with newspapers – the Southampton Daily Echo and the Daily Express appear regularly in the house. As children we have sufficient food to give us the energy to rush around and explore. We grow up fit without an ounce of fat and play outside in all weathers without feeling cold. Every morning we are lined up and given in turn, a spoonful of cod liver oil, orange juice, and malt, all from little bottles issued by the Ministry of Food. From time to time on a Saturday, the milkman lets me help with delivering milk to various doorsteps, with varying responses, sometimes a happy wave, sometimes cheerfully ignored. I am getting to know the local area very well and at the end of the milk round I get a free orange juice, and then walk home a mile from where I am dropped off.

Outside the house is a garden, backing onto a large copse of trees with a stream running through it. Most days my brothers take me out, exploring the paths, climbing over fallen trees, jumping over the stream, making dens with small branches. If we cross over the stream, we can make it up an incline to Mayfield Park with its obelisk and football fields. We return home, often mud-splattered, with scratches, bruises, and torn clothing, where we are sorted out and given yet another lecture by our harried mum and sent upstairs to the bedroom until we were called down for tea of bread and jam and perhaps a piece of cake.

Outside the house and family, world events pass me by. I understand the war, which I was not aware of at the time, is over and things will only get better. Dad mutters about atomic bombs and the tests going on in the Pacific Ocean, with the papers displaying mushroom shaped clouds of atomic debris. As children, we thankfully don't understand the significance.

After a year of mum taking me to the corner shop and beyond on her shopping trips, I am trusted with the housekeeping purse, some money, and a list for the shopkeeper. I hand it all over to him and watch in awe as he uses a wire to cut cheese, butter, and lard, ladles out loose biscuits, and uses a whirling machine to cut bacon. All are carefully weighed and wrapped in greaseproof paper and put into brown paper bags. He takes the ration books and cuts out the required coupons. He then writes down on the list the amounts, takes the money, puts the change in the purse along with the list, and puts it all in my shopping bag. I am amazed by the whole process, and hurry home as if on a mission. Mum checks everything and I get a pat on the head if all is well.

As children out playing, we met up with other children roaming around, sometimes going to each other's houses, sometimes playing games in the copse. Mum instructs us that if we were offered a plate of cakes or biscuits by a neighbour, to only take the one nearest to us and not reach across for the biggest one; also, listen and be polite to every adult, using please and thank you where appropriate. In other people's houses we are to be on our best behaviour.

Eventually it becomes time to go to primary school. Luckily, my elder brother John is still there, and we set off to walk a mile along a new street, with a view of a large ship being built at Woolston shipyard looming at the end. We pass a small park with children's swings and roundabouts. I resolve to try them out later. The school is of Victorian design, with an asphalt playground, surrounded by a wall with the school gate. In the classroom, seating about 30, we sit at desks with inkwells. In the corner there is a stove where the crates of milk ($1/3^{rd}$ pint each) are sometimes stacked to thaw out. We take some sandwiches for lunch in our little satchels. On the blackboard are our letters – a, b, c, in small and in capitals. We have our writing books to practice our handwriting, first with pencils and then with ink, with much ink blots and scraping of nibs as we work away. Most of our teachers are women; some are kind, some are sharp. At playtime we all rush outside and run around playing tag, sometimes playing hopscotch. We fall over frequently, dust ourselves down and carry on playing. Eventually a teacher appears with a big hand bell, and its ringing makes us rush back to the classroom. Over the blackboard easel we have rollover charts of the world, with the many red areas denoting the British Empire; maps of Europe with its capital cities; and maps of Great Britain, with mountains, rivers, and the complex coastline. Sometimes, when the classroom is noisy with activity, the teacher has to calm us all down. Despite the stove it is often cold in the classroom, and we wear our out-door coats at our desks; sometimes our gloves as well. Released from school by the bell, we all rush out and set off home, stamping in any puddles we find and scaring any cats relaxing on top of walls or fences. There is little road traffic and just the occasional sit up and beg bicycle. We take home our exercise books to show mum what we are doing; she is very keen on education and encourages us to make progress. At Christmas time the class makes paper chains and they are draped around the classroom. We do this at home as well, saving our efforts for the following year in a cardboard box under the stairs.

As 1946 ends, we hit a cold snap across the country that lasts well into 1947. For children, the snow means throwing snow-balls, building snowmen, creating slides along pavements, and stamping on frozen puddles to break the ice. Where icicles hang down, we pull them off or use sticks to break them. At home, coal is short and as children we are sent out into the copse to gather firewood – essentially, fallen branches – and after chopping them up with small machetes, bring them back home. Our war-time Anderson shelter is dug out of the ground and now serves as a garden shed in the back garden. Our pieces of branches are sawn into logs and then join the store of coal we keep under the house. Going to school means wellingtons, coats, balaclavas, and woollen gloves, as well as a satchel. The pavements are cov-ered in snow, so we make slides, not worrying about the adults who pick their way through the snow to the shops. At home the freeze is causing problems: pipes are frozen, then burst, with wa-ter everywhere; coal is short; vegetables are short; the house is cold; at night we have coats on the beds and in the morning the bedroom windows have frost patterns all over. As children it is a new experience and therefore exciting. The news across the nation is full of doom and gloom: railways and roads blocked, everywhere food and fuel shortages. As a family we come to-gether, coping with a common problem and accepting lengthy power cuts stoically, gathered in one room with only the light of candles and a coal fire and, of course, no mains-powered radio. We talk and, being the youngest, I listen to people's experiences. Mr Shinwell, the government Minister for Fuel, is apparently the man to blame. In some ways it is quite chummy, although for our parents, hoping for better times after the war, it probably is quite a big worry, as even potatoes now become rationed. At school our children's milk arrives frozen, with the cream pushing open the silver foil. The milkcrates are stacked around the stove to thaw out. One day at school we receive a shipment of large red apples from Canada. Each of us is given one to take home for our mothers.

"Don't eat them on the way home", comes the stern instruction, which I obey, and Mum is pleased. That evening we all share a segment, which is much appreciated. Mum increasingly looks at my exercise books and my copperplate handwriting, sloping to the right and not very round. Throughout life my handwriting is rarely legible to other people, but I can read it well enough. Perhaps I will become a doctor, writing prescriptions.

As I learn to read, I am told about the local library. On joining I am directed to the children's section. Soon I am into the Enid Blyton books, the Famous Five and all their adventures. When I have read all of those, I find books by Arthur Ransome, featuring children who sail little boats. I am truly jealous of the fictional children in "Swallow & Amazons", having adventures with their sailing dinghy on Lake Windermere. Soon I am reading up to three books a week, lapping up the nautical knowledge and a sense of adventure. Inevitably, I find "Biggles", by Captain W.E. Johns, and all his flying adventures. We are all encouraged to read at home; there was often little else to do in the evening except listen to the BBC Home Service on the big radio or on a crystal set, supplied by my brother Peter.

About this time, I join my brothers in attending Sunday school, which entails a walk through the copse and across the Mayfield

Recreation Field. It is a lovely little church, and I learn the Bible stories and the Ten Commandments. I learn to tell the truth rather than lies, though I do later learn some diplomacy. Over my flying career I learnt to distinguish between the facts as they were and the facts as portrayed by people with vested interests. Little did I know that, many years later when I am being positively vetted to receive state secrets, my Sunday school teacher and all other head teachers are formally approached and questioned as to my character. I am apparently a normal, mischievous, and active boy in every way, and therefore acceptable to be trusted.

Eventually it is time for junior school, about a mile from home and in a different direction, involving crossing the busy Portsmouth Road. The crossing code – look right, look left, and right again, and cross if clear – keeps me safe, and I often make the journey alone. This is a stricter school, with the cane for bad behaviour in class. I remember a number of sessions – no doubt fully deserved. One day, after a caning administered by the headmaster for talking in class, he utters the prophetic words: "David, you will either go a long way in this life or end up in jail."

The emphasis changes from reading and writing to rote-learning the times tables up to twelve.

The class chants in unison day after day. Those tables stick in the memory ever after. We began mental arithmetic; adding and subtracting are straight forward, while long division and multiplication require concentration. We start taking some work home to be given in the next day. I am lucky in that my elder brothers check over my calculations and frequently correct my work. Mum looks at my handwriting and spelling, and again there is room for improvement. However, our joint efforts sometimes earn a gold-star rating, which we all appreciate. Meanwhile, as boys, we become interested in comics, especially American ones featuring Superman flying around the place, always saving the world from the bad guys. We swap comics at break time, along with cigarette cards featuring famous sportsmen, famous cars, ships, and aircraft. Another good feature of the school is swimming lessons in the Lido, near Southampton's town centre. I learn to swim in the shallow end of the 25-metre indoor pool, using the breaststroke and keeping my mouth shut, as the water is full of chlorine. Within a few sessions I am diving in from the side and swimming underwater for several strokes, eventually completing lengths under water. After an hour the class climb out of the pool, have a shower, change, and go back to school by bus. En-route we compare our crumpled hands and fingers, where the chlorine had extracted the natural oils. Our eyes are often a little red as well, but we were all buoyed up as we were making progress. We can swim, and in the summer, if we behave ourselves, we will be allowed in the outdoor pool.

The outdoor pool, to a little boy, is huge, with a deep end twelve feet deep with a staged diving platform above it. As I grow in confidence with my diving, I look at the challenge of the highest board at 20 feet and contemplate how I could dive straight in with my arms forward and not do a belly flop. One section of the pool has lanes, where I can swim up and down, turning underwater at the ends. A length is 50 yards and every visit I clock up more and more, using a combination of the breaststroke, the crawl, and backstroke. I think I get up to half a mile eventually. Diving in from the side, bombing, and swimming underwater builds up my confidence in being in water, which proves to be useful later on. Eventually I come on my own to the Lido and swim up and down the lanes to my heart's content. During the school lessons we learn lifesaving, again very useful.

It is a mile from the house to the junior school and I walk it in all weathers, taking care when crossing roads, but looking out for specific vehicles as listed in my "I Spy" handbook. A rare motor car is worth 50 points, so it's worth checking vehicles as they go by. Soon I am 'I-Spying' aircraft, trains, ships, and trees. I learn to observe my surroundings, not just see them in passing.

On my various train journeys with the family on a day out to Bournemouth, I look out for locomotives and various types of wagons, the shock absorbing one with three vertical white stripes taking several years before the first one is spotted in a siding. My elder brother Peter, 4 years older, suggests one summer holiday that we buy runabout railway tickets that give us free railway travel within the local area for a week. We go out exploring; Lymington, Christchurch, Winchester and the New Forest, with maps supplied by brother Michael, 8 years my senior, who works at Ordnance Survey in Southampton. Michael is the only one of us boys to do compulsory military service, in his case the Army. He has a mix-up with other soldiers crossing an assault course, ending up with a boot in his stomach area. Three weeks later he is diagnosed with diabetes, and invalided out of the Army, told to have an office job but to get as much fresh air as possible with an outdoor hobby such as sailing. He takes up dinghy sailing and assembles a Mirror dinghy from a kit of parts. Later he buys a 16-foot open-deck sailing boat named Falcon, on which, over a few years, he builds a small cabin and joins the Netley Sailing Club on Southampton Water. He sails with me as crew from May to September then brings the boat ashore for winter maintenance, basically rubbing down and re-varnishing the hull with "Spinnaker" varnish. I learn a lot from him and from the other yachtsmen. Southampton Water is relatively sheltered, with reasonable waves and tidal currents, and clearly marked with red and green buoys are the shipping channels, which are dredged continually. My experience of sailing and the outdoor world builds up and without the intervention of my mother, looking at my schoolwork, I would cheerfully consider going to sea at the earliest opportunity, knowing that the Maritime Training School was close by at Warsash, on the River Hamble. Michael applies for the Royal Naval Auxiliary Service and eventually becomes a skipper of a 60-foot plastic-hulled minesweeper based at Hythe, which was designed to operate in shallow water. However, with 6 crew it is large enough, usefully, to visit the Chanel Isles and the Ports of Northern France.

Michael at the helm of Falcon,
Southampton Water.

In my last year at junior school, I become aware of the 11+ selection due in the spring. My brother Peter has passed his and is doing well at Taunton's Grammar School, a 5-mile bus ride away from home. Now it is going to be my turn. Mum is very keen on education, so I receive some coaching for the exam, in various subjects: English comprehension, problem solving, times tables, spelling, and geometric puzzles. With all this encouragement I do very well, passing the 11+ exam and going to the same school as Peter. I am put into Class 1A1, the top class of 4 for the year, each of which is 30 schoolboys keen to get going. That first morning, the Headmaster, in his flowing black gown, goes around all the new classes outlining the purpose of the school – essentially a stepping stone in our career of our own choosing. In those days you could pick your lifetime-career, whether academic, medicine, law, commerce, or the Armed Services. The school would ensure you had the right mix of O levels and A levels to get into the college, university or any training of our own choosing. Just like that!

Unusually, after the first year the class is split into a science or arts stream, starting A levels in year four without first taking those subjects at O level. The science stream concentrates on pure and applied maths, physics, and chemistry, taking some O level subjects for balance, such as Latin, French, English, English Literature and History along with a little sport. Interesting subjects like Woodworking and Art are dropped, as there was no space for them in the timetable. Sport and athletics find a niche for the first few years before they, too, are squeezed out of the programme. Homework is soon stepped up, initially to two hours a night with extra at the weekend. The one-hour bus journey to and from school sees boys with their heads in the textbooks the whole way.

By chance, one day in August, having achieved the age of twelve, my friend and I cycle down to Hamble to look at the yachts moored on the river. On the way home we pass the grass covered Hamble airfield and, seeing the aircraft take off and land from a distance, wonder if we can get closer. We draw up at the main gate of Air Service Training and, undaunted, go up to the man at the gate.

"Please, sir, can we go inside to look at your aircraft?"

"I don't know about that, I had better ring the chief instructor."

After a few minutes we are allowed in and told to report to Squadron Leader Webb in the Air Traffic Control Tower, a white square shaped building amongst the hangars. We find the building, find his office, and knock on his door. "Come in," booms a voice.

We explain who we are, and he decides to give us a short tour of the facilities, starting at the wooden marshaller's hut, complete with yellow batons and tea making facilities. He shows us the big hangar where the training aircraft were kept overnight, then the dispersal where there were many small single aircraft and a few large twin-engine machines, all lined up in neat rows. He takes us upstairs to the top of the tower, where through sloping green glass windows we can see the whole airfield, with the active runway marked out with white boards. We stay there a few minutes, watching the controllers directing the aircraft on the ground and in the air.

"I'll leave you in the capable hands of Mr Cummings, who will explain everything. Knock on my door when you want to leave." So saying, he goes downstairs and Mr Cummings takes over.

Between controlling aircraft, he explains the layout of the airfield, the signal square outside the tower, and the meaning of the coloured signal lamps that he is using. Aircraft are coming and going all the time and Mr Cummings names them: "That one taxiing out with the wing at the top is an Auster; that one which has just landed is an Airspeed Oxford, just returning from a cross country. In dispersal you can see several sleek shiny aircraft, they are Chipmunks belonging to the University Air Squadron."

My friend and I sit there for an hour absorbing every detail – absolutely spellbound.

Eventually it is time to go, so we knock on the Chief Instructor's door. "Come in," booms his voice. We say our farewells and ask if we could come to see the aircraft again. "Check in at the Entrance Guardroom first." As we are leaving, I ask if there was any chance we could fly – as ballast – in some of the aircraft in the future. "You can fly if your parents sign an indemnity form, which I will give to you both. They will have to sign over a half crown stamp."

Clutching the forms, we head for our bikes, check out at the guardroom and race the three miles back home. Much to my surprise, Mum reads the form and says, "You go and buy a stamp and I will sign the form when you come back." Within an hour the form is signed and after a quick glance through two pages of long legal words, I fold it up, ready for our return to the airfield the next day. Mid-morning saw us again at the main gates being checked in and cleared to proceed to Air Traffic Control. There we present ourselves to the Chief Instructor and flourish our completed forms. He checks them and puts them away in a filing cabinet. "Right, that's fine, you will be able to fly today. I will take you to the Marshaller's hut, where you can stay until I come down and collect you prior to your flight."

We follow him down the steps, out onto the dispersal and into a wooden hut, where we met the aircraft marshallers in their bright clothing. We stay for an hour as aircraft are guided into their required positions on the tarmac. Eventually the Chief Instructor appears and, pointing to me, says, "Right, David, we are going spinning in an Auster. Follow us out to the aircraft. I will strap you in, give you a sick bag in case, and you can sit there in the back while we go up to four thousand feet and prepare for spinning. You will feel the aircraft shaking as we pull the nose up and go into a spin. On recovery the nose will be pointing down quite steeply before we climb up for the next one. We will do three in each direction and then return to the airfield to do some circuits and landings."

I sit in the aircraft transfixed, noting every detail as the engine is started and magnetos checked. All is well and the chocks are waved away and with a flashing green light from the tower we taxi out onto the grass airfield towards the marked-out runway. More checks, then a steady green light from the tower, and we move out onto the grass runway and take off towards some hangers in the distance. After a few seconds of bumping over the grass we are airborne, and the ground drops away. We are flying above the hangers, the cars, and people on bicycles. Wow!

Ahead is the broad expanse of Southampton Water, the Fawley Oil Refinery, and beyond that the Isle of Wight. We turn left, bringing the Hamble River into view, with lines of yachts; and in the mid-distance, Calshot, with many moored flying boats. As we continue to turn, Portsmouth comes into view, with grey-painted vessels moored up in the upper harbour. Soon we are at the height of large white cumulus clouds. Some checks, then the nose comes up, the engine dies, and then we are spinning. Then it all stops, and we are in a steep dive. The engine comes back to life, and we climb up again. This time we enter the spin in the other direction and, after recovery, we climb up again.

Four more times we enter a deliberate spin and then recover; then we return back to the airfield, which we circle. Looking down, I can see the white runway markings on the grass airfield and the signal square by the white air traffic control tower. The arrow in the square indicates a left-hand circuit; I had learnt that the previous day. Now were approaching the airfield to land. We are descending over the River Hamble with all its yachts, big houses, and a double-decker bus. The engine increases power as I become aware that the flaps are lowered. We cross the hedge at the airfield boundary, the engine dies, and then we are down, rumbling along before the engine increases power, and then we are airborne again. Climbing up, we turn left towards Southampton Water and the then left again so we can see the whole of the airfield. Once again, we turn onto final approach, cross the River Hamble and, still losing height, cross the hedge at the airfield boundary to touch down. This time we come to a stop at the end of the runway, turning left between two white wooden markers before coming to a halt. Some checks are carried out and flaps retracted, then we are on our way back towards the tower, the nose swinging from side to side, allowing us to see where we are going. My friend the marshaller is standing amongst the parked aircraft holding his batons above his head. This is where we are going to end up, choosing our own path to get there. He crosses the batons above his head, and we stop, do some engine checks, and then it splutters to a stop.

The whole world goes quiet, and I am helped out from the back, still clutching my unused sick bag. The marshaller takes me back to his hut and makes me a cup of tea. He listens patiently as I told him what we had done. My companion was also flying, but in the twin engine Oxford. Later, as we cycle home, we work out what to tell our mums. We want to fly again, so nothing too exciting or we will be grounded. I am learning diplomacy at an early age! None of us realise at the time that this is the first day of a lifelong adventure in flying that will take me around the world at somebody else's expense! Not only were mums to be kept in the dark, but also our mates at school; we do not want any other enthusiastic chaps muscling in on the action.

Squadron Leader Webb who I have to thank
for starting my flying career.

Come holiday time, my friend and I cycle down to Hamble, spending our days either in Air Traffic Control or in the Marshaller's hut. We are learning all about flying, and about the role of Air Service Training (AST) in training up pilots, mainly university graduates, from the Commonwealth and from the Middle East. Before each flight that we are allocated, we listen to the pre-flight briefing by the instructor and after the flight listen to the debrief. We get to understand aviation maps, especially the half million scale map of the South of England, with its airways, control zones, and danger areas. We beg for old copies on their way to the wastepaper basket, which we treasure and take on every flight, identifying towns and cities as we fly around. With flights in the twin engine Airspeed Oxford, sitting in the back as passengers, we need a parachute. The chief instructor rings the parachute store to brief the chief packer of our imminent arrival. On presenting ourselves we sit down on a back parachute, the harness is adjusted around our small frames, and we are shown where the "D" handle is, which we were to pull only when clear of the aircraft. Although it seems to weigh a ton, we proudly carry our "chutes" back to the hut, where we are issued with headphones prior to each flight so we can be on the intercom and hear everything that is being said. We are learning fast, admiring the disciplined way in which flying is organised, on the ground and in the air. We also pick up weather lore, types of clouds, the importance of wind speed and direction on the ground and in the air. You took off and landed with the nose pointing into the wind for good reason. Most of the trainee pilots are training for their National Airline and have to complete a lot of flying and pass ground exams on air law, aerodynamics, and engine handling, as well as carry out instrument let-downs in a procedure trainer, an early form of flight simulator.

The trainee pilots are always smartly dressed and turn up in sports cars; they are not paying for their courses, after all. After they achieved their Air Transport pilot licences they would become first officers (co-pilots) for several years before they would be considered for captaincy. It will be a long slog, but they all seem happy with their prospective futures; after all, this was their chosen career. The instructors are all ex-RAF, some with handlebar moustaches, lots of grey hair, quietly spoken and very self-controlled. Some, like Tony Farrell, DFC, AFC, had flown on Pathfinder operations using Mosquitos during the war, but he would not talk about it, unless politely asked.

The situation as regards access to the airfield remains the same for a year or so, and other boys from Hamble turn up from time to time. Then one day when I was not there, an instructor and trainee pilot start up a twin-engine Oxford. As the engine starts, the undercarriage retracts, damaging the propeller, the engine and the underside of the fuselage. The cause of the accident is that the undercarriage lever is in the "Retract" position and when the engine started, the hydraulic pump provided power to retract the wheels. Notwithstanding the fact that the position of the undercarriage lever is part of the start-up checks, which the crew somehow missed, it was felt that little boys around the dispersal were a liability. They were to be banned unless they had a clear connection with flying, such as the Air Training Corps. This is a big disappointment for me, only to be overcome if I joined the Air Training Corps. I made inquiries at school and am told that the joining age is 14 and the Southampton 424 Squadron HQ is in some huts next to the Civic Centre. They meet in the evening on Tuesday and Thursday at 7pm for 2 hours. I could get there from home by No 5 bus, half an hour ride, so no problem. I duly report and express a wish to join and am accepted, even if slightly underage. I said that I had been flying at AST, Hamble, and I am issued with a uniform including a beret and little notebook which showed when I had joined and what courses I had attended, all in all a record of service and a form of ID. Duly qualified, I report back to AST, proudly wearing my uniform and carrying my flying maps. I am accepted back into the fold and continue to have access to all aircraft types and am now allowed to fly with solo trainee pilots on their cross-country flights.

The first one is a four-hour flight from Hamble to Exeter, north to Llandudno, east to Felixstowe, south to Brighton and then back along the south coast to Hamble. My job is to hold the maps, keep a good lookout and monitor the instruments. After take-off my pilot climbs to 2000 feet and sets off west along the coast. I call out the names of the places, speak about aircraft I can see around us, and check that the engines and systems instruments are reading sensibly. After half an hour, the trainee pilot explains that he had had a good time in London the day before and therefore he is going to relax and let me fly the machine to Exeter, where I am to alert him if he is asleep! As Exeter rolls up, I alert him; he turns the aircraft towards Llandudno, and hands over control to me, gently slumping and pulling down the visor on his cap. Some 50 minutes later the town came in view, and we turn right towards Felixstowe. The flight continues in similar mode, luckily with good visibility. We see military aircraft, mainly Meteors, flying around, some in formation. The countryside unrolls like a carpet, and we stay on track all the way.

Eventually, as we approach Portsmouth, my pilot takes over and we gently descend to 1000 feet. We circle Hamble airfield, looking around for other aircraft and noting the information in the signal square. Left hand circuit, as expected, runway direction as expected. We do checks, lowering the undercarriage and getting the green lights. As we turn onto final approach we get a long green light signal from the tower, so clear to land. The engines are hot after a long flight and begin popping as the throttles came back. The flaps go down, the power increases, and my pilot is using the flying controls quite a lot as we come down the final 500 feet. Over the hedge, throttle back, rumble, rumble from the wheels, pull back on the stick and some gentle braking. We turn off the runway quite close to the end, stop, and do some more checks. Another light signal from the tower, and we taxi back, looking for our marshaller. He is there with his batons above his head, indicating the spot for shutdown. More checks, then, with the throttles fully back, my pilot selects weak mixture for the engines, and they splutter to a stop. Then he switches off the magnetos and closes the fuel cocks. He opens the window to let in some fresh air and indicates to me to leave the cockpit first.

I cannot believe how stiff I am as I climb out of the seat and made my way down the fuselage to open the door. My ears are singing, my muscles are weak, my eyes ache. Slowly we walk across dispersal, looking out for other aircraft moving. I thank my pilot for the trip, find the marshaller's hut and flop into a chair, exhausted. Half an hour later I cycle home, thinking how much to tell Mum; not a lot, I figure, as I want to repeat the experience and not get grounded.

Ready for a flight in an Airspeed Oxford at AST Hamble.

At school, a few of us boys talk about the upcoming Farnborough Air Show and the latest aircraft that would be on display. One of our dads says he will take a carload of us up if we behave ourselves.

We arrive early but still join the queue for the car park. The tented enclosure is full of salesmen talking about their latest engines, radars, and electronic equipment. Surprisingly, when not talking to potential customers they converse with us boys about the capabilities of their equipment, even giving us brochures to take home and study.

Outside in the static display are a range of jet fighters and bombers with some crews alongside, the RAF pilots in slate grey flying suits, carrying silver-painted bone domes. The latest jets have swept-back wings, designed to delay the effects of shock waves when travelling close to the speed of sound. As the start of the flying show approaches, we boys find ourselves a good open area where we could see the aircraft taking off and landing. We are not disappointed with the flying show, with a range of jet and propeller driven aircraft taking off, displaying, and then landing. There are a few helicopters, but we were only interested in the jets and the daring test pilots who fly them. There is a lot of interest in the press about aircraft trying to break the sound barrier and the problems with control reversal and loss of control due to formation of shock waves over the wings. Eventually it is the turn of Lieutenant Commander Mike Lithgow to display the Supermarine Swift swept wing jet fighter. He roars down the runway, flames coming out of the jet pipe, and disappears quickly out to the West. A few minutes later the public address tells us to look out for him coming in from the left on a supersonic run. Sure enough, a loud double bang and then a small aircraft streaks down the runway, pulling up into a steep climb and disappearing from sight in a few seconds. Wow! That is impressive. A minute later he comes into land from the east, with smoke coming off the tyres as he touches down and taking the whole runway to stop.

Now it is the turn of the rival fighter, the Hawker Hunter, flown by Squadron Leader Neville Duke, a wartime fighter pilot with the RAF. He also takes off to the west and the public address says he is climbing up to 30,000 feet before pointing his aircraft towards the airfield, putting it into a steep dive and selecting full throttle on the engine. Sure enough, the double bang and the small aircraft streaking down the runway to disappear in near vertical climb. Sounds of clapping from the audience all round us. A moment to remember. A few minutes later he comes into land, undercarriage and big flaps clearly down, nose up attitude on touch down, rolls to the end of the runway and ends with a slow taxi back to the parking area on the other side of the runway.

Show over, back to the car and the queue to get out, but no worries for us boys, swapping brochures and impressions in the back of the car. That was it. This would be the life for me. I would tell my parents and my headmaster that I was going to join the RAF and fly its latest jet aircraft. At 14, you know, nothing is impossible, just ask for it and people will give it to you!

Who to tackle first – Headmaster or Mum? Problem resolved on Monday at school. It is lunchtime, and I am passing the Headmaster's room for the canteen. Now is the time, so plucking up courage I knock on his big wooden door.

"Come in," booms Mr Chalacombe. As I enter he says, "How can I help you, David?"

"I have decided that I want a career as a jet pilot in the RAF and would appreciate your guidance how to achieve this."

There is a dull pause – clearly not the normal career path for one of his boys. "The Air Force is very technical these days, so like your brother Peter you will need A levels in all your four science subjects plus say six O levels for balance, in fact the same qualifications you would need to go to university. Follow your elder brother, and get good A Level grades in Pure and Applied Maths, Physics and Chemistry. As regards to O levels, you will need History, English, French, Latin, and English Literature. To achieve that in the timetable of lessons you will have to drop

Geography." (A shame, as I enjoy it). He does not try to make me change my mind, and I now have something to aim at.

"Thank you Headmaster, I will get those results that you suggest." So saying, I leave his study, suddenly hungry for lunch and talking with my aviation-minded friends. Clearly it would have to be tonight that I tackle Mum.

It goes better than expected. If the School's Headmaster is giving his blessing and points the way in terms of subjects and required grades, effectively University entrance requirements, that is OK. She is keen on my going to university, like my elder brother Peter, and RAF Cranwell is spoken about as the University of the Air. Perhaps I might get in there at 18, if I tried.

So, next night at Air Training Corps I ask to talk to the Commanding Officer, a Squadron Leader in the RAF Reserve, and I outline my aspirations. He gives me the address of the RAF recruiting office in Southampton and suggests writing a letter outlining my plans and what I had achieved so far in terms of flying. I write and I am invited for an interview the following Saturday morning. I suggest to my mum that she comes along but she says, "No, its your life, but see what you can find out."

I mount the steps of the grand looking building on the Avenue in central Southampton, check in with the Secretary and am taken to the office of the Officer Commanding, a Squadron Leader, a tall grey-haired gentleman with medal ribbons under his RAF wings. He welcomes me and asks what information I am looking for. I outline my desire to become a jet pilot in today's modern Air Force. I run through my experience of flying with AST at Hamble, my joining No 424 Squadron Air Training Corps and the expectation that I would be able to go gliding at Christchurch in the near future. Finally, I tell him of my interview with my Headmaster and his advice.

"I don't see any problem with what you want to do. You are doing all the right things at the moment. With the phasing out of National Service shortly, the Services will need full career regular officers and no doubt jet propulsion will be the future for most new aircraft. I think the best thing we can do is to give you a range of leaflets about what the RAF does and some application forms for you and your parents to look at. Come back in six months if you are still keen."

I follow him into the adjacent room with shelving around the walls. He starts in one corner and picks up appropriate leaflets as he goes round, finally placing them in a big OHMS envelope, writes my name in large capitals on the front and finally stamps the address of his office.

As he hands me the envelope, he shakes my hand. "We get a lot of applications for RAF pilot training, which is long and expensive, and trainees have to reach a very high standard. We can afford to be very choosy when we select pilots for training. Good luck, see you in six months." I make my way out of the building, clutching my envelope, and head for the bus stop. At home I lay out the leaflets and begin to learn what the RAF is all about. I am being taken seriously, but clearly there are going to be a lot of hoops to jump through before qualifying as a jet pilot in today's RAF.

Back at school I see my Geography teacher and explain that concentrating on my science course meant dropping geography, a subject I enjoy. "Well, David, you can still study the subject in your own time. I will give you the syllabus, the textbooks, and some past exam papers. The school will put you forward for the O Level exam when you feel ready. I was looking at the list of subjects for our Examination Board and saw that Elementary Aeronautics was also on the list. If you would like, I will get you the syllabus and some past papers to study and you can take that as well. Your experience flying with AST and the courses you receive at the ATC will cover the subject, I am sure." *The next four years are going to be a busy time,* I think. Luckily, in my brother Peter I had someone who had been in the science stream, so if I had any problems, he would put me right.

Holiday time and I check in at AST, but there is a problem and I have to see the Chief-Instructor. "Sit down, David, and I will explain the situation. One of our Middle Eastern trainee pilots took a light aircraft away and flew to London and landed in Hyde Park and then took a taxi into the city. We were contacted by the Metropolitan Police and we sent an instructor up with some fuel in cans and he brought the aircraft back. We now have to account for the whereabouts of everyone on the flying side, including visitors like you. If you wish to go anywhere, like the hangar, the factory, or just look into an aircraft cockpit, you will need to be escorted. Understood?"

"Yes, understood. You mentioned the factory – what is being produced there?"

"During the War it was Spitfires, now it's producing wings for the Javelin all weather fighter. Do you want to have a quick visit? I can arrange it now if you like."

Five minutes later I am taken across to the big hangars and as we open the door, I can hear the high-speed drills zinging away. I am introduced to the manager, and he takes me round the production line. The internal structure of the wings looks very chunky, and the metal aluminium alloy skin looks half an inch thick as it is bent around and secured to the frames. The wing root looks three feet deep, apparently good for fuel tanks and retractable undercarriage. I spot the ailerons on the trailing edge of the wing, and they are squared off – apparently to stabilise where any shock waves might form at high speed. I am told that the aircraft has powered flying controls, again not affected by any shock waves or prone to flutter. At the end of the line the completed wings are being loaded onto an open lorry with the wing tips pointing up at least twenty feet and covered over. A special route is required to the final assembly plant at Gloucester, avoiding low bridges. I make a mental note of how big the finished delta winged aircraft will be and that it will be replacing the Meteor NF 14 Night Fighters based on the east coast. I could be flying it eventually, so from then I take an interest in all things fighter and air to air missiles, which are replacing cannons as armament.

I am amazed at the Air Training Corps. We parade at 7pm and ex-RAF Warrant Officer Brading takes us for parade drill with and without rifles – 303 Brownings, single shot with a bolt action. Thrown around, it makes a lot of noise. The cadets come from a wide variety of backgrounds, some already skilled in motor mechanics, others electrics, and others already into building. We meld together on parade, during lectures and in taking apart engines, radios and our guns.

I get particularly fond of looking after an ex-Bomber Command Marconi Type 1155 radio receiver. It is a sophisticated "Superhet" design with magic cat's eye tuning so you can pick up the faintest signal. Because the receiver is so accurate, the matching transmitter (Type 1154), normally in a stowage rack above, can be tuned accurately to the required frequency on the receiver, before transmitting. Not only can you hear voices and music but also you could receive morse code and I quickly get up to the required four words a minute after a few lessons with a morse key. What I appreciate is seeing the blueprint of the wiring diagram, complete with valves, variable capacitors, and colour coded resistors. I like it so much I get one at home, modified to run off the mains, with headphones to keep the noise down in the bedroom. Broadcasts from around the world are available; some from abroad fade in and out, depending on atmospheric conditions. Most nights I listen in to my favourite stations, hearing news and music from everywhere.

The lectures are on aviation-based subjects, meteorology, theory of flight, avionics, aircraft recognition, navigation, and types of aero engines. Also, aspects of the RAF are being taught: ranks, RAF history with films of WW 11, decorations, and command structures. Comprehensive handbooks are available on most subjects, and you can take them home. What I learn with the ATC chimes with what I am experiencing with flying with AST. All this information just soaks in and is retained until needed. As aircraft fly over, I strive to identify them and, if new, to describe them to my friends, i.e. twin piston prop, fixed undercarriage, colour blue heading for Southampton airport.

With my goal of flying with the RAF ahead of me, I just proceed through every exam, every piece of work, every encounter. Every day one more step, one more experience, some new knowledge to tuck away. Every day a new adventure. Time flies when you are busy. I begin a friendship with another ATC cadet, Alan Jones, whose elder brother, Ernie, is a pilot on a Hunter jet squadron. Later he would fly Javelins and be part of the Red Arrows team. Alan is interested in joining the RAF as a pilot, too, and we swap information about how to go about it. Alan is also interested in building a car from scrap parts, an Austin 7, so that when we are old enough, we can learn to drive. We save our pocket money and the money we earn from doing Sunday paper rounds. Eventually we club together and with £5 go to a scrap yard and buy an old pre-war example. A friend tows it to a little grass field out of view of the public. Then Alan and I begin work, dismantling it and working out what can be refurbished and what must be replaced. Luckily, Alan has the knowledge and flair. I provide some manpower and moral support. With a simple A-frame chassis, the body is secured on top and is easily removed by freeing up the nuts and bolts holding it all together. With liberal application of light oil and waiting a few hours for it to soak in, the nuts become easy to undo, and soon the body is off and lying in the field alongside the chassis. There is rust everywhere and we agree the body is too far gone to be repaired, so at some stage we need another body. Undaunted, we carry on cleaning up the chassis with a wire brush and lots of elbow grease. The wiring, unsurprisingly, just falls apart, so new wiring eventually. Now to get the engine out for Alan to take apart, clean and re-assemble. He seems confident enough and has the required tools and other friends who will help him put it all back together. He has a handbook for the car, complete with colour-coded wiring diagram; invaluable when we put the new wiring harness together. I look at the page on mpg versus speed: best at 30 mph and the graph stops at 50 mph, looks sensible to me. The project takes years, but eventually a serviceable, hand-painted black car is ready to drive. A friend who drives has offered to demonstrate it on some nearby rough ground. It starts up. Wow! I climb in the back, Alan in the front next to young driver Ian, and off we go in first gear, nice and slow. Ian gains confidence and we proceed along a bit of track, picking up speed, with Ian changing gear into top and now up to 30 mph. We come to a bend with a bank on the left. For whatever reason, Ian heads up the bank and then yanks the steering to the right. We roll over with a crash, some windows smash. Without seat belts we are thrown around and the newly painted car is lying on its side. We get out through the left-hand door with bodies not too bruised. While standing there, we hear a trickling sound and eventually locate the battery, where its contents of sulphuric acid are pouring into the car. We have to right the car and get it back home, so with the help of the many onlookers we roll it over onto its wheels again and push it back home. Alan says he can fix everything, which he does. It will be not until I am 21 that I get my first driving licence, and my first car, an Austin Minivan, all in Anglesey, and that six months after I have gone supersonic in a two-seat jet Hawker Hunter Trainer of No 56 Squadron with Ernie Jones over the North Sea, flying from RAF Coltishall in Norfolk.

Back at No 424 (Southampton) Squadron ATC, parades, classes, aircraft recognition, and socialising continue two nights a week. Every year in the summer holidays the Squadron goes to an RAF Station so those cadets considering a career in the RAF will see for themselves what the modern Service is all about. My first camp, in August 1955, is to RAF Wittering, near Stamford Lincs. The main aircraft on the station are the swept-wing Vickers Valiant bombers. Close up, they are huge, and painted white. I notice that the two-wheel undercarriage retracts outwards, and the leading edge of the wing has compound sweep from the root to the tip, where there is a long pitot tube. The five-man crew enter the cockpit via a ladder on the port side. The two pilots have ejection seats. The three rear-crew – Nav Radar, Nav Plotter, and Air Electronics Officer – have seats and normal parachutes and are considered at risk if a bail out is necessary below 2000 feet. They face backwards apart from when the visual bomb aimer position in the nose is being used. The cockpit is in a pressurised cabin, enabling the aircraft to fly to very high altitude. The navigator has access to a periscopic sextant in the cabin ceiling to take shots of the sun and the stars so he can navigate in any part of the world without ground facilities. As cadets we get to fly in an Avro Anson, looking down on a big station with a 9000-foot runway. On the ground I notice one Valiant with bulges underneath the engines. The liaison officer explains that they are De Haviland Sprite booster rockets, used to enable overweight take-offs. Once airborne they are dropped. In talking to the young pilot conducting the trials, he explains that only 60 seconds of extra thrust is available and his job during trials is to work out the optimum time for them to be fired up during the take-off run. He feels that 20 seconds after brake release is about right, so that the extra thrust is there for a while after the aircraft leaves the ground (many years later I learn that the trials are abandoned because of the satisfactory performance on normal engines without booster). I notice a red sports car nearby that I don't recognise. He takes me across to it and explains he is building it from a kit of parts. He is not happy with the recommended positions of the speedometer and rev counter. I suggest changing them over. Three days later, as we board the coach to leave, our liaison officer tells me the pilot did just that and is pleased with the result, and would I like to see the car in action during a test drive?! Another day, perhaps.

As we start 1956, I bid for the ATC Gliding camp at nearby Christchurch for the Easter Holidays. This is agreed, and Mum is happy, as my schoolwork is going well. On the due day I go down to Christchurch on the train with some fellow cadets, with our overnight clothes and some food to cook. We meet the Commanding Officer, a Squadron Leader of the RAF Reserve who had served during the War. He briefs us on what is expected from us; we need to be responsible and hard working. We meet some NCO cadets and are instructed on how to handle the fragile gliders on the ground. There are two types; the side-by-side seating Slingsby T21 Sedbergh, and the Kirby Cadet Mark 3 single-seater. Now, already briefed and ready, our T21 is hooked onto the mile long winch cable. The slack is taken in and as we begin to move the instructor calls for full power. We bump along on the skid underneath and in seconds we are airborne. Then the instructor pulls back on the controls, and we climb quickly with a high nose-up attitude. As we reach 1000 feet, the nose dips and the instructor pulls the cable release. We jump up a bit and it all goes quiet, just the noise of the slipstream over the wings. He points out the local landmarks, and where we need to be positioned to carry out our circuit back to the take off point on the grass runway. There is no power to affect an overshoot, so we need to judge our approach correctly; we have just the one chance. Now lined up with the runway on final approach, the instructor opens the airbrakes on the wings and we descend at a steeper angle and touch down with a gentle bump, just past the other glider waiting to take off. In seconds, willing hands secure the glider and drag it back to the take-off point. After twenty minutes it's my turn again, but this time I will be handling the controls as instructed – no problem.

As we get airborne the instructor shouts, "Pull back harder!" I do, the nose rises sharply, and we are climbing steeply as before.

37

I can feel the glider vibrating under the strain. Seconds later the nose levels off and we are not climbing any more. Time to drop the cable before it releases automatically.

It all goes quiet and, gently descending, I turn the glider across the wind and then onto the downwind leg. I can see the touchdown spot clearly and judge my turn onto final approach. I announce that we will make it and deploy the airbrake. We start descending quickly, but we have plenty of space in front of us. As the ground rushes up, I gently raise the nose and hold off touchdown until the glider sinks down on the skid and we bump along to a halt. As we stop the right wing slowly drops to the ground before willing hands can get to it – no problem, apparently. Another 10 flights and I should go solo. That's my flying for the first day. I help moving the gliders around until it's time for tea.

I go to Christchurch Airfield every weekend after Easter and convert to the Kirby Cadet. Eventually I clock up three solo flights and earn my certificate of competence. In so doing, that will be the end of my gliding for a few years. Between my flights I am checked out on operating the Winch and driving the big Bedford truck, dragging the cables back to the gliders at the other end of the grass runway. Now with gliding over for a few years, I concentrate on flying with AST at Hamble.

Gliding with the Air Training Corps, Kirby Cadet Mark 3,
Christchurch Airfield – 1956

In the autumn, trouble brews in the Middle East, with Israel initially invading Egypt with France and Great Britain joining in to "Protect the Suez Canal." The papers are full of our paratroops going in on the 5th of November and raids on Egyptian airfields by Valiants, Canberras, and Naval Sea Hawks. The war is brought to a close, British and French troops withdraw, and the Royal Navy helps with clearing the ships that were deliberately sunk in the canal at the start of the conflict. At AST, there is a small problem with what to do with Egyptian students currently on pilot training courses. I understand that they are removed for the duration of the conflict.

1957 opens with the prospect of going to the Lake District with the school at Easter. I am pretty fit with all my cycling and my elder brother Peter has been twice already. I apply and go through the list of kit that I will need, the main items being boots with commando soles for grip. The coach leaves the school full of excited schoolboys, aiming to reach Hassness Country House, Buttermere by evening. Along the roads I look out for rare vehicles, for my "I Spy" booklet, and appreciate the green hills as we approach Lancaster and Westmorland. In my hand are the maps supplied by my brother Michael, who works in the Ordnance Survey, and between glancing at the passing scenery I absorb the layout of the Lake District with its numerous lakes and mountains. We are given a list of possible walks that we will try and accomplish, depending on the weather. We arrive at our amazing destination on the shore of Buttermere, surrounded by mountains; bliss. Can't wait to get going.

Morning dawns with good weather, so our school group head off towards Buttermere Church, where we line up for the group photograph. We start off for the mountains at great pace, we are exploring, after all; the teachers have trouble holding us back. As we start climbing our first objective, Red Pike, the group spreads out into a long crocodile of toiling human beings. The gloves and scarves come off as we warm up with the hard exercise. Eventually we all reach the top and take in the view; we can see for many miles. Our next objective is High Stile, and we are warned about the scree slope, with small loose rocks ready to slide. We are not to run down, but to go down under control, sliding and jumping to keep balance. We all start with good intentions of course, but as confidence builds, we go faster and all too soon the scree slope finishes and we are on a steep grassy slope. We assemble at the bottom; everybody is OK, so after a short rest we toil up the slope to High Stile, then across to High Crag, where, seated around the summit cairn, we tuck into our packed lunches. The views are just breath taking, one could stay for several hours, but we have a schedule to keep, and the weather is good, so no reason to delay. We journey on to an area known as Haystacks, a roughly level area with little lochans, an area much favoured by Wainwright, the author of the Lakeland Fells guidebooks. From there it is a steep descent on pathways going towards Buttermere, alongside the mass of Fleetwith Pike on the right. Reaching the shoreline, we walk around to the right, cross a beck, and along the road we reach our House. Boots off outside, scrub them under the tap, then into the drying room, to be ready for tomorrow. The first day has gone well, as does the rest of the week. Lovely mountains, lovely valleys, lovely stone buildings. I resolve to return and explore.

Now the serious stuff begins. I have applied for a Cranwell Scholarship and now the papers have come through for aircrew selection at RAF Hornchurch in Essex. At school, the Geography master and two others give me coaching on interview techniques, running over what questions I am likely to be asked and what my ambitions might be if I am selected. I make it to the RAF Station and join around 30 other schoolboys from a variety of backgrounds, some public school, some grammar school. The rumours of what the selection board want to see circulate with close interest from all concerned. Apparently, they like "WASPs" – white, Anglo-Saxon Protestants, i.e. Church of England. Luckily, I fit into that category. At 15 years and eight months I recognise that I am a bit young for this process, but some old hands reassure me that I can reapply if I fail this time. The medicals go well; it is my first time with the book of numbers for the colour blindness test, and I confidently call out the figures that I see – blue 7 against a magenta background, green 5 against a yellow background. Now for hand and eye co-ordination tests, keeping a dot of light in the right place as a cylinder revolves. That was OK, apparently. Now the tricky part, the interviews.

There are five officers facing me across the table, headed by a Wing Commander. "Why do want to become a pilot in the RAF?"

"What do you hope to achieve?"

"What level of responsibility would you like to attain?"

"There is a situation in Algeria now with rebels crossing the border and carrying our attacks. If you were in charge of their Defence, what action would you take?"

The questions probe my commitment, my understanding of current affairs, and where I might fit into the current RAF. Apparently, I do well enough to join the group heading up to Cranwell for leadership tests. On the RAF bus we swap experiences and prepare ourselves for the next round. We are split into small groups and start with presentations.

"Give a 15-minute presentation on a subject of your own choice. We will start with you – David."

Luckily, having been in the ATC, I was used to presentations using a blackboard and chalk, so I started into describing the workings of the Calder Hall Nuclear Power Station, which had recently been officially opened by the Queen. I sketch out the layout of the Plant, Reactor, Steam Turbines, Transformers and Transmission Network. Having explained the layout, I rub off my efforts, and began to explain nuclear fission of the uranium atom, the role of neutrons, the moderator, the cadmium rods and the concrete radiation shield. Having fazed my audience with technical detail, costings, and the possible future of nuclear power, my time is up.

Another presentation is on the development of the Spitfire and Rolls Royce engines following the Schneider Trophy Float Plane races in the Solent. The RAF-piloted Supermarine S6B had won the contest outright. The competition had pushed aircraft and engine development, which was helped by a £100,000 contribution from Lady Houston. What followed was the Spitfire, designed by R.J. Mitchel, with its elliptical wing, and coupled with the Rolls Royce Merlin engine it enabled us to win the Battle of Britain. The Spitfire and its variants were so successful that it stayed in production right through and after the war.

Presentations over, it is time for the leadership tests; how to cross a mock river using planks, ropes, and carrying a box of delicate instruments. What the selection officers are looking for is how we work together in the discussion of how to solve the problem and how we work together in carrying out the task. We cross the river unscathed, so we are hopeful that we have done well. Close to where we are staying is the RAF College, where we all hope to go some day. We head home, waiting for the acceptance letter through the post within the next few weeks. My brown envelope duly arrives, I open it carefully, but it is not the news I want to read: yes, there is competition for places, and this time I was not chosen, but I could apply again in a year's time. After a few days I resolve to apply again next year. Now I understand the selection process, I know better how to approach it; meanwhile there are O Levels at school to worry about, the summer ATC camp to look forward to, and continued flying at Hamble with AST. There are not enough hours in the day as I go from activity to activity. As my head hits the pillow at night, I dream of a life of flying around the world, and I am soon fast asleep.

At AST a Douglas Dakota arrives, apparently to train students from Indonesia. It is a big aeroplane for a small airfield, but I ask if I can fly in it and the answer is yes. I will not need a parachute, I will be seated in a "jump" seat, just behind the pilots, and the training will concentrate on procedural let-downs at Southampton's Eastleigh aerodrome. I am given a piece of paper with the layout of the procedure on it, with its beam approach and two markers. This approach procedure enables aircraft to descend safely in cloud to a specified level and lined up with the runway in use. The beam has a defined direction, and the centre of the beam is achieved by turning towards the centreline according to whether you can hear dots or dashes in your headphones, having first identified the transmitter as being the one you want. We talk a lot to air traffic control – we are flying in cloud, after all – and obey his instructions. I begin to understand how it all works and am not surprised when we pop out of cloud with the runway in front of us, enabling us to land should we so wish. On every flight we overshoot the airfield and climb back up into the cloud, awaiting further clearance for another procedural let-down. I am growing to accept flying on instruments, directions by air traffic control, and descending through cloud on a published procedure. This experience will be invaluable in later years, as I fly in controlled airspace with other aircraft around me.

With another opportunity to apply for a Cranwell Scholarship I resolve to get all the qualifications needed, all the flying I could get at AST, all the information from my experience from the Air Training Corps, and further mock interviews at school. The pace of life is increasing; more hoops to jump through, more exams to take, but I now knew where my ambition lay – a life in flying. Suitably prepared, I apply in 1958 for a second time for a Cranwell scholarship and receive my papers to report to RAF Hornchurch in Essex, a former Battle of Britain Station. Knowing what to expect from the interviews, I express confidence in my ability to achieve things. Since my previous interview, I had clocked more flying hours with AST and passed several O Levels, including Elementary Aeronautics with 97%. When asked what rank and responsibility I am aiming at, I reply that becoming a Station Commander responsible for the activities of several operational Squadrons would be what I would like to achieve. The whole process goes well and at home a week later I receive a big brown envelope. Not only am I awarded a Cranwell Scholarship, I am also awarded an ATC Flying Scholarship. I will be trained on light aircraft to Private Pilot's standard at the Hampshire Flying Club, based at Eastleigh Aerodrome. This will take place during the school's summer holiday in August, so there will be no distractions.

Flying begins on the De Haviland Hornet Moth, with side-by-side seating making instruction easier. There is no radio fitted and we are controlled in the Aerodrome Circuit by light signals from the air traffic tower. After 10 hours dual instruction, I am sent solo for one circuit. That completed, instruction switches to the Tiger Moth, where the instructor sits ahead of the student, both in open cockpits, communicating by shouting down a

Gosport Tube! Once clear of the aerodrome circuit I am shown aerobatics, loops, rolls, and stall turns. With that completed we climb to 5,000 feet and, checking we are clear all round, I am introduced to spinning and the recovery drill. Between flights and ground instruction I make myself useful by helping to push aircraft in and out of the hangar.

Inside the hanger is a two-seat Spitfire painted blue, flown by the Chief Instructor Vic Bellamy. I understand he flew with a Spitfire Squadron during the War. Eastleigh Aerodrome was where the first flight of the prototype Supermarine Spitfire, K5054 took place on 5th March 1936, three months after the first flight of the Hawker Hurricane.

Flying away from the circuit, cross-country flights begin using the Hornet Moth, with its enclosed cockpit better for looking after maps and flight plans. I am used to cross-country flying, using aeronautical topographical maps, but always in good weather and well below any cloud. We fly a dual cross country to Exeter Aerodrome, land, taxi to a dispersal next to the flying club, and shut down. We are welcomed with a coffee, refuelling is arranged, and we contact air traffic control about our flight back to Eastleigh via Christchurch. The flight goes well and there are no problems, except a practice engine failure 30 minutes into the flight. I select a large, level grass field for an emergency landing and make a glide approach into wind. When it is clear that we will make it, my instructor instructs me to overshoot, so I open the throttle fully and we climb back up to cruise altitude. I am familiar with Christchurch Aerodrome from my gliding days, but it is my first visit to their Flying Club. The weather remains good while we return to Eastleigh and in joining the circuit pattern we look out for other aircraft and signal lights from the tower.

The next day the weather remains good, so I do it all again, this time solo. A few days later it is time for the flying test with the Chief Instructor for the granting of my PPL (Private Pilot's Licence). He selects the Tiger Moth, saying that if I can fly that well I will be able to fly anything in the future. We take off and leave the circuit, climbing up for aerobatics. These completed, it's time for some steep turns before returning to the aerodrome, where we do a roller landing – touching down then taking off using full power.

After one hour, when we are positioned downwind for the runway in use, I hear "Practice engine failure," and my instructor closes the throttle. I turn towards the runway and ensure that when descending below 500 feet I am lined up into the wind, and we touch down about halfway up the large grass aerodrome. We taxi in towards dispersal, swinging the nose from time to time so we can see past the engine blocking our forward view. Approaching dispersal, I slow down; we have no brakes, after all, and we need to use full rudder and propellor wash to turn into our shut down spot as indicated by our marshaller. At the de-brief Vic Bellamy runs through the exercises that we carried out, commenting where improvements were possible. Finally, he pronounces that I have reached the required standard for the Private Pilot's Licence; he will send away the documentation and I will receive the Licence from the CAA in due course.

His parting remarks are: "You will be responsible in the air for yourself, your crew and any passengers. Aim to learn from every flight you are involved with, at any level, until you retire. Good luck."

*Happy to be next to the Tiger Moth in which I took
my flying test, Hampshire Flying Club,
Eastleigh Airfield July 1958*

Chapter 2: The Cranwell Years

(September 1959 – July 1962)

The initial months at Cranwell are spent in basic brick huts, with 8 beds to the room and a pot stove in the middle that would glow at night if the vent was left open. Most days are spent doing drills, PT, kit inspections, and learning about the RAF: history from its formation in 1918; achievements; and ranks, decorations and equivalent ranks in the other two Services. There is a chance to fly gliders on the grass north airfield, which I take up whenever I can. In the sky are Vampire T11 trainers, taunting us flight cadets square bashing. The initial year goes quickly without any major hiccup, though occasionally when returning from the library doing private study I find that a bunch of Senior Flight Cadets have rampaged through our accommodation huts, turned over all the beds, scattered our clothing and then exited through the back windows. Good training for meeting enemy action at some future point – unpredictable random destruction! To cope with hut inspections, I have one set of toilet kit that I do not use, and it stays immaculate. The other set, which I do use. stays out of sight.

Luckily for me, I had done four years in Southampton's Air Training Corps (No 424 Squadron), so I am experienced in basic drill using the 303 rifle. Also, information given on RAF history, ranks, and medals is already known to me. A similar story is in place for my having been streamed onto the AFRAeS course (B Stream). I know basic aerodynamics, meteorology, airframe structures, piston and jet engines, radio, radar, and navigation aids. I am keen to crack on with the academic course and, naturally, the flying. We know that our course will be the first Cranwell course to start our flying training on jets from the word "go." We will start on the Jet Provost Mk3, with wing tip fuel tanks and Martin Baker ejector seats. Again, I am fortunate that I have arrived with a Private Pilot's Licence, having flown light aircraft during my ATC Flying Scholarship at Eastleigh Aerodrome, as well as gliding at Christchurch, and the many hours flying in Airspeed Oxfords at A.S.T Hamble.

Eventually our Entry moves from the brick huts into accommodation blocks around the Parade Square, entitling us to our own rooms. We can study if needed or prepare our kit for drill. My rifle is cleaned most nights, and to make more noise during rifle drill certain items are loosened. Our drill sergeant, Sgt McDill is a slave driver; we look straight ahead as we are castigated for our turnout or performance on the drill square.

His favourite castigation is: "The next time you have a shave in the morning, stand closer to the razor Sir!" Good discipline training no doubt, just taking criticism without response.

I join two societies: the mountaineering club and the caving club. Both will enhance my skills and confidence. The mountaineering club uses a minibus to take us to Stanage Edge in Derbyshire, where we tackle difficult and very difficult climbs on hard Millstone Grit, ideal for reliable hand and footholds. I learn not to progress up a rock face unless I can reverse every move, even though I had a top rope for safety. I learn to trust the experience of my leaders and never fall off a climb. Having got to the top, we abseil down the cliff face. During the Easter holidays we head off to the Isle of Skye, Glencoe, and Snowdonia, doing mountaineering in summer and winter conditions. This experience of operating in the mountains will be invaluable to me later in my flying career.

Abseiling at Stanage Edge – Derbyshire 1961

The caving club leaders take us underground, where it is dark, wet, and cold, and in places quite narrow. One afternoon we take down one of our Flight Commanders to show him what we do. He is not impressed, being a big burly chap, becoming stuck in a narrow passage with water flowing past him. We have to cajole him into pulling on the boots of our leader ahead while I push on his boots from behind while he squirmed his shoulders through the narrow passage. We made it to the surface, where he says very little, except he was looking forward to a hot shower and a good meal. Whether he was impressed with caving, I cannot tell, but he never comes again.

After one year we all move up to the main College building; our own rooms, good batting, splendid dining room, large library, and a parade ground outside the front door. Life is getting more hectic during the week, though we have weekends off to do our own thing. I spend some time at the Nottingham's University Campus meeting up with Ann, a young lady undergraduate reading Mediaeval and Modern History. On our first meeting over a coffee, I explain that she should realise that I was aiming to be a career officer in the modern-day RAF and flying jets wherever that might take me. Somehow, surrounded by undergraduates who have no idea what they might do, she is attracted to someone who has ambition and is prepared to work to achieve it. Ann teaches me to play tennis over several months and slowly I get up to her standard. We walk around the main university buildings, and the adjacent lake and open areas. When I have an overnight pass, she arranges for me to doss down in a men's accommodation block and to join the queue for breakfast, hoping my short haircut will not stand out too much. I meet many of her contemporaries; their aim was to enjoy themselves for three years before the serious business of earning a living will have to be faced. For me it is very relaxing, meeting other young people with a different range of attitudes and experiences to me.

It is suggested to me that I might resurrect the Amateur Radio Club, as I am proficient in sending and receiving Morse. I make enquiries about the whereabouts of our old equipment, a Marconi 1154 transmitter and 1155 receiver, and find both in a bad condition. I contact the Station's Radio Section and ask that if the items are on charge, could they be repaired? They are taken away, and a few days later brand new items turned up, with a note requesting that we should not allow our equipment to deteriorate to such a state in the future.

Flying begins with a bang at the start of term 5, January 1961, Ground School started, flying kit issued, pilot's notes signed for, and ejection seat training complete, including a half power ride up the ramp. I was fortunate in that my initial instructor is Master

Pilot Jackson, with rows of medal ribbons on his chest. At our first briefing, his first words are:

"My shrivelled ear was the result of an encounter between a Zero and my Beaufighter in the South China Sea in 1944. Professional flying depends on skills, knowledge, discipline, and experience. Aeroplanes bite fools."

Clearly, a man to learn from and to copy. Throughout my flying career he is proved right on many occasions. I note the Air Publication No. of his instructor's manual for the Jet Provost Mk 3 and got a copy that afternoon. It is invaluable knowing what is important for instructors to look for during various manoeuvres. Knowing what is required I am able to concentrate on the key points of every exercise.

The day dawns for the first flight. Mr Jackson gives me a short briefing along the lines of, "I will show you what the Jet Provost can do and how nice it is to fly." We have discussed my flying background, so as we walked out to our allotted aircraft, he says, "You may as well do the take-off. It is quite straight forward. I will talk you through it and do the appropriate checks." We start the engine and taxi out to the runway. "You have control, open the throttle, release the brakes, keep it straight down the middle; as we get to 65 knots, pull gently back on the stick and she will lift off the runway. Let the speed build and I will raise the undercarriage as we pass the airfield boundary."

In seconds we are airborne, good view forward with having a nosewheel, and no need to use the rudder to keep straight. As I lock onto best climbing speed he runs through the after take-off checks and changes frequency from tower to approach. Within minutes we are at 10,000 feet with oxygen check and HASEL checks before aerobatics.

"Let's try level turns, 30 degrees of bank, and roll out on this heading." Using the outside horizon and glancing at the flight instruments, I complete several. "OK, let's try steep turns, 60 degrees, and roll out on North and then reverse it." As I roll on the bank, I instinctively increase power to counter the drag increase. With 30 degrees to go I roll out level, reduce power and hold North for a few seconds before rolling in the reverse direction.

"OK, that went well, let's try some loops around these cumulus clouds. I'll talk you through. OK – that one dead ahead, full throttle now, dive down, get the speed up to 360 knots and as we pass under the base, I will tell you when to pull up. Right, that's good, pull 3G now. OK, as we go up the side, reduce the G so we follow up, keeping out of the cloud. As we go over the top take the G right off – we are following a ballistic curve as our speed drops below 60, the engine will keep running for twenty seconds at zero G. Nose is going below the horizon, speed is increasing quickly, so throttle back, airbrakes out, pull to maintain contact. Nearing the base, airbrakes in, full throttle, same again please."

After a few more we try barrel rolls and then slow rolls, which feel uncomfortable with the negative G; we are hanging in our straps but fully secure in our ejection seats. The dust comes up from the floor momentarily. As we roll out level I glance across the cockpit for approval and notice Mr Jackson with his head slumped on his chest. OK – oxygen problems, most likely. I start descending rapidly and he comes back to life.

"Good – these connections can come loose – this was just a practice, let's look at what this machine will do at low level. We are in the Low Flying Area, so take me down to 200 feet and follow that long straight drainage ditch going southeast, leave the throttle fully open."

The flat Lincolnshire Fens come up to meet us and I pull out of the dive and settle at 200 feet, with telegraph poles racing by on both sides. The airspeed builds to 360 knots. "Fast as a Spitfire, pretty good for a basic trainer. Now pull 2G and set 15 degree angle of climb." We climb like a rocket; the rate of climb indicator on the dash stops, exceeding 4000 feet per minute. In seconds we climb through 10,000 feet – another oxygen check, then we climb at the optimum Mach No., the rate of climb reducing as the engine gives less thrust at higher altitudes.

Approaching the airfield, we change to tower and call to join the circuit. We join on the dead side, looking out for others in the circuit. Again, I retain control as I am instructed around the circuit for a touch and go landing and then a full stop, rolling gently to the end of the runway before turning off for dispersal. As we shut down, the ground crew insert the ejection seat pins in the top of our seats. We insert our own at the base of the seat – now we are safe to get out. Mr Jackson signs the Tech Log – Satisfactory – and we walk back to the crew room.

"Good start. The work begins tomorrow – circuits, turnbacks. and practice forced landings, probably two sorties."

As weather and aircraft availability allow, we fly one or two trips a day, building up my skills and awareness and practicing emergencies, engine failure, flap failure, artificial horizon, radio failure…in the end, quite a long list, needing the pilot's reference cards which I keep in my flight suit pocket. No time to relax and enjoy the view, it is all go. What is very exciting are "turnbacks," where the engine fails just after take-off where the aircraft has built up sufficient momentum to be traded for a steep climbing turn back to the runway. Decision height is 500 feet minimum, and the turn needs to be into any crosswind. Don't forget to call "Turning back," to warn other aircraft possibly on the runway. Don't lower the undercarriage until you will definitely make it, also the flaps. As you come in downwind, your ground speed will be high, but it's your airspeed that keeps you airborne. If in doubt, eject!

It was all going too well. Coming back from a weekend in Nottingham, three of us strike calamity. I was passenger in the front seat of the car, my trainee navigator colleague, Phil Hawken is driving, and George Wade is in the back. As we speed home, it is getting dark. I remember that bit, and then waking up in Newark Hospital, face bandaged and feeling bruised. In adjacent beds are my colleagues. I must have fallen asleep, followed by the driver, and we went off the road at a corner, hitting a vehicle parked in a layby. Not being strapped in, I must have hit the windscreen with my head. The driver was punched in the chest with the steering wheel and George was thrown around in the back. Within days we are back at Cranwell, billeted in the medical centre. My face does not look good – stitches everywhere, black eyes developing – but nothing important damaged. Lucky escape for me, and lessons learnt. If there are seatbelts, use them. If you are next to the driver, keep him awake.

Four weeks later I am deemed fit to fly and allocated another instructor, Flt Lt Lees. Mr Jackson had been sent back to CFS to train up more instructors. Fortunately, all my flying skills come back, and I have not suffered any long-term effects. So, on 14th March 1961, I am entrusted with a Jet Provost Mk 3 for my first solo, one circuit and full stop landing, ten minutes. My instructor looks pleased and within a few days we are all celebrating and are handed our First Solo Certificates, now proudly displayed and secure in my logbook.

A visiting artist comes to the College, showing us caricatures of officers he had met, in best rig, flight suit, or flannels and striped jacket. I go for the flight suit. Somewhere in my loft is his framed drawing.

Now the hard work begins: acquiring accuracy; awareness; scanning the flight instruments; radar talkdowns; learning the emergency procedures off by heart; touchdowns on the runway at the correct point, correct speed and pointing straight. We may fly swept wing types in the future, where we need to understand and be ahead of what is happening. I am worked hard by a mix of instructors, some ex-Hunters, some ex-Canberras; somehow, you can tell them apart, although the patter is the same for any exercise.

Cross country flights to other airfields are planned, including solos. I plan to go to RAF Leuchars in Scotland, climbing to 25,000 feet en route and diving down the last 50 miles for a level break into the circuit. This is not appreciated, even though I have practiced it dual at Cranwell. A smack on the wrist on return by the Flight Commander.

Having finished flying, we cadets jump on our RAF bikes and race each other back to the College. Sometimes with John C. J. Thompson (later ACM) I would win and sometimes I didn't. We do stop and look before crossing the main road to Sleaford before racing the last 300 yards.

Instrument flying is relatively easy, as the Jet Provost has natural stability, and all our let-downs were controlled from the ground. One day, however, we call for a radar approach, stating our position. We carry out a turn for identification and think all is well until reaching 600 feet in the final descent.

The controller announces, "I see you overshooting, climb straight ahead to 2,500 feet!" At that moment we emerge from cloud and ahead us are flat green fields and no runway! Apparently, another aircraft had carried out an ILS approach to the same runway on a different frequency and we had been misidentified. Cautionary tale. Another time I am carrying out aerobatics solo above cloud and at the end I request a QGH let-down, homing to overhead Cranwell before descending on the outbound leg. I enter cloud and continue descent to the cleared altitude. Passing what I perceived to be 12,000 feet it becomes lighter in the cockpit and glancing outside I can see the ground rushing up to meet me. I level out and check my three-pointer altimeter; 1,500 feet, with the flag showing I was below 10,000 feet. Not the first one to be caught out with misreading the altimeter, nor the last. Luckily, no harm done, and lesson learnt: double check vital items!

This philosophy saves our bacon one Friday afternoon. My instructor has taken control and is showing me a quick way onto finals. As we are the last aircraft returning, we're late, with the runway caravan already being moved. He pulls onto the final turn, calling, "Finals, three greens."

"Clear to land, expedite taxi in," is the reply from the tower.

I glance down at the undercarriage indicator, expecting to see three green lights. The sun was streaming into the cockpit, so when I cannot see them I shade them with my hand. Still no green lights. We are rolling out on runway heading.

"I don't see three greens!" I shout.

"OK, going down." My instructor pushes the down button. Within seconds, clunk, clunk, clunk, and three bright green lights.

"Three greens," I announce. Seconds later we touch down and roll to the end. The instructor says nothing. Was he checking my awareness, or was this a genuine error? Whatever the situation, from there I had good empathy with that instructor to the end of the course.

At Easter in our third year, I ask to go on a Service Visit to 56 SQN, flying Lightnings at Coltishall, where I have a contact – Flt Lt Ernie Jones (later Wg Cdr). Under his wing I spend a few days at the squadron drinking in the atmosphere, admiring the huge twin-engine machines that take off like a rocket and on landing thump into the runway at 150 knots with a braking parachute fluttering behind. Ernie takes me airborne in the SQN taxi – a Hunter T7 – and we set off over the North Sea, climbing briskly to 30,000 feet. I had asked if we could go supersonic, so having cleared it with radar, we dive at a steep angle, and full throttle gradually reaching Mach 1. Throttling back, the speed decreases quickly. At altitude Ernie shows me high speed stalls in steep turns, with the speed reducing even at full throttle. The fuel gauge suggests time to return, and we feed into a precision radar approach to the southwest runway. Even with undercarriage down and full flaps, the approach speed seems fast, but we thump down on the runway and the brakes stop us in good time. Clearly, a lot to learn.

Boarding the Hunter T7, 56 Squadron RAF Coltishall

One day, with another instructor, I am criticised for not getting the nose wheel off the ground at 65 knots during a take-off at Barkston Heath in a cross wind, flying a Jet Provost Mark 3. He emphasises the point during my pre-flight briefing for a solo trip for general handling. Being keen, as I race down the runway approaching 65 knots, I pull back hard on the stick. The nosewheel lifts, followed by the aircraft. I am flying at stalling speed, crabbing along the runway about 10 feet up, running out of runway and ideas. Fortunately, Barkston Heath is on a hill, so as I pass over the boundary fence, I push the nose down and gain precious speed, reappearing to the air traffic controller about 20 seconds later climbing away normally. He checks all was well. With heart racing I assure him I am in a normal climb and changing frequency to approach. No harm done, no enquiry, another lesson learnt. Lucky boy!

In the final year at College, things get very busy. During the day the academic staff are talking aircraft stability, stick fixed and stick free, supersonic airflow, and all the equations that go with that. On the flying side we are converting onto the more powerful Mark 4, with night flying until three in the morning. I kept going on strong coffee, every hour on the hour. I stay awake until my head hits the pillow, having set an alarm for the morning drill parade. The pace is too much for some of my colleagues. Some bow out of the Science specialist stream to concentrate on flying and officer studies, some leave to go to University, having found flying not to their liking. I am fortunate in that by going to Nottingham some weekends I can relax and get my breath back. The finishing line is coming into view, and all around us is encouragement to keep going. The exams are coming up, on the ground and in the air. On the ground we sit the exams for AFRAeS, myself and Tom Sawyer being the only two to reach the required standard. In the air I complete a pre-final handling check that is so good that the examiner says it would do as the final handling check.

Only the Instrument Rating on 18th July to go, and, with that complete, no more flying for me. The three refresher sorties are not required, and no, I cannot fly them! The chief instructor says of my flying that if anything I was verging on being over-confident in the air. However, I will be going on to advanced jet training at Valley, Anglesey, possibly on the new Gnats, possibly on the old Vampire T 11s. This is the next step if I want to be a Lightning pilot. Life is a blur, until suddenly we are all told we have completed the course and to concentrate on getting ready for the Passing Out Parade and the Graduation Ball. Apparently, I had done well on the science studies and would become the Course Science Prize Winner.

A different routine now ensues:practice for the graduation parade, with a fly past of the station's aircraft; accommodation to be booked for visiting parents and girlfriends coming to the Ball; finding a slot for that final short back and sides; sorting out clothing and buffing boots till the toes were like mirrors. My mother and my oldest brother, Michael, come up for the events and we are able to team up with my main flying instructor Paddy Hine. Together we head for a dinner in the Green Dragon in Lincoln, where champagne flows during the many toasts. Mum had been dubious about my becoming a jet pilot but now, with the Graduation Parade the next day, all is smiles.

No problems with the Graduation Parade, where we are inspected by Sandhurst Drill Instructors as we form up away from the Main Parade Ground. Afterwards my Flight Commander informs me I am the smartest cadet on Parade, much to everyone's astonishment. My batman grins as I pass over a fiver later that day.

Graduated at last with proud mum beside me.

The Graduation Ball goes very well and with all the hard work behind me I am able to thank my ground and flying instructors for getting me into shape. My friend Martin Herring and his girlfriend turn up in an open horse drawn carriage – wow! He too is going to Valley for advanced jet training. My Ann, who had encouraged me to keep going throughout the course, is getting a flavour of service life. There are dance bands in three ante rooms and a delicious meal. It is a night to remember.

A few weeks off, then off to RAF Valley, Anglesey, with Snowdonia on the doorstep.

I am to report to the Station mid-August – another course, another adventure in prospect.

Time off and living in Woolston Southampton makes me realise that the new jet trainer, the Folland Gnat is being made a few miles away at a factory at Hamble. I write a letter to the manager requesting a visit to the production line as I am a potential trainee pilot. I can make my way to the factory by bike and in uniform with my RAF identity card – Form 1250. He writes back a few days later with a date a week ahead. I snap up his offer of a visit and present myself to the security guard. He looks at my letter, makes a call and a young man turns up to collect me.

I am introduced to the managing director, who explains that the RAF is insisting on several modifications that need to be incorporated on the aircraft on the production line. It will be several months before Training Command gets its first aircraft and then instructors will need to be trained. However, I am welcome to view the production line, meet some workers and see a publicity film. The factory is ringing with high-speed drills as I see several fuselages being worked on. I am introduced to some workers, and we go into a room and close the door. I ask some questions and get comprehensive replies. The Indian Government is interested in it as a single-seat fighter, as well as Finland. The RAF want it as a two-seat trainer. I am told that it is very encouraging for them to see a young, enthusiastic RAF pilot, as opposed to the long faces of the men in suits from the MOD. After a few handshakes the workers go back to the production line and the manager takes me to a conference room and signals to a projectionist to run the Film. It covers the concept of the "lightweight fighter" and the development of the Folland Gnat and its own lightweight ejector seat. It is very impressive, and I would certainly like to fly one. It will be several years, however, before I get a back seat ride in the back of one based at RAF Valley. By then I will be firmly a helicopter pilot, flying happily up to 100 mph and at times hovering 30 feet above the sea.

Chapter 3: Advanced Jet Training

August 1962 – December 1962

Mid-August and we trainee pilots from 81 Entry assemble at No. 4 FTS RAF Valley, Anglesey. We are welcomed by the Squadron Commander, Sqn. Ldr. Lee, and are informed that we are the last course flying the Vampire T11, as the Folland Gnat was not yet ready for us. The Vampire T11 has 2 Martin Baker ejector seats, side by side, with a canopy that opens up, hinged at the back, which must be jettisoned before the ejector seats can fire. The safe limits for ejection were above 200 feet from the ground, level or climbing, and at least 100 knots airspeed. Descending on final approach don't eject below 500 feet, you will not make it. We start Ground School with lectures on the systems in the Vampire. Simple jet engine with centrifugal compressor, inefficient but robust. Something new – pressurisation keeping cockpit pressure at half ambient atmospheric pressure. Select "ON" before take-off and select "OFF" before opening the canopy after landing. It's noisy and hot on the ground, but above 30,000 feet (minus 55°C outside) the canopy will ice up gradually, leaving just a small clear patch on the windscreen. The wide track undercarriage and nosewheel mean it is stable when taxiing, although the brakes are weak, so just walking speed in dispersal. Top speed low level, around 460 knots. Limiting Mach No .8 above that and control is difficult. The aircraft is cleared for aerobatics, including spins and tail slides. If you are descending out of control, eject before reaching 10,000 feet. Suitably impressed, there is a lot to learn for us student pilots; a new cockpit layout, new checks, and a new way of operating. To cap it all off, the airfield is being worked on, so every day there may be a different way of taxiing to the runway in use; check the airfield map in the briefing room before flight. We are taught theory of flight again, and basic aerodynamics, and yes, there will be an exam at the end of Ground School before we start flying. We need to learn the checks by heart – start up, taxi, pre-take-off, post-take-off, climb, cruise, pre-aerobatics, descent, pre-landing, finals, post-landing and shutdown. Write them down in a big notebook and recite them until you can recall them when required. The Pilot's Notes are a slim volume compared to the Jet Provost, but there are limits to learn, so again, they are written down in the big notebook. There is an emergency check list in the form of flip cards that fit into a flight suit trouser pocket, so always available to confirm actions already taken and to list considerations. The engine fuel system has no acceleration control unit, so great care is needed when opening the throttle from idle rpm as the engine might stall/lose thrust and the jet pipe temperature will exceed limits. This is especially important on final approach – keep high engine rpm until crossing the boundary hedge, when the throttle can be safely closed. (I notice that on the first flight with a new instructor their fist is behind their throttle on final approach, in case I try to close it too much).

Eventually we begin flying. My first flight is with F/O Pavey on the last day of August. As we accelerate rapidly down the 9,000-foot runway, you can see that the Vampire was designed as a fighter. We leave the circuit, climb rapidly, and at 20,000 feet take a look at the local area. Underneath, the flat expanse of Anglesey, to the east, the mountains of Snowdonia, minimum safe altitude if in cloud 5,500 feet. Most of Wales is a low flying area, and we will spend some time there navigating at high speed at 200 feet above the ground. Out to the west, the Irish Sea and the coast of Ireland, and to the north, the Isle of Mann. To the south a large Danger Area, where air to air guided missiles are being tested and pilotless aircraft are flown as targets. Not active every day, so check the briefing board before you fly. Returning to base, we join the circuit on the "dead side," noting two others in the circuit.

We join the downwind leg at 1,000 feet QFE and call "Downwind roller," before carrying out the pre-landing checks, including undercarriage down and partial flap. Coming abeam the runway threshold, we turn towards the runway and start a gentle descent, aiming to be pointing at the runway by 500 feet. This achieved, "Finals three greens."

"Cleared roller landing."

We continue down, lowering full flap and closing the throttle as we cross the boundary hedge at 105 knots. We touch down and the throttle is opened slowly to full power, while keeping straight down the runway. A few seconds later the ground drops away and we climb to 1000 feet and turn onto the downwind leg. This time it will be a deliberate overshoot on finals, simulating runway blocked.

At 500 feet, nicely lined up, we call, "Overshooting." The throttle is slowly opened and I feel the surge of power. Once we are climbing, the undercarriage comes up and flaps are retracted. Levelling off at 1,000 feet we continue ahead and then turn onto the downwind leg, calling, "Downwind full stop." Pre-landing checks again and continue to Finals. Throttle closed as we cross the boundary fence with 105 knots, touch-down with 8,000 feet of runway left, so as we slow down the throttle is opened a little so that we can vacate the runway at the end as quickly as possible. Clear of the runway, we stop and carry out the after-landing checks. Pressurisation off, noticeably quieter. Flaps retracted, clear to taxi back to dispersal, checking the brakes, and bringing the speed back to walking pace as we enter dispersal with all of its activity. We see the marshaller ahead with his bats. He points to a shutdown spot, and we turn into the line using the brakes, come to a halt and begin the shutdown checks. Engine shut down, canopy open, the ejection seat pins are inserted. Ladder is alongside, time to get out, make coffees and then debrief.

"This flight was your familiarisation flight to show you the local area," intones my instructor. "With the mountains nearby, if in cloud stay above 5,500 feet until air traffic control instruct you to descend. From now on your instructor will expect you to come up with the checks when required. Also, he will introduce you to emergencies. We generally have very few and the aircraft as a whole is very robust. The engine uses a lot of fuel, especially at low level, and without engine power you will descend at 4000 feet a minute. Our sortie flight times are usually 45-60 minutes duration. You will be shown how to recover to the airfield if the engine stops and you are in cloud in the local area. You will also be carrying out instrument flying under the hood and you will also practice talkdowns to 200 feet above the runway, guided by a GCA radar controller using Precision Radar. You will also see the missed approach procedures should you not see the runway approach lights."

The days pass quickly, in good weather at least one flight a day, sometimes two. Something new every day, with at least two circuits at the end of each trip, sometimes using the engine normally and sometimes with the engine throttled back, so zero thrust. Like this, the aircraft descends rapidly, and judgement is needed to decide when to lower the undercarriage on final approach and to engage the drag inducing flaps, always aiming to touch down about a third of the way up the runway. Like the rest of our course, I am flying with a different instructor most days, but the pre-flight briefing, instruction during the flight, and post-flight debrief for the same exercise are always the same, thanks to "Standardisation." Eventually I am deemed safe enough to be launched into the circuit on my own, my first solo on type. This is my 3rd flight on 2nd October, just 40 minutes in the circuit, practicing roller landings with the final full stop landing at the end. I forget about the empty seat next to me and concentrate on where I am in the circuit, what calls to make and what checks are required. It goes without a hitch, but I feel pounds lighter when I climb out of the aircraft back in dispersal. That evening I am celebrating with others our first solos on type and speculating on which OCUs we might be going to at the end of the course. But, far away in the world, events are happening which are unknown to us young keen aviators, will affect control our destinies, nevertheless.

By now I had spent 2 weekends with the station's Mountain Rescue team, there to go out and find aircrew who have ended up in the local mountains, for whatever reason. The team is comprised of volunteers drawn from all trades of the station and they go out to Snowdonia every weekend to practice their skills. I am picked up by the lead truck of our small convoy of vehicles at 6pm on a Friday night and we head off to Snowdonia. When we meet congested traffic, our driver puts on the siren and flashing headlights and the traffic parts like magic. Reaching our campsite, the requisite number of tents are erected, including the cookhouse. Everyone is allocated a camp bed, a sleeping bag, mess tins, and metal mug and KFS, and a roster is drawn up for essential duties. It is first name terms for everyone, but we all respect the team leader's requirements and plans for our exercises, all dependent on the weather. The first day out we practice stretcher lowering over a cliff face above Betws-y-Coed. I volunteer to be the casualty, so I am given a crash helmet, goggles, thick gloves, and a heavy duty overall to protect me from falling rock fragments as they are prised off the surface by the numerous ropes. It takes a lot of time, is slow work, and needs good cooperation from the whole team. Below me, someone is controlling the stretcher, making sure it isn't snagging on the rock face as it is slowly lowered. That evening we all walk to Betws and go to a barn dance with our heavy boots on. The young ladies keep well clear and shout encouragement in Welsh as we struggle manfully with the sequences. With the fun over, we partygoers make our way back to base in bright moonlight, walking up the main road singing Welsh songs and hymns. I sleep well that night and wake to the smell of frying bacon and coffee. The sky is blue. Life is looking good. Daybreak, and another adventure beckons. Today, navigation between grid references using map and compass.

Some weekends I can get a lift across to Nottingham with F/O Phil Langrill, an instructor, where Ann is attending University, reading Medieval and Modern History. As before, her fellow male students are willing to provide me with a mattress on the floor of a room in their hall of residence so I can stay overnight. In the morning I join the queue for breakfast, and at a big table I enjoy talking to students about their way of life – having as much fun as you can, while you can – a big contrast to my disciplined existence. During the day I walk with Ann in the local park and explain what is happening with my training and what my future is likely to be. At the end of my current course, it will be off to an OCU for further training on jet fighters or bombers and then possibly an overseas tour; Germany, Middle East, or possibly Far East. She is in her final year, so she is working hard for those exams next summer. There is a lot to learn, and the exams involve written essays. A cosy and secure world for the moment, and it is a very different world from the being involved with the military, which is exciting, strenuous, and unpredictable.

Flying becomes more interesting as we move away from the confines of the circuit and the local area. Instrument flying begins, under the hood, so you can only see the flight instruments and nothing of the outside world. You are in the hands of air traffic controllers; they can give you "steers" to get you back to base, or "true bearings" to help you navigate. When the weather is bad with a low cloud base, you can request a GCA (Ground Controlled Approach), where you receive instruction to get you to half a mile from the runway threshold, at 200 feet above the runway. From this position you should be able to see the runway approach lights and make a landing. If you don't see the lights, open the throttle fully and climb away straight ahead initially. There are procedures to ensure you don't hit the ground or collide with other aircraft in the vicinity. For your part you need to obey the instructions of the controllers and achieve and maintain speeds, headings and altitudes as needed. Power will need to be adjusted, the aircraft trimmed, and appropriate checks carried out.

Initially I have trouble with the basic engine fuel system; the rpm tends to overrun my requirements. I need to develop patience, make a throttle movement, and wait for the rpm to stabilise. Similarly, I need to accurately trim the aircraft in level flight, as altitude needs to be kept within 100 feet and airspeed within 10 knots of the requirements. It is hard work, needing concentration, a continuous scan of the flight instruments, and anticipation of the next change or check list requirement. However, it is uplifting when the instructor tells you to "look up" at 200 feet on a ground controlled approach and there is the runway, dead ahead. "Head down and overshoot" are usually the next instructions. Slowly open the throttle, gaining height, undercarriage coming up, gaining speed, adjusting flap, reporting 2,000 feet to ATC, change of altimeter setting. The more you do the easier it seems. Another 3 years and I will have got it mastered ...

Ann makes it across to Snowdonia for a weekend. She has not seen mountains close up before. However, starting at the Pen y Pass car park in the Llanberis Valley, we set off along the footpath towards Crib Goch, a prominent ridge that connects to the summit of Snowdon. It is a popular route, and we are overtaken by youth groups, striding ahead. The path steepens and becomes rocky, now more a scramble than a walk. We stop many times to catch our breath and admire the view. Eventually we make it to the top of the ridge, gasping for breath, and squat down on boulders, drinking in the spectacular view of the lakes below and the knife-edge ridge stretching towards the Snowdon summit. The leader of a youth group offers Ann an orange, as she appears exhausted. Eventually she is happy to descend, and we pick our way down until meeting an area of scree, which we start running down. As we slide down, more or less in control, something tells me there is something wrong. We slither to a stop, and I look further down the scree and see a sharp line across our proposed route, a sign that the scree is above a drop. We move slowly sideways off the scree onto steep grass, making our way slowly down past a precipice. We learn later that two lives were lost when a scout group ran down the scree and fell over the drop. Cautionary tale.

However, at a later date Ann and I make the transit of the Snowdon Horseshoe, Crib Goch, Crib y Ddysdl, Snowdon Summit and Y Lliwedd, descending to Llyn Llydaw, and then the broad Miners' Track back to Pen y Pass. To this day, when we see an aerial view of the area, Ann wonders how she did that. After that, on further visits to Snowdonia it is more strolls around lakes than scrambling up mountains, challenging though they were. Things are developing quickly in our relationship. We both realise that if I am posted overseas and we are not married that will probably be the end; so we get engaged on 21st October in the village of Nant Peris in the Llanberis Valley, meeting up with two of Ann's friends from university for a celebration dinner in the famous Tyn y Coed Hotel in Capel Curig. With that settled, I concentrate on my training, course after course, exam after exam for the next six months. Ann works on getting her degree, and we meet up from time to time as events allow.

I am so busy with flying, learning to drive and pass my driving test in Holyhead, and operating with the Mountain Rescue Team, that the Cuban Missile Crisis in late October passes me by. I learn later that aircraft and crews of Bomber Command on quick reaction alert (QRA) were brought up to cockpit readiness, ready to scramble, and held for several hours until the crisis was over. I am told that Russian diplomats who monitor the bomber bases raced back to London to tell Moscow what was happening. Nothing I could do about it, of course, so being in a state of cheerful ignorance was helpful, as I was busy from dawn to dusk with more mundane matters.

Surprisingly, in the middle of our course we trainees are given notice of our OCU slots, some to fighters, some to Canberras, and some to the V Force. I am to report to the Valiant OCU in the first week of January at RAF Gaydon in Warwickshire. The next day, before flying starts, the Chief Instructor calls me into his office; something important, obviously. For me to finish my course in time to meet the start date for my OCU, there will be changes to my course. All formation flying will be dropped, but I will be given priority on a daily basis and, weather permitting, I would fly up to 3 flights a day. My course would be tailored for the Final Handling and Instrument Rating Test to be scheduled for mid-December. I would fly with any instructor, but the flight briefings should be the same. Some of my colleagues are going to V Force OCUs, but I am the only one going to the Valiant in January. Others are going on to the Hunter OCU in north Devon at RAF Chivenor, with possible postings in the Middle East. Their courses start in March and April, by which time I should have finished my OCU and be on an operational squadron. With enhanced status as a "priority" case, my name features on the flying programme every day and I am offered a weekend away at a "Jet Meeting" at RAF Middleton St. George (now Teeside Airport). I fly the trip with instructor Phil Langrill and learn a lot about the "real" Air Force, outside the training regime. En-route to Middleton St. George at 25,000 feet, we look up their radio frequencies. With our 10 fixed channel (fixed frequencies) VHF set, we can only get them on "RAF Common," which is a babble of messages cutting across one another. We have to communicate as we want a let-down and GCA for practice, which I am to fly. We call Middleton with our details and requests. Amazingly, they come back loud and clear, and we are identified and begin a descent to the overhead. All goes well with the GCA and at 200 feet on the final approach I am instructed to look up. Ahead is the long runway, so I aim for the threshold, throttle closed over the boundary fence and 105 knots, touching down a few seconds later. We taxi in slowly towards a mass of aircraft in a big dispersal. As expected, we spot the first marshaller and get handed on eventually to a third, who points to our slot in a long line of Vampires. As we leave the aircraft for the "Line" office in a nearby hangar to sign in our aircraft in, we are mixing with other crews from Meteors, Vampires, and

Canberras, in their slate grey flight suits with squadron badges on the shoulders. Later in the bar before dinner, still in our flight suits, my instructor and I are on the fringe of a group of gesticulating pilots, handwaving to describe their manoeuvres. We hear the Canberra pilots boasting how high they can go in their machines, 50,000 feet plus, putting our Vampire to shame. However, getting down from very high altitude is a problem for them as the axial compressors on their Avon engines need high revs to prevent compressor stall, and if you put the machine in a dive you run into control problems with limiting Mach No. Clearly, I have a lot to learn and realise how well protected we trainee pilots are in our closely supervised environment. OK, for me, then, it is clearly going to be new knowledge and experience every day for the next fifty years.

Next morning, as we go in for breakfast, a notice on a blackboard shows the start-up, taxi and take-off times for all visiting aircraft, sequenced at five-minute intervals. Flight plans for our return to base have been submitted; plenty of time for a good breakfast and listening to the conversations. The return flight goes to plan, and we call Valley for a GCA on recovery to make good use of a training flight.

Life is hectic, big decisions are being made, and around me the system is working hard to get me through the course on time. One day, having flown two trips by lunchtime, I notice that I am not scheduled for a flight in the afternoon. Plucking up courage, I ask the Chief Instructor if I could carry out a solo cross country followed by aerobatics. He grins, and writes the trip into the authorisation book for take-off at 3:00 p.m.

He briefs me on the sortie and then says, "You are costing the taxpayer £10,000, so make good use of the trip."

I plan out a route that I have done before, with easily identified turning points and the final leg being along the A5 and exiting the LFA at Bethesda. I take things slowly to get everything right and get off on time and head for Snowdonia at 5,000 feet. I can see the boundary of the LFA and begin descending, adjusting the speed to 360 knots, as I pass over Porthmadog. My eyes are scanning the horizon – no use looking out sideways, as everything is a blur. Nicely on track, correct speed, trimmed slightly nose up so if I relax on the controls the nose will start to come up. The turning points are coming up on schedule, no other aircraft seen so far, so concentrate on the final leg, starting at Capel Curig and following the A5 to Bethesda. Up comes Lyn Ogwen, roll on 60 degrees of right bank and pull hard to get round the corner, avoiding high ground. Ahead is Bethesda, the boundary of the LFA, so full power and enter a steep climb, aiming for 25,000 feet for aerobatics. Hassel checks, then loops and barrel rolls, ending with a tail slide. You seem to wait for ages before the aircraft flips nose down; don't move the controls until the airspeed is above 150 and increasing. Everything stabilised at 20,000 feet, fuel check, 25 minutes remaining, so time to go home.

Visibility is good, I can see the whole of Anglesey with the airfield in the far corner. Nose down, I want 2,000 feet initially; I swoop down, airbrakes out, looking out for other aircraft around Mona airfield. Nothing seen. Slow down to 250 knots and drop to 1,000 feet, aiming to join the circuit on the dead side. Change to tower frequency and call, "Joining dead side."

"Runway 15, left hand, QFE 1012, 2 in."

Checking the fuel, we have 15 minutes endurance, but I feel that landing straightaway is best, so call, "Downwind full stop," and am cleared to final approach and complete the pre-landing checks. Concentrate now on achieving the correct speeds, don't throttle back to idle until over the boundary hedge. Gentle touch down well up the long runway, but I still need to apply power to keep going to the end of the runway before turning off. Thankfully, I can now switch off the pressurisation; much quieter and cooler.

Flaps up as well, slow taxi back to dispersal, checking the brakes and dead slow as I spot the marshaller. In my slot, time to shut down and open the canopy; with seat pins inserted, I can get out. I sign the aircraft in, 45 minutes flying, no snags. In the crew room I fill in the authorisation form "DCO" – duty carried out.

The Chief Instructor comes across the room. "Everything OK?"

"Yes – good flight."

"Well done. I have you down for 3 flights tomorrow, mainly instrument flying."

First coffee doesn't touch the sides as it goes down; the second one disappears quickly too. The Hangar is a mile from the Officer's Mess, so this time I will walk back and get some fresh air and exercise after all those hours breathing pure oxygen from my face mask.

An advert on the notice board catches my eye. "For sale – green minivan, 1 year from new, with 2 pop up passenger seats. Owner posted overseas at short notice so good price of £330." I contact a young airman, and agree to the price if I can get a £300 loan from my bank in London. It takes 10 minutes on the phone before a personal loan is granted, with a £20 arrangement fee and £20 a month payment until the loan is paid off. Being a van, I should not exceed 50 mph, so I keep an eye on my rear-view mirror for patrol cars. I have windscreen wipers, no wash/wipe, no heater/no rear demist, but I can get to the engine if needed to fix things. Good sense of freedom; having got my licence two weeks earlier driving the examiner around Holyhead in the driving school car, and now my first set of four wheels of my own, with a large flat space for carrying kit. I notice other small vans in the Officer's Mess car park; young trainee pilots, no doubt.

The mountain rescue team are camping in the Idwal Valley, close to the Idwal Slabs rock climb. The Slabs are a smooth rockface at an angle of 60 degrees, best climbed in trainers rather than boots. Our team leader leads the way on the first 100-foot pitch, belays on a strong point, then watches us as we almost walk up the slope with our weight on our feet as much as possible. Being safeguarded by a rope from above gives you confidence to try things. It works well, so later we try a long, difficult route on Tryfan. We need our climbing boots for this and a range of climbing techniques before we get to the twin pillars on the top. We take the easy way down and meet up with the Idwal Valley civilian volunteer mountain rescue team. They invite us to their hut near the main road and an open area on which helicopters can land. The civilian teams are called out by the police to look for missing walkers and to help fallen climbers. Their source of funds is public contributions, and they are clearly well financed, being equipped with stretchers, ropes, first aid kits, cold weather clothing, and radios.

The course now concentrates on instrument flying (IF). It is easy to enter cloud, not so easy to descend out of cloud without hitting the ground or losing control. With myself under the hood, the instructor does the take off and hands over to me in the climb. I call out all the checks and on handover start making all the radio calls. As we gain height, my instructor reminds me to keep scanning the flight instruments and not concentrate on one and forget the others. Also, it is very easy as a solo pilot to become anxious when flying procedures and to overbreathe (hyperventilate). Unfortunately, if you do this you can lose consciousness for a few seconds and lose control – the cause of several jet crashes, it is thought. So, as far as possible, relax and breath slowly. When flying procedures, plan your mind to expect to overshoot the approach, and that seeing the runway is a bonus. I fly as instructed and soon we are over the Menai Straights at 25,000 feet, ready for unusual attitudes. The exercise involves the instructor mishandling the aircraft, after which you are required to recognise the problem and then, recover the aircraft into a full power climb, all with minimal height loss. Starting with a spiral dive, and then a gamut of nose up, near stall situations, steep turns, sometimes with power applied, sometimes with low power, sometimes clean, sometimes with undercarriage down, flaps down and airbrakes out. With that completed, I am instructed to return to Valley and request a GCA and overshoot. On speaking to Valley Approach, I am instructed to steer certain headings and make turns. These show up on his radar screen and we are identified. Only then do we get instructions to descend to 3,000 feet on the airfield QNH 1018 and set speed at 250 knots and initial heading of 300 degrees. While descending, my instructor reminds me not to get into bouncing above and below the glide slope on the GCA; just adjust the power slightly to change rate of descent. Keep the airspeed constant until you see the approach lights. When instructed, I carry out pre-landing checks and, on setting the QFE 1,016 (altimeter figure), check my altimeter is lower than my instructor's by the elevation of the airfield above sea level, 60 feet. We are instructed further to descend to 1,500 feet QFE, reduce speed to 200 knots and prepare to turn onto final approach heading. On turning onto 150 degrees heading, I am requested to complete my landing checks and confirm three greens. I do the final checks and my instructor sets QFE on his altimeter and cross-checks it reads the same as mine.

As we approach the three-degree glide slope from underneath, the controller instructs, "Begin descent now for three-degree glide slope."

I throttle back and we begin descending. I receive a continuous commentary on my progress down the glide slope, using rudder to make small changes in heading and very small changes in power to keep on the glide slope. Passing 500 feet, I cross check our altimeters. They both read the same.

My instructor tells me, "When you are instructed by the controller to look ahead for the lights, look up, then carry out an overshoot."

I look up as we pass through 220 feet and the whole airfield and main runway is ahead. I slowly open the throttle to full power, calling, "Overshooting."

"Clear straight ahead to 3,000 feet on QNH 1018 and maintain, call Valley Approach with intentions."

I set the QNH 1018 on my altimeter. As we are climbing, I lift the undercarriage and, checking airspeed is sufficient, retract the flaps.

"Request another GCA and we will land off this one," intones my instructor. So doing, the Controller takes me north of the airfield to let two aircraft into the circuit to land ahead of me. A few minutes of straight and level before I am turned back to the airfield. This time I will be landing, so quickly run through in my mind what I will be doing in the last 200 feet before touchdown. I am aware that my mind is tired, and I try to relax. Do things slowly and deliberately, that's the trick. It all works well, and I feel my shoulders relax as I look up at 200 feet to see the 9,000 foot runway ahead. Throttle back a little, aim for the threshold, throttle right back crossing the hedge, 105 knots – on the button – rumble rumble from the undercarriage – I need not have worried; all that training is now paying off.

Back in the crew-room, my instructor debriefs me on the flight. "You clearly understand the main points, but you are capable of flying more smoothly, with very small movements on the throttle, and being ready for the next check, procedure or ATC instruction. A few more trips and we will put you up for your Instrument Rating and then after that, Night Flying, Cross Countries dual and solo. We plan your Final Handling Check around 20th December. That's the plan. Keep at it, you are doing well."

I sit down for five minutes getting my act together. So far so good. Just carry on the good work. More of the same. Keep learning. Now a gentle walk back to the Officer's Mess; my batman will have sorted out my bed, my room, my shoes and laundry. At 5:00p.m., toast and jam, tea and coffee will be available in the Ante room ready for tired trainee pilots. At the weekend the mountain rescue team will be looking at Snowdon and the various routes up to the summit. This the non-flying side of the RAF. I am learning a lot about the trades that my rescue colleagues are involved with and the circumstances in which they work. I feel very privileged to be a jet pilot under training. One day I will be doing a useful job after more than three years of training so far.

I am now concentrating on instrument flying, just the same procedures; nothing new, just building up accuracy, awareness, and anticipation. I understand one of my colleagues has been chopped off the course, as his instrument flying is not good enough. He is leaving us for a career in the Provost Branch. I happen to be in the Chief Instructor's office and see the names of our course on the big board and how we are progressing. Given priority, I am well ahead of the field, and the frequent flying ensures that my flying skills and airmanship are continuously improving.

I am down to fly my Instrument Rating Test with Flight Lieutenant Vickers. I have not flown with him before. His briefing – what he wants me to demonstrate – is straightforward enough. I have done all these exercises before. Just a question of keeping calm and producing the goods. The flight goes well; everything I am asked to do, I have done many times previously, so no anxiety there. The flight is complete after 45 minutes. My standard is acceptable, but I should look to improving my accuracy, the smoothness of my flying and to taking every opportunity to practice procedures so that they become second nature. Now, I will go on to night flying and to fly cross countries, including land aways, dual and solo. Another tick on the big board; the end of the course is coming into view. The instructors are very encouraging, talking about life after training, on an operational squadron, possibly based overseas. Just keep going, keep learning, keep improving. I sleep well at night and need the alarm in the morning, welcoming another day, another memorable experience.

The course moves on to night flying, circuits, roller landings, dual and solo, not aided by work on the airfield, which brings in taxiways not lit with normal edge lighting but with goose neck flares, and at times having to cross the active runway to taxi to the start of the runway in use. Also, if you are planning to leave the circuit, that take off clearance is given on approach frequency to save you taking your eyes off the instruments just after take-off to find the radio frequency selector, which is tucked away in the dark cockpit. We are instructed to land well up the long runway and try not to stop descending just prior to touch down but just fly it on. We should look ahead for the runway edge lights, allowing our peripheral vision to give us height judgement. It will feel like the runway edge lights are coming up to your shoulders just before touchdown. With that advice, the touchdowns are quite acceptable, no heavy landings and no "I have control" from my instructor. These chaps must have developed nerves of steel watching their charges feeling their way down to the runway. The cockpit lighting on the small instruments reflects 1940s technology, and I have a forward-facing service torch clipped to my life jacket as a back-up should the lighting fail. The outside world with its street lighting in towns and villages is very pretty, but does not provide a horizon or any indication of your speed through the air – both parameters you need to know to fly safely. Some strips of road lighting mimic runway lights, so you need to identify the airfield beacon with its light flashing an ident in morse code. Other aircraft in the circuit can only just about be seen amongst all the other lights, so you need to keep a mental picture of where they all are and where they are going. Danger points are when joining the downwind leg and on finals, when the temptation is to look out towards the runway, neglecting the flight instruments and risking stalling at a low height. Awareness is the key, practice makes perfect, another three years and 100 hours should do it. However, I need to concentrate on my night

79

flying test, carried out by our CO, Sqn Ldr Lee. He apologises for the difficulty in getting round the airfield, with work bring carried out on various taxiways. My standard of night flying is acceptable, and I listen carefully to the debrief. Again, I need to work at improving my awareness of what is happening to the aircraft and where it is going. Either you fly the aircraft, or it will fly you. Valuable lesson learnt.

That night at three in the morning, when we have completed night flying, fellow trainee Frank Hoare offers a lift to three of us back to the Officers Mess. On arrival we all feel hungry and decide to try the kitchen for some "night flying supper." Using our initiative, we find cold cooked chicken legs, salad, bread, butter, and the wherewithal to make brew of tea. While discussing our recent hair-raising moments, I agree that one weekend I will walk them up to the top of Snowdon from the Railway Station at Llamberis. I arrange accommodation at a climbing cottage in the Idwal Valley, run by a mountain guide.

We set off early Friday afternoon with the aim of walking the next day. The forecast is dire, however, there is a big parade being planned for the station. So, having arrived at the cottage, we decide to go up at night. We have the gear, and our host knows when to expect us back. We start in daylight and make swift progress up the good track, with the light from just one torch being sufficient for all of us. Eventually we arrive at the café at the top but, being now in cloud, there is no view. Martin Herring pulls out his handkerchief and there is a tinkling sound.

"That's the car keys, nobody move." We search around our feet amongst the gravel with our torch and luckily, they glint. Having found them, they are secured deep in a zipped rucksack pocket. We head back down the mountain and are soon back at the car, and heading for the cottage for a late supper. Next day, rain and gales from dawn and the parade is cancelled. We trainees head for Nottingham to meet our other halves.

The pace of flying hots up with high level navigation, not in sight of the ground, using true bearings from various RAF Stations along the route. Finally, a descent from overhead RAF Valley, descending outbound and turning inbound, continuing descent to a check altitude, all being monitored on the ground using bearings on a cathode ray tube (QGH). All RAF airfields can offer this form of descent through cloud or at night, not using ground-based radar, so useful to practice them to build up experience. Emergencies are thrown into every flight when there is a quiet moment. The instructor wants to see what initial actions you would take and draws your attention to the emergency flip cards you carry in your flight suit trouser pocket.

Cross-countries take a new purpose, with a land away at RAF Linton-on-Ouse in Yorkshire. It goes well, with our aircraft being turned around and refuelled while we sign in, grab a coffee, and check the weather forecast for our return. Returning to RAF Valley we work Midlands Radar, a surveillance radar, and they hand us over to RAF Valley without the need to be identified. We request a controlled descent through cloud (QGH) and I follow the instructions. We pop out of cloud at 4,000 feet with the airfield in sight and join the circuit for a full stop landing. Although the flights went well, my instructor, Flt Lt Poulter runs through all the important points again in a long debrief. I will be doing the trip solo in the next few days, so he is ensuring I understand what I need to do. On 18th December, with good weather, I am sent solo to Linton-on-Ouse and am back by lunchtime. All has gone well, so I get another solo trip just doing circuits and landings. After 50 minutes fuel runs low, so a full stop landing then back to dispersal for a shutdown. I glance at tomorrow's programme; one dual flight, general handling, then an hour later the Final Handling Check with the Chief Flying Instructor, Wg Cdr Edwards ...

Chapter 4: Final Handling Check

19th December 1962

"Good morning, David. For today's trip I would like you to plan a low-level cross-country in our local Low Flying Area (LFA). Here is the route. When we have completed that, we will climb up to 25,000 feet for some handling and aerobatics and then return to base."

Wg. Cdr. Edwards, Chief Flying Instructor (CFI), is briefing me on my Final Handling Check on the Vampire T11 at the end of my advanced jet training course at RAF Valley, Anglesey. It is the 19th December 1962, the end of five months of hectic activity. No time to reflect as I lay out my map, draw in the route, using a sixpence coin to give the right curve at the turning points at 360 knots, 6 miles a minute, a mile every 10 seconds. Ten minutes later the planning is complete, the flight plan written out with the salient leg headings and times scrawled onto my kneepad in chinagraph pencil.

He glances at my flight plan and my map and hands them back. "OK, let's go." I stuff the map into my flight suit leg pocket and follow him out to the Dispersal hut. He glances through the Form 700 – the servicing document for our aircraft, XD 445. "The pre-flight inspection has been done, there are no deferred defects, no limitations, and the fuel is full. Let's go to out to the Line and find our aircraft."

We leave the hut with our bone domes on, as it is noisy outside, with two ground crew, who will assist us with the start-up and initial taxi. Time for me to start talking.

"When we get to the aircraft I will do an external inspection, starting at the nose and working my way around in a clockwise direction. Then we will climb in, start up, check the brakes, and turn right onto the taxiway towards the threshold of runway 15."

As we arrive, I start my inspection with the CFI watching and listening. Going round the bulbous plywood nose, I am looking for damage, ducking down to examine the nosewheel for obvious damage, that the tyre is inflated and there are no hydraulic leaks. The engine air intake is clear and there is no sign of foreign object damage. Underneath, the starboard wing all looks normal. The leading edge of the wing looks undamaged. The wing tip is undamaged, as well as the green navigation light. The trailing edge is undamaged and the aileron is secure as well as the flaps, and the airbrake is stowed. The twin booms look normal, tail scrape bulges undamaged, and the elevators are secure. The engine jet pipe looks normal. A minute later the external check is complete, and I climb up the port side, step onto the ejection seat, noting the safety pin is still secure at the back of the seat. The ground crew are helping us to strap in. Firstly the parachute harness, ensuring that we insert the spring clip below the round rotating plate on the quick release box (QRB) after all straps are locked in . This will prevent premature releasing of the parachute straps should the QRB experience a shock loading during an ejection. Next the ejection seat harness is secured, with its QRB situated above the parachute QRB. When strapped, in the ground crew check that we are happy for the ejection seat safety pins to be taken out and stowed. All secure, I close the canopy, ensuring the lever is in the locked position. On intercom at last, I call out the pre-start checks from memory so that the CFI can both see and hear what I am doing.

Pressing the start button, the engine winds up slowly, and on reaching the minimum rpm I open the High-Pressure Fuel Cock. The engine lights up, does not surge, and accelerates to normal idle rpm. Unlike the Jet Provost I have just trained on, this engine has no acceleration control unit so it is easy to mishandle it, especially at low RPM. All systems working, so more checks on equipment, controls, oxygen, and radios. All is well, so chocks away and calling for taxi on ground frequency using my instructor's own callsign, 20 Alpha. We are cleared to taxi to the holding point, runway 15. I am marshalled forward, checking the brakes work before we go many yards, then right turn onto the taxiway, acknowledging the help of the ground crew as we set off at walking pace. Once clear of the line we increase the taxi speed and are soon approaching the holding point. On reaching we are directed to tower frequency and request line up and take off. We are cleared to line up but must change to approach frequency for take-off.

As we move onto the runway I complete the pre-take-off checks, turning on the noisy, hot pressurisation, and call, "Approach, 20 Alpha ready for take-off."

"Clear take-off – climb initially to 3,000 feet on this heading. Call reaching."

So cleared, I gently open the throttle. When I feel the brakes slipping, I release the brakes and open the throttle fully. I feel the push in the back as we accelerate along the newly resurfaced 9,000-foot runway. 80 knots airspeed, time to lift the nosewheel. A few seconds later the runway drops away; I'm waiting for the airfield boundary before lifting the undercarriage. Three clunks later the three red lights go out and I start the post-take-off checks. Passing 200 feet, our Mk 1 ejection seats will now work effectively. Calling three thousand feet, we are cleared for en-route navigation and set the QHH at 1018, crosschecking altimeters and levelling at 5000 feet heading for the first waypoint – Porthmadog. Soon we are approaching the Welsh coast in the vicinity of Caernarvon and the boundary of the LFA. More checks then, setting the airspeed at 360 knots, we begin a rapid descent to below 500 feet above the ground, but not going below 200 feet – difficult to assess as there is no radio altimeter, so it's the Mk1 eyeball for that judgement. The weather is fine, good 20-mile visibility, and cloud just on the peaks of the high mountains. If we get trapped below cloud going into a valley, it's full power and a steep climb to minimum 5,500 feet to ensure clearance of all mountain tops. There are enough crashed aircraft wrecks in the mountains, as evidence of past misjudgements. The countryside is flashing by in a blur, the sheep are not scattering because they don't hear us coming. I adjust the elevator trim so if I relax on the stick the nose comes up automatically. I can see the first waypoint, Porthmadog. When I reach it, I will turn onto a new heading for Dolgellau and start the stopwatch. Overhead. 60 degrees bank, turning onto next heading, starting the watch. So far so good. Don't relax. Keep focussed.

We are barrelling along across lumpy country. I can see Dolgellau in the distance, so set the heading marker for the next leg on the compass, ready for the turn. Overhead. Steep turn onto heading, pick a spot on the horizon straight ahead and keeping heading for it. When steady – quick glance at the Ts & Ps. All is well. The lake is coming into view and the waypoint – Llanwddy – is there slightly right of nose, so turn gently towards it. I can see the town and the dam clearly now, so turn in the overhead for Bala. All the time my head is turning left and right, looking out for low flying aircraft, helicopters, and birds. The big reservoir is coming into view, and I need the eastern end of it. Got it, turning on, seconds to go. On course, on speed. Good. Overhead the dam, turning left. On the new heading, I can see mountains on the horizon – Snowdonia. Familiar ground. Next waypoint, Betws y Coed. Did stretcher lowering over a cliff edge there with the mountain rescue team, but no time to identify the spot. There is the little town nestling in the valley with the main road – the A5 – snaking through it. I can see the famous Falls as we come overhead, turning below high ground on the right heading for Capel Curig, with its climbing centres and Outward Bound School.

We are flying along the A5 valley, between high ground, and need to turn early and lift up over high ground on track. After we pass Capel Curig, the distinct wedge shape of Tryfan mountain comes into view; I can see Lyn Ogwen coming up on the nose. Luckily, I did this last week with my instructor, so as we reach the lakeshore I roll on 60 degrees of right bank and pull 2G for five seconds to get us round the corner. This is the exit route from the LFA. Rolling level, we are pointing down a wide valley with the town of Bethesda at the end. Time for a sharp exit from the LFA. Full power and, selecting 15 degrees, nose up. I can see the huge hole in the ground on the left, a former slate mine, as the ground quickly drops away and we are climbing up towards the clouds.

"Valley Approach 20 Alpha climbing to Flight Level 250 overhead the Menai Straights for General Handling."

"Copied – QNH 1018, weather state Green, runway 15, left hand (circuits) surface wind 180/ 15."

"Copied."

As we climb, ice starts to form on the rear of the canopy, in spite of full heat being selected on the pressurisation system. After fifteen minutes at altitude only a small patch on windscreen remains clear, so flying on instruments becomes necessary. Approaching 25,000 feet, time for the pre-aerobatic Hassell checks. I run through them, ending with lookout – so a steep turn to check the skies are clear and we have a distinct horizon for use as a visual reference when recovering from manoeuvres. First, stalls and recovery, clean, then with gear and flaps down. Recovery to the climb. No surprises. Then some spins, first to the left. I still can't get used to the rapid entry as I pull back on the stick and push the left rudder pedal fully forward. Within a second, we are whirling around, nose down, and with 45 degrees of bank.

"Recover."

I push the right rudder pedal forward and progressively push the stick forward. With a lurch we stop spinning, I centralise the controls, and we are now in a steep dive. I look for the horizon, level the wings and, checking the airspeed is increasing, gently pull out of the dive and recover to the climb. We have lost three thousand feet in seconds. Our minimum altitude to eject if we can't recover is 10,000 feet; we are sitting on Mark 1 Martin Baker seats, after all. These aircraft were first flown without ejector seats, a sobering thought.

After a spin to the right and recovery, some aerobatics, starting with loops. Another good look round, then full power nose down, required airspeed, a 2G pull and up we come. As we go over the top, slacken off the G to prevent stalling, and as the nose goes down, reapply. Pointing straight down I recognise Caernarvon Castle between the clouds, confirming we are staying in the local area. Straight into another loop and then some barrel rolls. Then we need to climb to 30,000 feet to experience flight at high Mach numbers. A good look round again, temperatures and pressures are normal, fuel is down to half full – sufficient. Luckily, I did this exercise with my instructor this morning, so I am mentally prepared. It takes a long time to reach the required height; the D.H Goblin centrifugal engine, reliable though it is, is low on thrust at altitude, so patience is required. Eventually we get there, another all-round look out then, heading away from the sun, we enter a steep dive at full throttle. Slowly the airspeed and Mach No build up. Then, around Mach 0.8, the effects of shock waves generated over the wings make their presence felt. The aircraft is shaking, rocking, and pitching uncontrollably; the controls are ineffective. It is unpleasant.

"Recover."

I throttle back and gently pull back on the stick, we are in a steep dive after all. Suddenly, all is well. The Mach No has dropped as we enter warmer air and although the airspeed is high, we can recover normally to a climb. This aircraft was designed during the war, when there was little understanding of the effects of high speed at altitude. It must have been an unpleasant shock for fighter pilots when they lost control, or worse still, experienced control reversal.

"While we are here, we can look at max rate turns, the first one to the left – keep turning until I give you a roll out heading."

Setting full power at 250 knots, I pull into a 60-degree banked turn and pull G until I feel a gentle buffet as we are getting close to stalling. There is more drag as we pull G, so the speed drops and I ease the G and angle of bank to keep height. Eventually the situation stabilises at 200 knots and 30 degrees of bank, just nibbling at the buffet – good stall warning.

"Roll out on 360 and climb to 25,000 feet again and we will look at Tail Slides," (or Hammerhead Stalls).

A few days ago, I practiced these with my instructor, so I am ready and know what to expect. Another good look around, all clear, nose down, full power, I want 250 knots before pulling up into the vertical. I look out sideways at the horizon, making small adjustments to keep going straight up. The airspeed reduces quickly and dropping to 50 means we are now sliding down backwards. Holding all the controls central, I start counting. One, two, three. We lurch over backwards, and for a few seconds fishtail as our vertical descent straightens out. Watching the airspeed, I need 120 knots before levelling the wings with the horizon and pulling out of the dive, initially only gently, looking out for the buffet should we approach the stall. Within seconds we are climbing back up to 25,000 feet. Looking over the side I can see the Menai Straights, so we are still in our local area. A check on Ts & Ps and fuel; down to one third, so must be returning to base shortly. I was not expecting that.

As we level, "Practice engine failure." My instructor closes the throttle and I need to push the nose down to prevent a stall. I also need to turn towards base somewhere on our right.

"Valley Approach, 20 Alpha, practice engine failure, request homing and let down."

"All copied, make your heading 290, call passing 20,000 feet."

"Assume you can't restart the engine on the way down. I want you to make a glide approach and landing."

"Valley Approach 20 Alpha passing 20,000 feet, 2 souls on board, request descent in the overhead for glide approach and landing."

"20 Alpha set QNH 1018, weather 4 eights at 8000 feet, runway 15, left hand, surface wind 180/20 knots. You will be cleared for descent in the overhead, call visual with the field." With things settled I check Ts & Ps, the engine is at idle rpm (so I can only open the throttle slowly if needed), fuel is one quarter full, so enough for an approach and one circuit if required.

In the overhead, above broken cloud, I can make out the coast but not yet the airfield. With the circuit being left hand I need to circle to the left. Need to conserve energy, height, and speed, and need to stay close to the airfield. We are descending like a streamlined brick towards broken cloud. For a successful approach and landing I need to achieve "high key," starting the downwind leg at 4,000 feet, and "low key," turning onto finals at 2,000 feet. Emerging from broken cloud with 300 knots I am too close to the airfield to make an immediate approach to the runway in use, but I have sufficient height and speed to join on the dead side at 6,000 feet plus. I can see the airfield clearly now under the port wing. That will be plan A, trading speed and height for the distance to the start of the downwind leg. Decision is made for me, good. Quick check, engine is still running at idle, there if needed, reassuring. Concentrate now on getting the required parameters of position, height, and airspeed.

Looking good as I call, "20 Alpha visual with the field."

"QSY tower."

"Valley tower, 20 Alpha, request join dead side 6,000 feet for glide landing." Clear join, one in, downwind for full stop landing, set QFE 1016, call downwind. 30 seconds later, "20 Alpha downwind, high for full stop landing."

"Clear to final, one clearing the runway."

Pre-landing checks, but undercarriage staying up, flaps remaining up, QFE set at 1016 descending through 3,800 feet, crosscheck, harness check secure. Abeam the runway threshold, height passing 2,000 feet, time to turn onto finals and reduce airspeed to 200 knots, aiming to be lined up with the runway at 1,000 feet. We are high so would land long, so undercarriage is selected down, three clunks, three green lights.

"20 Alpha finals, three greens."

"20 Alpha, clear land, one joining."

Still very high, so selecting half flap and adjust the trim. After a few seconds we are still very high, so full flap, the nose dips, and I trim back. I want to land about 1,000 feet into the runway so dive for the threshold at limiting airspeed for the flaps. At 200 feet I begin the round out as we are descending fast. The airspeed reduces immediately. I am aiming for 105 knots at 50 feet above the runway centreline. Normal touch down abeam the 1,000 foot marker, good.

We are slowing down quickly, so gently open the throttle to keep the speed up; we have several thousand feet to go before we can vacate the runway and there is an aircraft calling downwind. Turning off we come to a stop; post-landing checks; pressurisation off, the last of the canopy ice clings on but I can see well enough. All checks OK, and on ground frequency we are cleared back to the line. Fast taxi back to the yellow line at the entrance to the line, then braking to walking pace we are marshalled back to our slot. Handbrake on, chocks in, we can shut down and open the canopy. The ground crew insert the ejector seat face blind pins so that we are safe to get out.

Still pumped up with adrenaline, I greet my instructor as he comes around the nose. "No sign of obvious damage, no obvious oil leaks, no unserviceabilities."

"Right, I will sign in, then debrief." The CFI signs the authorisation sheet – 55 minutes, duty carried out. "Right David, that FHT is satisfactory. You will be going on to the Valiant OCU early next month. You will recall that to get you through in time we had to tailor your course, we chopped your formation flying and some general handling. We gave you two, sometimes three flights a day. That good continuity showed today. Some of your colleagues will not be going to their OCUs until March or April, so they are being held back. Your instructor F/O Wells will want to debrief you now. Congratulations."

I manage a smile, "satisfactory" is all I want to hear.

D.H. VAMPIRE T11 – Two seat Jet Trainer, RAF Valley, Anglesey. DEC 1962.

Postscript:

"White with one sugar, I believe." My flying instructor, F/O Wells waves me down to a seat in the crew room and pushes a mug of coffee in my direction. "How did it go, any surprises?"

I get out the map and show him the route and the planning. He wants to keep them (could be useful for other students, I'm thinking). We run through the exercises that the CFI had lined up and what I did. Luckily, I had done them all with him in recent days, so I was well up to speed. I knew the parameters that were required, and I was able to produce them to order. He seems very keen to hear of my experiences – *was I his first student? He seems very pleased that I had satisfied the CFI. Was I the first of our course to do a Final Handling Check?* The good result is going down well with the instructors and my colleagues, so smiles all round.

The Squadron CO comes in and shakes my hand. "Lanigan, your course is finished, report to OC Admin this afternoon, and collect your Clearance Chit. With luck you will be off the Station within a few days and you will get Christmas at home. Some of your colleagues may be here still in April."

I could hardly say then that I had enjoyed the course, the enthusiasm, the aerobatics and the low flying. The Vampire T11 was certainly robust, I never did tail slides in any other aircraft before or since. In the hectic few months at Valley, I had completed the course, spent weekends in Snowdonia with the Station Mountain Rescue Team, passed my driving test in Holyhead and got engaged. I talk to my instructor about his conversion next year onto the Folland Gnat, which had been designed for our course. I explain that I had been to the factory at Hamble in August and met the workers on the production line. They were struggling with the number of modifications that the RAF were requiring to be incorporated on the production line. They seemed pleased to see me and I was amazed how small the aircraft was. It would be some years before I got a flight on one of them.

As a parting shot, my instructor warned, "In the air what matters is skill, knowledge, experience, and discipline. Good luck."

I complete the Valiant OCU in April 1963. On debriefing the course, the Station Commander presents me with a letter from Valley, saying that now all students had completed the course, they were awarding the prizes, and I had secured two – for my flying and my ground studies.

Little did I expect that I would be coming back to Valley a few years later to train as a helicopter pilot, as the Valiants I had flown were being chopped up for scrap on the orders of the then Prime Minister – Mr Harold Wilson. My future was now to be operating at low level over land and sea. No more aerobatics at altitude, no more strapping into ejection seats, no more oxygen masks or pressurisation. The future was going to be operating below 10,000 feet often close to the surface, land or sea, in all weathers, by day and by night.

Chapter 5: VALIANT OCU

(January – April 1963)

"Welcome to RAF Gaydon, home of No 232 Valiant OCU." So speaks Wg. Cdr. Flying on Monday 7th January 1963, to an audience of training aircrew and OCU staff. "While here you will fly mainly as formed up crews of five. Once you have finished the course you will go to your respective squadrons and become part of an established crew. Flights are conducted always using Standard Operating Procedures and standard language. You will have two weeks ground school in this classroom, followed by the procedure trainer and the flight simulator for pilots. In that machine we can practice start-ups, shut-downs and emergency procedures. After that will be flying the Valiant on a number of exercises by day and by night. We plan to finish your course in early April. Your postings on completing the course are on the noticeboard. Good luck."

I meet up with our Captain, Flt Lt Jock Wingate, ex-Navy (Sea Hawk fighters) – his medal ribbons allude to various campaigns – very easy to talk to, and seems relaxed all the time, possibly because he has seen it all before. Coffee and biscuits are being served and I meet up with members of our temporary crew.

Jock says, "I have checked the noticeboard, David, and we are both going to Marham, you to 49 Squadron and me to 207 Squadron, both Bomber I'm afraid, so we will end up doing QRA," (Quick Reaction Alert). "Our Air Electronics Operator is Flt Lt Trembling and our two Navigators are Flt Lt Ward and Plt/O Lane."

Looking round the room I appear, as a 21-year-old Plt/O, one of the youngest here. Most of the staff have medal ribbons, grey hair, and glasses, and lots of experience around the world, no doubt, with the post-war RAF. Jock produces the training schedule for the week, pretty much systems, systems, and more systems, and this is the earliest and least complicated of the 3 V Bombers. This afternoon we start on the D/C electrical circuits with their bus-bars, circuit breakers, generators and batteries. Tomorrow it's A/C electrical systems. I will need a good night's sleep before tackling that. The days in the classroom pass quickly; outside there is deep snow. We are not flying at the moment, so no problem, but walking from the Officer's Mess to work you need to watch your step. Plenty of breaks for coffee and lunch and we get the weekends off to relax. Compared to the Valley Experience this course is very gentle.

During our 2 weeks of ground school we learn that that the max speed is 0.82 Mach and the range 4,500 miles with underwing tanks. We take our exams on what we have learnt. There are multichoice answers and we use a pencil to tick the appropriate box. Afterwards, our tutors run through our mistakes so we can make a note of them; a voltage here, a frequency there, and yet another oil pressure to remember. Lots of these systems are covered by the emergency checklists and warnings displayed on the Central Warning Panel. Another 3 years and I will understand it all …

Now we pilots progress on to the Emergency Trainer, a part of the fuselage containing the pressurised cabin within which we all work. To get to our ejector seats, we have to climb up a few feet from the main cabin. We have a good view forward but will not be able to see the swept-back wings on the real aircraft. The cockpit is quite spacious, and all the important levers and switches are located in the middle so either pilot can reach them. For me, as co-pilot, I have to monitor brake pressures during taxi, and they are behind my right shoulder so I have to squirm my way round in order to see them every few minutes. Between the seats on the cockpit floor is enough room for 2 pilots' Nav Bags, plus a stack of inflight meals in cardboard boxes. The rear crew sit in

3 seats facing aft with a long tabletop and various screens, dials, switches, and angle poise lights. It is not my responsibility, so I am not told anything about what goes on. Their seats house parachute packs should they need to bail out. For safe escape crewmembers require a minimum of 2,000 feet above ground and they need to pull the parachute ripcord once clear of the aircraft. Up front, to escape as pilots we need to jettison an overhead hatch by pulling up on a lever which triggers explosive bolts. As it departs it pulls out a safety pin on the top of our ejector seats, allowing them to be activated using the face blind handle above the head. The face blind provides protection from the slipstream as the seat leaves the aircraft at 84 feet per second. This should be enough speed to clear the fin and tailplane. Also in the roof above the Navigator Station is a hatch that can be opened if we ditch and need to deploy our multi-seat dinghy. For astro-navigation, which works anywhere in the world, there is fitted a periscope sextant, which luckily can also be used to view the top of the aircraft from outside, should it be felt that damage has occurred, say, following a multiple bird strike.

The flight simulator is good for practicing all the drills, normal and emergency, on the ground and in the air, using the "Challenge and Response" system, nothing left to memory. It takes a long time from strapping in to get 4 engines started and all systems functionally checked before being ready for taxi, then yet more checks during taxi, besides pre-take-off checks and checks on the runway before opening the throttles for take-off. The acceleration seems slow after the trainer jets I have flown, but eventually we lumber into the air and climb away. After take-off checks, air traffic instructions, climbing checks, and then radar handovers with change of squawk, so we can be identified and our altitude monitored. Once we are straight and level, we look at handling emergencies, starting with engine failure, then moving on to engine oil pressure failure, engine fires, autopilot malfunctions, and many others. Clearly, we can accept a lot and still carry on, or return to base or divert to an airfield with a 9,000-foot runway. We practice airfield approaches using ILS with two engines throttled back and then overshooting using full power on the two good engines, countering the expected roll and yaw effects from the asymmetric power. If not correctly flown the aircraft will roll over and crash so I need to remember that ...

On 4th March I eventually get to fly. As our crew bus trundles out onto the snowbound airfield, I am looking out for a white painted aircraft parked in a remote dispersal. Our made-up crew of 5, headed by Flt Lt Court, QFI, step out into the cold and with no external check climb straight into the cockpit. Already the external power is on and our "Chief" is on the ground in front on the external intercom, ready to monitor our start up. Ten minutes later we are starting the engines and with the cabin door closed and locked we can switch on the pressurisation, and with it some heating. All is satisfactory on start up, so I call for taxi and within minutes we line up on the snow cleared runway, looking up at a grey sky. The take-off is uneventful and soon we are at 20,000 feet heading out towards the North Sea. I am given control of the aircraft and practice 20-degree banked turns rolling out onto specified headings. As befits a bomber the control response is appropriately slow and with powered controls, no effort to control. The tailplane trim system, in coarse and fine mode, is immediate and effective. We engage the autopilot, selecting the various modes we might use in future. The time in the flight simulator has not been wasted. Behind us the two navigators are practicing using the nose mounted ground mapping radar, looking at the coast and its communities, which are "painting" well on their cathode ray tube. Sometimes they go into "conference mode" so their conversation does not drown out the standard crew intercom. Up front we can recall them at the push of a button. After 2 hours at altitude, we descend back to base requesting an ILS approach. The ground-based radar vectors us onto final approach and our Captain flies the first ILS approach and overshoot, calling for checks when needed. He carries out another ILS approach for a roller landing.

At 200 feet on final approach, he requests "Flaps fully down." As the flaps move I can see the airspeed dropping back 15 knots and he corrects the nose down attitude change with nose up coarse trim. We touch down and he requests 100% rpm for the engines. I feel the surge in power and within seconds the ground drops away. "After take-off checks."

I call out the checks and carry out his instructions. Soon the undercarriage is up and the flaps retracted, and approach radar is vectoring us round for anther ILS and another roller landing; this time it will be my go on the controls as handling pilot. Happily, it all goes smoothly, and I call out the checks when I need them and our Captain responds straight away, acting the role of non-handling pilot. All the time I am watching the fuel consumption and managing fuselage and then wing tank consumption to keep wing bending stress to a minimum. Over time the centre of gravity moves forward, and I need to ensure it stays within limits. After 4 hours, it's time to land and shut down. After landing about 1000 feet up the runway, our Captain waits for 80 knots airspeed before applying the brakes and we reach the end of the runway at walking pace, turn off and carry out the after-landing checks. Back in Dispersal the crew bus is waiting, and we are soon back in our Operations building, drinking coffee and going through a debrief of the flight we have experienced. A number of flights are scheduled along with simulator trips for the next 4 weeks, weather permitting. The aim is that the course finishes early April, when we will go to our Operational Units where we are apparently sorely needed.

Two days later and we are scheduled for another flight, concentrating on take-offs and landings as well as emergencies in the circuit. Even for this flight, close to base, we carry a full five-man crew. We brief for me to do most of the flying with some demonstrations by our Captain, Flt Lt Court. During take-off I begin to lift the nosewheel at 100 knots; at 140 knots the ground drops away. I hold the aircraft in a shallow climb as airspeed increases, calling for after take-off checks as we climb through 500 feet. Reaching 2,000 feet, Radar vectors us around for an ILS approach which will be for a roller landing. It goes well as I maintain the appropriate speeds for the weight of the aircraft at the time. These landings are into wind and using 4 engines so relatively straight forward. I carry out 4 roller landings and then our Captain takes control for to demonstrate a few emergencies.

Now in the visual circuit and "Downwind," at 1,000 feet he pulls two circuit breakers to remove hydraulic power from the flying controls. They feel rock solid, but with both of us straining and pushing hard on the rudder pedals we achieve 10 degrees of left bank and the aircraft is turned onto finals a long way out. He demonstrates how effective the coarse trim is as an elevator, so no straining there, just anticipation. The undercarriage is lowered, and flaps lowered 20 degrees, while pitch is controlled using his trim switch. We overshoot that approach at 500 feet and level at 2,000 feet when he restores hydraulic power to the controls. Wonderful to have full control again.

The next landing will be our final landing and our Captain positions the aircraft downwind at 1,000 feet, and then pulls back 3 throttles to idle, advancing the remaining one to 100% rpm. At this low weight we maintain height on the power of one engine, albeit on full power. As we apply bank to turn onto final approach, we begin a gentle descent, maintaining speed. We roll out on finals at 500 feet, then lower the undercarriage. We begin another gentle descent. As it becomes clear that we will land well up the runway we lower 20 degrees of flap. At 200 feet we lower the flaps to 40 degrees and at 50 feet close the throttle to idle. The airspeed comes back quickly, and we touch down about 1000 feet up the runway, braking normally at 80 knots and slowing to walking speed to leave the runway. At the debrief our Captain emphasises that these are demonstrations to show what can be done with the aircraft with these problems but not to be repeated by ourselves on serviceable aircraft in the future. The

Valiant was designed so it could be flown without hydraulic assistance to the flying controls, the only one of the 3 V Bombers to be able to do so.

After the "Emergencies" flight, our made-up crew are now allowed to fly a four-hour cross-country, more than 2000 miles, in UK airspace to gain experience for the Nav Radar (NavRad) and the Nav Plotter (Nav Plt) to work together. At altitude, the nose mounted radar can see more than 100 miles, both forwards, backwards and sideways, working well when we are flying in cloud or at night. The navigators spend most of their time in "conference" so the rest of the crew do not hear their deliberations. Up front, my job, as non-handling pilot, is to talk to the ground-based UK Surveillance Radars, part of the Air Defence System. Sometimes, when we plan trips, if we add "Embellish" to our submitted flight plans, we are advised of fighter aircraft coming up to intercept us for practice. Even though we are informed of their proximity and we can see them on our own radar, often we can't see them visually unless they are "trailing," making condensation trails. Even large aircraft such as a B52 Bomber can't be seen when passing underneath by 2,000 feet, much to their anxiety. Apparently at altitude, the eyes focus on the nearest solid object – the cockpit window frames, about five feet away – and therefore cannot see another object outside, which is out of focus, a mile away, against a continuous grey background where sky and sea merge with no clear horizon.

After 4 hours we are close to our "Top of Descent Point," a position the navigators have assessed for us to start descending from 36,000 feet at 1,000 feet per minute, at 250 knots airspeed, in order to arrive at 5,000 feet 20 miles from our airfield. With the strong wind at the aircraft's altitude, today a tailwind of 150 knots, we start descent over Northern Ireland, more 250 miles out. The Surveillance Radars clear our route with other traffic and hand us over to our own "Gaydon Approach" about 50 miles out. They vector us for an ILS for the active runway and we request a roller landing and further ILS. Checks, checks, and more checks as we prepare to make an approach. Depending on the weight of the aircraft I determine the initial approach speed and the other speeds we will need later. The lighter the aircraft, the lower the speeds. Often in bad weather the captain will get the co-pilot to fly the approach down to 200 feet (which can be hard work) and then take over, fully refreshed to make important judgements of height and speed during the landing. Sometimes we get the autopilot to fly the ILS approach down to 200 feet, while still monitoring the controls, which are moving, and the ILS centreline and glide slope. It is annoyingly good, but we are still in a job.

One day I notice on the flying programme that there is flight with another crew that only has four crew on board. I make enquiries and am told that the Nav Rad is not required so I make my bid to fill the spare seat. Within minutes that request is agreed, and I am given a quick briefing on how to exit the aircraft and deploy my parachute. I meet up with the crew and the Nav Plt says he will instruct me on the use of the aircraft's ground mapping radar. It feels strange taking off sitting in a dark space, no view outside, hearing the engine noise and watching a few dials change their readings. Once clear of the circuit, my colleague switches my intercom to conference and he begins to instruct me on the radar screen in front of me. Certainly, the system is very flexible; the aircraft can be placed at the bottom or the middle of the screen or move up the screen as we progress over the land. He shows me the strong returns on the screen from Scarborough and by putting a cursor on that point of the screen and dialling in the Lat and Long for that point, he shows me on another dial our current position in Lat and Long. Also, he can change the use of our radar screen so that we can see returns from aircraft near us; the higher we are, the further out we can see them. The aircraft also carries a Doppler system, which gives us ground speed and drift and can be used anywhere in the world. To get this information, the aircraft needs to make transmissions, so in wartime it is unlikely to be used. To be able to navigate anywhere in the world without needing ground stations and without transmitting from the aircraft means that the time-honoured system of astronavigation is taught and practiced. Too quickly we are returning to base for circuits, and we switch the radar to standby. I have learnt a lot about what goes on down the back in the darkness and how to navigate and bomb targets in cloud and at night. On the debrief I mention how useful it has been for me to understand what goes on down the back. Apparently, I have been lucky to have bagged that slot as few opportunities occur. I notice that the rear crew members are reluctant to talk to me about their job. Is everything they do still new and classified? As I don't "Need to Know" how they do their job in order to do my job, that is probably why they clam up when I start asking questions. However, my trip reaches the ears of Wg Cdr Flying and he is very supportive of my actions and says that my experience will be invaluable in working with rear crew members in the future.

The course progresses with long cross-countries, by day and night, out over the Atlantic towards the Faroes so that our navigators can practice their astronavigation. We are so far away from Highland Radar's head that they can only see us on their screens by our secondary radar response from our IFF equipment. We are advised many times about the proximity of other aircraft, but we don't see them and they, in return, don't see us. With an hour to go before the planned end of the flight, crews feel comfortable about having a drink from their own carton of fruit juice, as facilities on board are somewhat limited. Most trips return with enough fuel for an approach, overshoot and then another approach for the final full stop landing. I am getting used to the standard procedures and the numerous check lists and can usually anticipate what the captain needs next. All the time I am noting down the fuel usage, checking centre of gravity and, on approaches, working out the correct airspeeds for the weight of the aircraft at that time. Eventually on 3rd April I carry out my final flight and I become qualified as Co-Pilot, day and night.

A day later the Station Commander debriefs me on my course: well up to standard for attitude, my flight in the back of the aeroplane drawing particular praise.

"All being well," he says, "you will be back in three years' time for your Command Course." I am on the first rung of a very long ladder, and conscious of how much I need to learn and understand about the Valiant, operating on a squadron with an established crew, and about the Air Force generally. But I have made a start in the fixed wing jet world, after three and a half years' training. An operational squadron beckons at last.

Chapter 6: No 49 Bomber Squadron RAF Marham, Norfolk

"Good morning Lanigan, sit down. Welcome to No 49 Sqn and RAF Marham." It is mid-April 1963. "Our mission is to support the NATO commitment to Deterrence against the Warsaw Pact Alliance." So speaks Wg Cdr. Langston, Navigator, CO of the unit. "This station supplies four aircraft and crews to maintain the QRA around the clock. On average you will spend one day in seven on QRA when your crew are designated "Combat Ready." At the moment the Squadrons are autonomous, meaning we have our own aircraft and ground crew, though the station is looking at Centralised Servicing which, on paper, should be more efficient. Security is very tight here, so you will have to get used to necessary procedures. Firstly we operate on the "Need to Know Principle," so you will only be told enough to do your job. Don't be tempted to ask your crew members or other crews any questions about what they do or how they do it. Almost all information that you have access to is classified, and not to be discussed outside the room where you receive it. No classified material is to be taken off the base without prior authorisation. When you are on base, wear your ID badge and carry your F.1250 at all times. When you are off base, don't wear your ID badge and don't tell anyone that you have access to secrets or what you do and where you fly. Most days the base is monitored by diplomats from the Soviet Union using cars with CD plates, parked near the airfield boundary fence. The RAF view is that the USSR needs to know that the Deterrent Force is real and ready to react if needed. The Squadron has recently switched to attack at low level and the aircraft are now camouflaged. Our Squadron aircraft are dispersed around the airfield, and we only use this hangar for inspections and rectifications. We share this hangar and offices with 207 Squadron, which is another bomber squadron. In the next hangar is 214 Squadron, which specialises in air-to-air refuelling, which does not involve us at all. You will be part of a new crew captained by Flt Lt Baldwin, who has just completed his co-pilot tour here. Previous to that he flew Canberras in Germany. Good luck."

I meet up with my captain in the crew room and meet other crew members: Flt Lt Kingdom, Nav Rad; F/O Dale, Nav Plot; and Sgt Foster, AEOP. Our captain takes us for a tour of the Operations Centre. At every department our ID badges are examined and the door shut before any conversation begins. Our first room is the Operations Room, where all flights are authorised and flight plans checked before we walk out to the crew bus to go to our aeroplane. The Planning room is vast, with plenty of space for navigators to lay out their maps edge to edge. Their favourite plotting chart is a Mercator projection, scale 1:1 million, white, a grid of Lat and Long, no relief, just coastlines and a few major cities. As a co-pilot I am not to take part in the planning process, as this is the domain of the Nav. Plot and Nav Rad. As we head up the corridor, we pass the target study rooms and the aircrew flight kit locker room. Eventually we reach the restaurant, where the duty chef immediately offers to make a pot of coffee for us and conducts us to a table where we can sit down and converse. Bomber Command has learnt that its crews function best if fed well before, during, and after all flights; ours can be up to six hours long. As coffee arrives, we are presented with menus so that we are aware of the range of food that is available for pre-flight, in-flight, and post-flight meals. There are normal and low cholesterol options, all cooked to order; very impressive, and available 24/7. My job will be to look after the in-flight rations, in white cardboard boxes marked with our names, and ensure they taken aboard the aircraft and secured. The cartons of fruit juice are not normally opened until the last hour of a flight. At the end of a flight, we are to leave our boxes on the aircraft so that the groundcrew can make use of uneaten food and drink. Another facility my captain and I will be training on is the flight simulator, where I am made aware that my capability as a pilot in command might be called upon if the captain becomes disabled for any reason. We will practice emergencies which we cannot do on the real aeroplane, such as engine fires, autopilot malfunctions and tailplane trim runaways. We will carry out approaches to various airfields and overshoots, some using asymmetric power. If we crash the simulator through mishandling, our instructor can press a reset button and all the lights come back on and we are airborne again. Just before we leave the building for a flight, we would empty our bladders, as on board facilities are basic. Also, there is a test rig for checking our oxygen mask and intercom are functioning correctly before flight. Small crew buses will ferry us around the airfield as needed.

My Captain talks me through a typical flight. This could be high level navigation, followed by descent to low level, to the start of a Route (1, 2, 3 or 4) at 500 feet above the surface, judged by rad alt, at 250 knots airspeed to place minimum stress on the wings (designed for high level flying with no turbulence.) Route 1 runs from the north coast of Scotland down the eastern side and then down the spine of England, ending at the Wash and its practice bombing range. Navigation is done by using radar returns from the aircraft to the surface. The navigators give headings to fly and altitudes above sea level to be maintained. We should cross high ground with minimum 500 feet rad alt. It is important to stay on planned route as we are a big and noisy military aircraft and there will be complaints if we deviate from the authorised route. We might enter the low-level bombing range on the Wash, dropping 25-pound smoke bombs on a target amongst the mud flats. We get a score for accuracy from the range controller in code over the radio. Another flight might all be at high level, where we cruise at 0.73 Mach up to 40,000 and attack targets using our aircraft radar and speaking to a range controller who is watching our progress on radar towards the target on the ground. We transmit a radio signal when we would have released a bomb and he gives us a score, in code, in terms of range and bearing from the target where he judges our bomb would have fallen.

Finally, on 1ˢᵗ May, we crew up for our first flight together. At the pre-flight meal the rear crew point to me and say, "In the event that the aircraft is going to crash, and we have no chance of escape down the back, you are to eject. We feel that our gallant captain will stay at the controls, fighting the aircraft until impact. But if you survive, you can tell the Board of Enquiry what went wrong, and that information might prevent another accident."

I murmur, "I hear what you say and I will bear it in mind if it happens."

This flight is planned to carry out high level navigation and then request a practice Diversion to RAF Waddington, carry out an overshoot and return to Marham for final landing. All goes to plan, and most of us are having steak and chips for our post-flight meal, our appetite boosted by 4 hours breathing 100% oxygen. Training flights continue through May, several days apart, giving time for simulator rides and target study. I am nominated as Squadron Adjutant, and because I can't type, all of the CO's correspondence goes off to the central typing pool. I see a lot of paperwork around the movement of people in and out of the squadron. We have many crews, and the CO's office has a curtained off board showing the status and whereabouts of all crew members. Because of the QRA commitment, crews have to take their annual leave together, and only a few crews can be on leave at one time. Our captain plans at least six months ahead so we all know our situation. I volunteer to take over the Station Sailing Club. We have six small sailing dinghies in which we can teach people to sail. We have water access to a long and wide drainage dyke at Denver Sluice, so we can practice all manoeuvres. At the end of each session, we pull the dinghies out of the water and park them on a grass area. Everyone is on first name terms, which is relaxing after the atmosphere in which I work. There is a pub nearby serving excellent beer and chicken in the basket. Great activity to unwind, just the wind and weather to contend with.

Eventually our crew are deemed "Combat Ready," which means we can be rostered for QRA. Our 1st day on QRA we report to the Operations Centre and change into flight kit, boarding the crew bus for the QRA compound. On arrival we have a meal first, cooked to order before taking over our duty from a squadron crew. I see in the readiness room a number of tables with comfortable chairs and stacks of magazines and books. An hour later the scramble bell rings, and all crews are rushing towards the double doors and the four aircraft in the compound. Our aircraft door is open; we climb in and plug into the intercom.

"This is the Bomber Controller, Readiness state 05," comes a steady voice. This indicates "maintain cockpit readiness to start engines." After 15 minutes, the Controller announces, "Readiness State 15," so back to our readiness room, walking slowly between the guard dogs and their handlers with revolvers strapped to their waists. Another few hours with our magazines, books, and hobbies, before waiting for the next meal.

With the prospects of getting married to Ann, I need to secure accommodation. This is achieved by renting the "Courtyard Flat" in a big house in Kings Lynn, 10 miles away from the base. We are married on 24th August 1963 in her church at Shrivenham, near Swindon. The church is packed with villagers turning out to see who Ann had managed to secure. They approve of the fresh-faced youth in Air Force Blue wearing wings on his chest, and the members of my crew who have driven down from Norfolk for the day. We drive off after the Reception in the Village Hall down to Devon for a week's honeymoon. We move into the Flat and Ann is able to take up a job teaching in a school in the Fens using the local bus service. Flats were in short supply at the time and, being under 25, I have no entitlement to married quarters; there are none available, anyway, with Marham being a busy base with 4 Squadrons. For various reasons, the flat is not very good, and Ann and I look round to buy a house. We find a builder constructing two-bedroom bungalows in Downham Market and we put our cross on plot 5, becoming No 9 Trafalgar Road, watch it being built and work with the builder to get the best facilities built, since we would need for a long occupation. We move in July 1964 and Ann gives up teaching. When completed with garage and central heating, the cost is £2620. We look forward to a long occupation. However, news of the Valiants' problem gradually leaks out as we sort out the garden, meet our neighbours and explore Downham Market.

Outside the Church at Shrivenham where
we were married. 24 AUG 1963

After 6 months I am told that the Squadron is looking for a Survival Officer to teach survival techniques to the SQN crews. I am young and available, so I get nominated. As such, I am sent to the RAF Survival School based at Plymouth and team up with 11 others for a one-week course. There are classroom lectures and practical demonstrations of the kit in our single-seat and multi-seat dinghy packs. We spend many hours in single- and multi-seat dinghies in Plymouth Harbour, pumping up the floor, closing the canopy and deploying the SARBE radio, which enables rescue aircraft and helicopters to home onto us in open sea. We train using the RAF rescue launches of WWII vintage and get rescued by yellow RAF rescue helicopters. Then, a whole day being briefed for a three-day "Escape and Evasion" exercise on Dartmoor. We are given boots, cold weather gear, old parachutes, and equipment from survival packs, and then dropped off near a stream by a wood. We have to make our own shelter, find or fish for food, light a fire, cook, and make our own sleeping bags. After 2 nights we are given a message that we must get to a rendezvous with the local resistance movement by 6 a.m., travelling 10 miles across the moor by night, evading soldiers who will be looking for us. If captured, we will be interrogated for the information that we might possess. Not a pleasant experience if you are cold, tired, and hungry. By luck or good navigation, we all make it to the rendezvous unmolested and are rewarded with lots of hot coffee with a splash of rum, and sausage sandwiches. Teamwork matters in these situations, along with knowledge, experience of the outdoors and the instinct to survive in any situation.

Later, as adjutant, I see a letter from the MOD stating that there are two slots for a two-week Winter Survival Course with the Norwegian Air Force based near Oslo. I apply and get sent tickets for a BA flight from Heathrow and meet up with my co-survivor, who is a Canberra navigator. We are met at Oslo Airport by a representative from the British Embassy and get taken to their magnificent building. We are taken downstairs to a large room lined with bottles of drink. It is suggested that we will be popular producing a bottle after dinner, wherever we are. We both buy 4 bottles of spirits each very cheaply, destined for gatherings up-country. Suitably prepared, we are taken to a five-star hotel for the night and meet up with two crewmembers from the local Air Force Base. Over a good meal in town, we are briefed for our survival course. Next morning, we are driven some 30 miles north of Oslo to check in to a Ski Lodge alongside a Ski Resort Hotel, where a group of SAS air stewardesses are having a break from looking after their passengers. There is a lot of snow about, and we are taught how to use cross-country skis. We are shown their ejector seat parachutes, which have coloured panels; orange, white, and dark green. If you want to be found, you display the bright colours. If you want to hide, you cover your shelter appropriately. A-frame shelters can be made using long pine poles and branches. Shelters can also be made from packed snow – igloo style. We all have a go at constructing one, but eventually settle for a parachute as the roof. Not used for anything else, the parachutes can be folded to make good sleeping bags. The parachute cord is excellent for securing everything.

Next day we are taken to a frozen lake and each issued with a packed parachute. With our cross-country skis lashed to our boots, we open the parachutes, which fill like sails. Soon we are being pulled downwind across the frozen lake at walking pace, nice and controlled. Then we are instructed to turn our skis across the wind, dig in the edges, and pull hard on the billowing parachute. Now we are doing 30 mph, bouncing over the rough surface and heading for the shoreline at speed. 50 yards to go, we get the instruction, "Release." The parachutes crumple into a heap and we ski at walking pace to the shore, where we are met by a truck and a recovery crew. All is sorted as we are offered mugs of coffee to calm our nerves. After a big meal at 6 p.m. we are told we can spend 2 hours at the nearby hotel before being taken to our "temporary" shelter to enjoy the wind and the cold overnight. There is a good party atmosphere, everyone speaks English, everyone enjoys the whiskey, and everyone is enjoying the good life. At the magic hour our instructors drag us away to our Lodge, where we put on every stitch of outdoor clothing and boots. At our nearby shelter, he issues us with parachutes, and we make up our own sleeping bags and bed down for the night, remembering to have twice as many layers underneath us as above. I don't remember going to sleep, but I do remember waking up cold and stiff at 7 am. Time to trudge back to the Lodge for a hot shower, clean clothes, hot coffee, and a fried breakfast. Our instructors arrive and we head off for cross country skiing, and demonstrations of survival kit. The principles of survival, everywhere in the world, are the same: "Protection, Location, Water and Food" – in that order.

At midday a light aircraft is flying in circles above our location. We wave, of course, and a little package on a small orange parachute floats down. Inside is letter from Ann, sent to the Base and brought out to me as a morale booster. That is being looked after! Back at the Lodge for dinner, then having to cope with another party. Let's try out my bottle of gin. I don't remember anything about it, so it must have been a good party.

A few weeks later, back at Marham, I am giving a demonstration of how to control a parachute if you are being dragged over the ground by a strong wind. As a precaution I tie my parachute harness to a stout tree with strong rope. With half the Squadron around me I confidently pull the ripcord, and the chute spills out and fills. There is a twang as my safety rope parts, and suddenly I am being pulled across the ground on my back. Everyone to the rescue, pulling the bottom lines so as to spill the air. I come to a halt, am released from my harness, and my chute is gathered up. Congratulations – best demo for a long time. I am unsure whether my fellow crewmembers are being kind or are genuinely impressed with the power of the wind. Sensibly, RAF parachute harnesses have an easy to operate Quick Release Box (QRB) to undo the harness – positioned on the chest, so always accessible.

From time to time, Bomber Command holds "exercises" to keep crews alert. One day we are briefed for a Low-Level Flight over the Netherlands and Northern France to test the NATO Air Defences. We are one of several flights on the route. We coast in over a sand dune coast and fly over miles of flat country. Eventually we turn west towards France, crossing small hills and acres of vine-yards. Then we receive many dummy attacks by French fight-ers from all directions, the fighters pulling away steeply at the last moment. Flying straight and level at 250 knots, we must be an "easy target." Coasting out at Dieppe we climb up over the Channel under Radar control and carry out a practice bombing run on a target in central London from 36,000 feet. We are on our own up there.

Another day, another exercise. This time we are to carry two 2,000 pound dummy bombs, full fuel, with a big schedule of cross-country flying and hitting a target at a specified time plus/minus one minute. It is tough test for the navigators and pilots to have to fly headings and speeds very accurately. The navigators' work will be assessed after the flight. We set off along the 9,000-foot runway, accelerating at our usual slow pace. As non-handling pilot I call out the relevant airspeeds so the Captain knows what to do if we have an engine failure, and cross-check we both have the same readings.

I call "80 knots, 100 knots."

Out of the blue, a call from Air Traffic Control: "Take-off cancelled."

"Abort take-off," instructs my Captain, "Throttles closed, full flap."

I will be braking at 80 knots. We are slowing up, but at max all up weight of 80 tons, we have a lot of momentum. "80 knots," I call out. "Braking." I feel the aircraft shuddering as the Maxaret braking system applies then releases the wheel brakes. We slow to walking pace, and the Captain turns off the runway at the very end towards the dispersal that we have just left. Still moving slowly, he asks for the after-landing checks. With those completed he calls Air Traffic for an explanation.

"Your exercise was cancelled and we called you soonest."

"OK, but there will be a report. Please send over a fire truck to monitor the brakes and tyres for the next hour, they are going to get very hot."

As we get out, we keep our protective bone domes on as we walk to the crew bus, in case a tyre explodes. The crew bus moves off quickly, leaving the ground crew and fire truck in charge. At our post-flight meal our two navigators are very upset. They have put a lot of work into the planning, but they will get zero marks because we did not get airborne. I keep quiet, as I realise that if this incident had occurred a few seconds later we might have run off the end of the runway and broken up, as had happened to a Valiant in the US some years before.

A few weeks later we are climbing through 10,000 feet and as I look forward my main windscreen begins to craze, blocking my view. I inform my Captain and he asks me which layer of the windscreen is affected, the nearest or the furthest? I think the nearest; it is five feet away, and strapped in, I can't reach it.

"That's OK, that is the weakest layer. We can continue to fly with that problem, and I will do the landing at the end of the flight."

We continue up to 36,000 feet. It's minus 55 degrees outside and we continue with our Nav Ex, no problem. Returning to Base I fly the approach on instruments; down to 200 feet, our Captain takes over and lands and we taxi into our dispersal for shutdown. The windscreen problem is snagged and it is replaced. However, the message comes back that it was the strongest layer that had crazed, leaving the weakest layer to take the strain – obviously strong enough!

It is the morning of the 7th May 1964 and our crew are assembling in the crew room prior to starting to plan for our flight. Our flight is cancelled. There was an accident last night when a Valiant of No 207 Sqn crashed near Market Rasen, Lincolnshire and all the crew were killed. All training flights are cancelled pending inquiries. After an hour my Captain takes a call. We are both wanted in the flight simulator. The instructors are tight lipped about what is going to happen, but we are briefed for our asymmetric approaches and overshoots.

On the 3rd overshoot the Captain calls for "Flaps fully up." As the flaps come up and the aircraft pitches up, he trims nose down in the normal way. Then, "Tailplane Trim Runaway Emergency Checklist." I run through the checks and carry out the actions, but to no effect. We dive towards the ground and pulling back on the controls has no effect. There is a bang, the lights go out and the intercom goes quiet. We have crashed the simulator.

"OK Jim, just press the reset button and we can try that again," asks our Captain.

"Sorry, but your time is up, and you need to get out." As we climb out, we are met by a very grim looking Station Commander. "You are Crew No. 5 this morning. You all have taken the same action and crashed. No Mayday call, no attempt to eject. Don't tell your crew or others, as we have other crews coming through and we don't want them alerted to what will happen to them." Our crew are upset that we won't say what happened and whether it was linked to the accident.

From time to time, we are allowed to fly abroad on a rare Lone Ranger Flight. On June 19th we head off to RAF Idris in Libya with Chief Tech Brooks on board. Flying over France we get handed over from one Radar Controller to another with no difficulty and land at RAF Idris (now Tripoli International) after 3 hours, 45 minutes. As we open the crew door, we are met by a blast of hot desert air. We are welcomed on our arrival and after checking on aircraft servicing arrangements we are taken to our accommodation and are well looked after. We have two days on the ground before we fly back to UK. The first day we get a tour of the base, which is a staging post for aircraft flying out to the Far East. It also is a base for aircraft using the nearby bombing range in the desert. Touring round we meet many people, who openly discuss their jobs. In the big dispersal we see a number of Argosy aircraft from the UK. Apparently, when they were night flying around their base at Thorney Island near Portsmouth, people complained to their MP because their TV signal was interrupted; so aircraft and crews have been sent out to practice over the desert. Nobody here to make complaints. Next day we are taken to the Tripoli to experience the marketplace, and we are briefed to bargain hard for the price of the goods offered for sale. We can't take much back, as we only have a crowded cockpit to stow stuff. So, after five minutes hassle, I get two sheepskin rugs at a good price – rolled up, they will fit in OK. We have been briefed to eat only hot food at a restaurant, and only drink from a sealed bottle or can and don't add an ice cube. Precautions successful, we all get back to the UK with no tummy problems. Next morning an early take off, while the air temperature is reasonable. Even so, we use most of the runway before the ground drops away and soon we are climbing up over the azure blue Mediterranean in a cloudless sky. Some four hours later we touch down at Marham, where it is pouring with rain, but mercifully cool.

Away from Marham, on 6th August 1964, back at RAF Gaydon, a Valiant lands after the crew hear a loud bang in flight, but everything seems to work. On inspection on the ground, a cracked wing spar is found. Inspections show wing spar cracks in other aircraft. Flying becomes limited as aircraft are taken offline for inspections and some are grounded. My last flight is on 25th November, with Flt Lt Cartwright as Captain. The Valiant Fleet of over 100 aircraft is grounded in early December, though QRA continues for several weeks afterwards. The upshot is that only reliable repair is to fit new wings. This is ruled out by Prime Minister Harold Wilson and the Cabinet, and the decision is taken that all Valiants are to be scrapped. This is bad news for Bomber Command, and it is followed later by cancellation of the TSR2 Project, announced in the Budget speech on 6th April 1965. From January 1965, crew members begin to be posted as the Squadron disbands. There is no social event to mark the occasion, no parade, just people being posted out one by one. Our own crew dissolves.

To keep pilots in flying practice, some Chipmunk aircraft are brought in, and I am checked out on 12th November by Flt Lt Edwards carrying out circuits, aerobatics, stalling spinning and forced landings. Where the programme allows, I grab the opportunity to fly solo, practice aerobatics, land in a short space on the 9,000-foot runway, and work with air traffic control. After a few weeks a notice goes up stating that volunteers are needed to act as glider tug pilots for the UK Gliding Championships to be held at RAF Bicester near Oxford in July. There will be a dress rehearsal in April. I sign up for that opportunity, as I have been towed up in a glider several times when at Cranwell and understand how it is done. I get checked out for glider towing at RAF Feltwell on 27th March, so becoming qualified for Bicester in April.

A few days later and news of my posting comes through; report in mid-May for a five-month Basic Helicopter Course at RAF Ternhill, Shropshire. Lots of my fellow co-pilots on the Valiant Force are also being retrained on helicopters. I won't be available for the Gliding Competition in July, but I am welcome to participate in the Dress Rehearsal in April, as they are short of glider tug pilots. I go down and participate. I enjoy good basic flying, with lots of aircraft and gliders in the sky. I need to keep a good lookout and observe circuit discipline. It is good also to meet lots of pilots and talk freely about the upcoming competition. Because I am available, I am sent to RAF Manston for two weeks to help set up a demonstration of a new aircraft crash fire truck, using dry powder to knock out flames. RAF Manston, in Kent, was a "crash strip" during the war and continues to provide crash facilities 24/7 to civil and military aircraft. The usual problems are failure of the undercarriage to lower properly, so the Crash Fire Team can lay a foam carpet on the wide runway in 20 minutes to cushion a wheels-up landing. The foam suppresses any sparks and prevents a fire starting. An old Hastings is flown in and towed to the "Burning Area," where mock aircraft are positioned for firefighter training. Air Attachés from around the Commonwealth are coming for the day, so they will need a briefing room, food, and transport. At 10 a.m. the aircraft is set on fire, and when the fire is raging the experimental truck is deployed. It knocks out the flames, but when it stops spraying in the dry powder, metal hot spots ignite the petrol vapour and the fire rages again. Eventually when the dry powder runs out the fire reignites and the standard foam vehicle is used to douse the flames; the liquid cools any hot spots, preventing reignition. After lunch another demonstration is laid on, just using the standard RAF Foam Fire Truck. It is completely successful.

The Valiants are being dismantled in our hangar. It is noisy, dusty and dangerous work and, quite rightly, the contractors will not allow anyone near. Very sad to see. Only one aircraft is spared, XD 818, as a future gate guard for the station. It took part in the nuclear weapons trials in the Pacific (painted in anti-flash white, it is now at the Museum at RAF Cosford). I am unsure of what the future of the station will be, so I bring the sailing dinghies back to a storage area for safekeeping. The station is like a ghost town, very bad atmosphere, as most aircrew had put in many years of service on the Valiant; now all that experience is wasted and they might be made redundant in middle age, a frightening prospect. As the Squadron disbands, as adjutant I am instructed to incinerate all Squadron files and photographs accumulated over the years, including photographs of the Squadron's Lancasters in 1944, still stamped Secret, still having to be incinerated. My job is to submit a list of the files destroyed; a thankless task, taking all day.

With news of my course date in May, Ann and I look to renting a flat near RAF Ternhill, Shropshire during the 5 month long course and putting the bungalow up for sale. That will be the end of my flying jets, as another flying experience beckons. Another day another adventure ...

Chapter 7: Basic Helicopter Course RAF Ternhill, Shropshire

(1965)

Our basic helicopter course is assembling on Monday 10th May 1965. We are six pilots from different backgrounds, different ages, but all ex-fixed-wing jet pilots. The training of helicopter pilots in the RAF is being ramped up and we wonder if we are destined for the Far East, where the US is fighting in Vietnam and Commonwealth Forces are fighting in Borneo. We will know our postings at the end of the course if we successfully learn this new way of flying. No more worries about runways being long enough, or getting close to the stall during manoeuvres. We are being briefed by the Chief Instructor. We will have two weeks of ground school before we start flying the Sycamore. Lessons kick off with how helicopters fly and how they are controlled. We are introduced to a new flying control, the Collective Lever, which is moved up and down by the left hand while the right hand controls the Cyclic Stick and one's feet work the Yaw Pedals. While flying, if you want to gain height you raise the collective lever and increase power to keep the rotor rpm (Rrpm) within limits. If you want to increase your air speed, you push forward on the cyclic stick. The yaw pedals work naturally: pushing forward on the left pedal, the nose goes round to the left. At the same time, you could be using a manual twist grip throttle for controlling engine power. Increasing power means offsetting the torque effect and you may have to push forward on a yaw pedal to keep straight.

"It will all come naturally," our instructor says, "just handle the controls delicately and try and relax; if you have ridden a bicycle, then you can do it." *That's all right then!*

Helicopters use most power when stationary, in the hover, 20% of the power used being needed by the tail rotor to compensate for the torque of the main rotor. Hovering close to the ground benefits from a cushion of air trapped underneath (this is called "ground effect"). Hovering at 100 feet or more is out of ground effect and requires a lot more power. As airspeed is increased when taking off into forward flight, more air begins to pass through the rotor, it becomes more efficient, and more lift is generated. The rotor becomes more efficient up to the designed minimum power speed (70-80 knots), thereafter becoming less efficient with increasing speed up to the designed maximum (not to exceed) speed, Vne. There is a danger of loss of control if this airspeed is exceeded. The rotor and engine become less efficient with altitude and with higher ambient air temperature. Most helicopter use so far has been below 2,000 feet, so reasonably efficient, though still 10 times more expensive, mile for mile, than fixed wing. Thus, helicopters are only used where it is necessary to come to a hover at some stage of flight. Helicopters have been used for evacuating casualties from confined spaces, such as jungle clearings. Also, helicopters are being used for Search and Rescue, typically picking up aircrew out of the sea. Increasingly, helicopters are being used to move the Army around, including its guns and vehicles as external loads.

Eventually flying starts. All checks from now on are from memory. My instructor, Flt Lt Hooper starts the Leonides piston engine and, after checking all is well at idle rpm, gently opens the throttle. There is a clunk as the clutch engages and the main rotor begins to turn. He continues opening the throttle, and the Rrpm settles in the middle of the required range.

A few more checks, then, "I am lifting the lever and opening the throttle as well as we come up on the main wheel oleos. We don't stop when we are light on the wheels as we could get ground resonance," a low frequency oscillation involving the main undercarriage, leading to a roll over. We rise slowly into the air, staying in the same position in relation to the ground. "We normally hover with 10 feet wheel clearance, well within the ground cushion. Holding our throttle at the same setting, we will maintain this height and we are stable."

After a few minutes he pushes the left yaw pedal forward a little and the nose moves to the left. We are turning on the spot and not moving away from our start point. "We will go completely round, staying on the same spot, and I will adjust the controls so that we stay where we are as we turn our tail into wind." We go round slowly, and I feel the helicopter shaking as we face downwind. We arrive back facing into wind. "Now, David, it is your turn. We will try one control at a time. Let's start you on the collective lever, just small movements needed. Just look well ahead for your attitude."

I maintain height quite well, then try out the yaw pedals, followed by the cyclic stick.

"Now try all the controls together, small movements only, don't squeeze the stick and look well ahead." Surprisingly, it goes quite well. These instructors must have nerves of steel to sit there as we students try out the controls. In no time our 45-minute flight is over, and we go through the shutdown checks, switch off the engine and brake the rotor to a halt. Inside for a coffee and a debrief. *Another three years should do it,* I'm thinking.

Next day, we are moving slowly over the ground (hover taxi), forwards, sideways, backwards and obliquely, maintaining our 10-foot wheel clearance from the ground and looking out for other helicopters nearby. Just small movements on the controls are needed, along with looking forward at the horizon for attitude. I am worn out after 45 minutes' concentration. This afternoon we are going to try flying some circuits, which involves transitioning from the hover to the climb (a ground cushion take off), levelling at 1,000 feet, turning downwind and then descending towards a given spot on the airfield. We need to keep the landing spot on the same position on the windscreen as we make our final approach (sight picture approach) until we need to slow up as we come to the hover over the spot. A quick lookout behind and we are off for another circuit; this time it is my go, so not so smooth as my instructor's circuit, but getting there.

There is more to learn, especially if the engine fails. My instructor demonstrates a practice forced landing from being on the downwind leg in the circuit and after saying "Practice engine failure." We start descending and turn steeply to get round into wind for the approach. At about 100 feet above the ground, he raises the nose, the Rrpm increases, the ground speed reduces, and we level off. He lowers the nose and applies full power, and after a bit of swaying we climb away. Small helicopters can land safely in small, level, spaces if the engine fails, it just needs constant practice to keep up the level of skill required. Compared to my Chipmunk days, the Sycamore descends a lot faster and a lot steeper, but needs a smaller space in which to land. On single engine helicopters this is going to be a necessary skill to acquire and keep in practice. As the days pass, we are all flying two flights a day, different exercises, building on what we have been taught. After 10 flights my instructor is changed to Flt Lt Smith and I stay with him for the next 15 flights. He sends me solo on 15th June, just one circuit, back to dispersal and shutdown. Next day more circuits, dual 45 minutes, and then solo for 45 minutes. Thankfully, the engine keeps going, so nothing too alarming.

The exercises take us away from the circuit and one sunny day we climb to height to demonstrate the early stages of "Vortex Ring" and how to recognise it and recover from it with minimum height loss. To initiate it we need to descend vertically at low airspeed and then slowly raise the lever. The rate of descent increases, and the controls become ineffective. To recover, we lower the lever fully and select a steep nose down attitude. When the airspeed rises above 45 knots, we can feed in the power to reduce the rate of descent and end up in a climb. From the moment we start the recovery to the moment we stopped descending we have lost at least 2,000 feet. Clearly, a situation to avoid in future.

We start practical work by looking at operating into clearings at Folly Wood, just to the east of the airfield. There is a landing pad there, so we are going to make an approach into wind, land on the small pad, explore the size of the clearing, and then depart using a "Towering" take-off. The new problem for me is the fact that we can't see the clearance between the tail rotor and the trees, so we need to keep the tail rotor in the centre of the clearing as we move around. Precision work.

We position ourselves at the end of the clearing, facing into wind, ready for take-off. Applying full power, we begin to rise and, as we get to tree top height, the cyclic stick goes forward, and we are moving across the clearing. As we do so, translational lift comes into play, and we begin to climb away quite steeply above the trees. Speed, and with it rate of climb, increases and we are soon at 1,000 feet, ready to join the circuit to land.

I report to the CO, Sqn Ldr Garwood on the morning of 8th July for a mid-course check. He briefs me for what he wants to see on the flight; nothing that I haven't flown already, so I just need to produce what I have done before. My standard is satisfactory, but there is room for improvement in awareness, which will come with experience. My instructor changes again, to Flt Lt Osborne, and I stay with him until the end of the course. Now we embark on cross-countries, planning the route on 1:¼ million scale maps and jotting down on my kneepad the important headings and leg times. We have to bear in mind the change of C of G (centre of gravity) as fuel is used. Also, when we spot electricity cables we need to cross them at a pylon, the highest point. Some cables are painted green to merge with background trees, and others cross valleys from side to side, difficult to see if looking up-sun towards them. Only three months later a Whirlwind Mk 10 from the base is involved in a "Wire Strike" with cables strung across a valley. The damaged helicopter spirals down and impacts with the ground going backwards. Both instructor and pupil survive to fly again. Cautionary tale.

As experience is gained, I progress into night flying circuits and approaches to the hover using a "T" of lights on the ground. Flying very gently, all goes well. The next exercise is flying on instruments, under the hood, the trick being to keep the scan of the flight instruments going all the time and not to focus on one and forget the others. That exercise goes well, and after 3 revision flights I am ready for my Final Handling Flight.

On 28th July, Sqn Ldr Garwood briefs me on what he wants to see. I am to do everything including operating the radio, navigating, all checks, and handling any emergencies. Nothing that I have not experienced before, so just a question of demonstrating what I have learnt to date. The test goes well enough, and I score a "Satisfactory" standard, good enough to proceed onto the next phase of the course – on the Whirlwind Mk 10. As a reward for passing my test, I am briefed for a one-hour low level cross-country – solo. The weather is good, and I plan a trip away from the hills and high-tension cables. I fly at least 1,000 feet above the ground, with a marker on my compass showing me the wind direction. If I have an engine failure, I know which way to turn to get into wind before picking a field for a forced landing. After an hour, with no problems, I join the circuit, make my way to dispersal, and shut down. This is my last flight on the Sycamore, and within a few years it is withdrawn from service because of 2 rollovers while sloping ground landings were being practiced dual. It is replaced with the Bell 47 (Sioux) with a skid landing gear. My logbook shows 47 hours on type, of which 15 are as captain.

Another day, another helicopter, another ground school. All of our course moves on to the Whirlwind Mk10 and we learn new checks by heart. This is clearly a more modern helicopter, with automatic control of the Rrpm, a gas turbine engine in the nose, and hydraulic assistance on the flying controls. This type is currently in front line service in the RAF in the SAR role, so quite an effective helicopter.

Ground school finished, we all start flying on 20th August. My instructor is Flt Lt Richardson, recently back from operating the Whirlwind Mk10 in Borneo with the SAS. He will be the main instructor while I receive training at Ternhill. We start flying with the same exercises; hover work, circuits, and practice forced landings. The whirlwind is much easier to fly than the Sycamore – the power controls are light and need only a gentle touch, the cyclic stick needing to be held all the time, but the collective lever can be secured in a given position by applying friction. The noise and vibration levels, again, are low, making it a pleasant experience when flying. Three days later I am sent solo for one circuit, 15 minutes in control. It feels very good.

We begin to practice more delicate manoeuvres, such as limiting the power used for take offs and landings, both "Computer in" and "Computer out" (using the twist grip throttle on the collective lever to control the engine). We brief for a "Height Climb" to 10,000 feet, the power requirements and handling changing with altitude, and of course instrument flying becomes essential. With that completed, we progress to instrument flying under the hood, including running landings guided by my instructor. It shows me what can be done in an emergency.

Most trips are incorporating an engine off landing (EOL) at the end of the flight after we have used up some fuel. The airfield has a strip of grass allocated to these manoeuvres close to the runway, so a good lookout is necessary before crossing the strip as there are minimum radio calls when operating in the circuit. One is impressed that a soft touchdown can be achieved, moving forward at walking pace, when no engine power is available. At the last second, as the helicopter is descending towards the ground, just by lifting the collective lever, the angular momentum in the main rotor is converted into extra lift, which cushions the touch down as long as all four wheels touch simultaneously. Clearly, another skill that has be acquired and maintained when flying single engine helicopters.

Before going to RAF Valley in Anglesey for SAR training, a mid-course check is scheduled for 15th September. My standard, as judged by Flt Lt Whitton Hayden, is good enough, and along with my colleagues I head off for Anglesey that weekend to learn about Search and Rescue out at sea and in the mountains.

Another phase, another series of briefings, another list of checks. Search and Rescue, both at sea and in the mountains, is taught at this dedicated Search and Rescue Training Unit (SARTU), which has been operating for many years. We are introduced to the "patter," the specific words that our winch operator will use to guide us when we are winching. Pilots can't see underneath the helicopter, so need to be guided by the winch operator, who can see not only below but back towards the tail as well. His words have specific meanings, requiring appropriate action by the pilot. This crew cooperation is crucial in most SAR operations, a skill that needs constant practice. We start with dry winching, just getting used to moving slowly over the ground, holding the required height and position as instructed. With the casualty in the rescue strop on the end of the winch cable, the instruction might be "Up gently." The pilot lifts the lever, and the helicopter moves upwards lifting the casualty, assuming sufficient power is available and the casualty is not attached to anything below. Sometimes the instruction might be "Hold your height. I am winching in." The winch operator operates a switch so that the casualty is lifted slowly, as the winch winds in, and he can check that the casualty is not attached to anything such as a dinghy or snagging up on obstructions. The pilot maintains the same position and height over the surface until cleared to fly away. Over land the pilot has got visual contact with a solid surface, so it is easy to maintain a hover and make adjustments as needed. The problems for some pilots begin when hovering over open water. Somehow, by looking at the horizon and picking up visual cues with peripheral vision, a pilot can assess where he is in relation to say, a casualty in the water beneath him, and the height of the helicopter above the average wave height. Not all pilots are able to acquire this skill and one of our number, Bill, is "chopped" for lack of progress. A few months later we get a letter from him in Switzerland saying he is a First Officer with Swiss Air and living in Zurich. Happy ending!

With hovering over water mastered, we practice with real survivors in real dinghies. With the dinghy below the helicopter, it can be affected by the rotor downwash and begin to move around erratically. Our winch operators instruct as necessary to stay overhead. To effect a rescue we lower a winchman on the end of the wire, and he has a NATO strop which he loops around the survivor's shoulders. All secure, the winchman holds his arms out to signal that he is ready to be lifted with the survivor. On receiving the instruction "Up gently," the pilot lifts the lever, and as the helicopter rises the winchman and casualty are pulled out of the water. The pilot automatically adjusts the flight controls for the weight coming on the winch cable on the right-hand side. Extra power is needed to cope with the extra weight and the pilot checks that the fuel flow to the engine is within limits.

With that exercise carried out successfully, the course moves on to practicing "Decks" – that is, working with vessels of all sizes, some under power and with directional control and some without. It helps a lot if the helicopter can fly pointing into wind and the pilot has good visual contact with the vessel. This can be achieved if the vessel takes up a course of the wind direction plus 30 degrees and maintains a speed of 10 knots. The pilot and the winch operator, both being on the right-hand side, have a good view of the vessel and can use the fore and aft axis of the vessel for guidance (boat's axis). Where the vessel is not able to maintain a course the pilot will state, "Aircraft axis," for guidance and use the sea surface for height control and maintain heading into the prevailing wind. In rough water vessels can roll, pitch and heave, and the winch operator has to select a safe operating height so that any tall masts do not strike the bottom of the helicopter. Clearly, good standard operating procedures and good crew cooperation is necessary for successful SAR operations at sea.

The next part of our training involves operating in the mountains of Snowdonia. We get a briefing on mountain flying and a comprehensive CFS document, "Mountain Flying", outlining what you might expect as a helicopter pilot and what techniques you need to fly safely. My first flight is on 27th September and my instructor is Flt Lt Whiteley. We head to an area just to the East of Bethesda on the A5 in Snowdonia, where we look at operating into bowls, valleys, peaks and ridges. We will experience the difficulty of not being able to see a flat horizon in the distance, the difference between airspeed and ground speed, and the danger of flying up a valley with a covering of cloud overhead.

As we arrive in the area, he points out the aircraft wrecks on the high ground, mainly from World War Two and from various Air Forces. On open ground our crewman drops a smoke canister, and it shows us that the local wind direction is 45 degrees different from the forecast wind and a lot stronger. We see how easy it is for fixed wing aircraft to get trapped by flying up a valley, running out of turning space and airspeed, and crashing, especially with a following wind. We make our way to the bowl and as we fly over the landing pad, our crewman drops another smoke canister, and we note down the local wind direction. As we circle around, we note our flight instruments are giving us our airspeed, height above sea level, rate of climb or descent, our compass heading and attitude in relation to the horizon. My instructor points out how disorienting it can be with the side of a mountain filling the windscreen and with the wind behind us, how we have a high ground speed but only 70 knots airspeed.

After making a landing on the landing pad in the bowl, we move on to the valley situation. It certainly feels strange on finals to the landing pad in the bottom of the valley to see the ground beneath not getting any closer as we descend towards the landing pad. One's senses are telling you to push the nose down to follow the ground down as you progress down the valley. This can lead to excess airspeed and loss of control – the cause of many helicopter accidents around the world. *Must remember that one.* Moving on to peaks, we experience updrafts, downdrafts, and turbulence. Flying at our minimum power speed of 70 knots give us maximum flexibility as regards power requirements and very good control of the helicopter as we get thrown around in an unpredictable way. The stronger the wind, the more powerful the effects, so there is clearly a limit for every type of helicopter, within which you can fly safely. On this flight I see the necessity for an "escape route," generally to the right, if an approach is going wrong because of downdrafting or turbulence. We are approaching the sharp-edged peak of Tryfan. About 100 yards to go to the summit; down drafting air is pushing us down in spite of full power and we are sinking below the peak.

"Taking escape route," announces my instructor. Right yaw pedal, 30 degrees of bank to the right, and we are dropping rapidly into a wide valley with a lake at the bottom. Having quickly lost a thousand feet, things stabilise, and we find that we can now climb back up to look at a ridge situation. There we experience the opposite problem; updrafting air. Sometimes in strong winds, rising air over a ridge prevents a helicopter descending to land – very awkward. Vital lessons to be learnt. If you are operating in mountains, you need lots of excess power and very effective flying controls. With today's conditions our Whirlwind is clearly struggling with power and my instructor is working hard trying to keep a level attitude. Lots to bear in mind for the future.

The weeks pass quickly, with two flights a day. When the weather allows, we head for the mountains, returning to valley low level along the Anglesey coast. Very pretty. When the weather is poor, we are flying "Wets and Decks" in Holyhead Harbour, working with RAF Marine Craft launches. To avoid conflict with the fixed wing training jets, we use a low-level route to get to and from the Harbour. Sometimes we can continue flying in the wind, rain, and low cloud, while they are grounded because of the weather. My last flight is on 8th October with Flt Lt Dixon, our exercise low flying, 100 feet above ground level, around Anglesey – and I get paid to do this!

Back to Ternhill, and the pace quickens. The syllabus widens to include underslung loads, day and night, as well as carrying soldiers (trooping). Having boarded, my five soldiers shut the cabin door and tap me on the leg when everything is secure in the cabin, ready for lift-off. On landing at the drop-off point, they leave the cabin, closing the sliding door, and after I have given them the "thumbs up" they clear the helicopter disc in a safe direction. We practice this exercise at night as well. Also at night, we get a chance of firing some pyrotechnics, Schermuly flares. These are very bright flares suspended below a parachute that illuminate the ground for at least 30 seconds to enable you to do an engine off landing, should the need arise. Most single engine helicopters carry these flares when operating at night over land. On the Whirlwind, two are mounted on the starboard main undercarriage leg and can be fired off by the pilot at the touch of a button. We also practice tactical formation, keeping the leader in sight while flying at low level, avoiding trees and various obstacles like radio masts with supporting wires stretching out sideways to the ground.

All good things come to an end, and I am put forward for my Final Handling Check by the CO, Sqn Ldr Trevenack on 25th October. All goes well and my standard is "Satisfactory." On the debrief I am told to keep learning, look to improve skills, knowledge and to acquire as much experience as possible, as soon as possible. In the helicopter world there is a lot to learn, and you can learn from other people's mistakes. As a parting gesture, on the next day, those who have passed the course take part in a solo low-level navigation formation flight, culminating with a flypast over the station. The next helicopter course, on the tandem rotor Belvedere, will start in a week's time for Max Sceats and I, while Harry Joy, a fellow trainee, is joining the Navy and will be going to an aircraft carrier, initially for a year. Another ground school, another series of cockpit checks, another way of flying and operating and possibly going abroad at the end of it. Keep going and one day I will become operational …

Chapter 8: Flying the Belvedere

(1966 – 1969)

With the Basic Helicopter Course at RAF Ternhill completed, in October 1965 it is off to the Belvedere Operational Conversion Unit at RAF Odiham, near Basingstoke in Hampshire. The two weeks' ground school, learning systems, is followed by a dull pause; the two machines are both seemingly permanently unserviceable due to vibration. Numerous ground runs, ground flag tracking and a few short air tests are all that is available to myself and Max Sceats, my fellow student. This situation persists to the end of the year. We are told about the advantages of tandem rotor helicopters – all installed power is available for lifting in the hover, as opposed to 20% being needed to keep straight, as is the case for conventional helicopters. This means achieving a good payload for the installed power, whether carried internally or externally. Both main rotors are robust and can withstand bird strikes, as opposed to the delicate tail rotors of conventional helicopters. Tandem rotor layouts allow a large centre of gravity range fore and aft, and the cabin has the same cross-section throughout its length, without needing to taper towards the tail. Clearly there is a need to synchronise the rpm of the rotors, so they do not clash. In the case of the Belvedere, each engine drives its respective rotor with a synchronisation (sync) shaft carrying the balance of the power from one gearbox to the other. In the event of an engine failure, power from the remaining live engine passes along the sync shaft to power the other rotor at the same Rrpm.

We are told the history of Belvedere accidents. In at least two cases, co-pilots had switched off the remaining live engine after an in-flight engine failure. This was thought to have been cause of an accident in Germany where all on board were killed, including many Whirlwind pilots hitching a lift as passengers. Also, an engine-off landing had to be made into the desert in Libya containing a WWII minefield after one engine had failed and the remaining live engine was switched off. After these accidents the small electrical engine HP cock switches were changed to large paddle-type switches and named: "No. 1 ENGINE – FRONT" and "No. 2 ENGINE – REAR." The co-pilot was not to move either switch following engine failure until the captain had confirmed that the failed engine had been correctly identified and that the co-pilot had his hand on the appropriate switch. There had also been cable failures in the Yaw Control System, which had presented the pilot with severe control difficulties. In Aden this had caused a Belvedere to crash land, and in Borneo a recent failure had resulted in the loss of the machine, three crew and many soldiers. We learn that the Belvedere had acquired a reputation as the "Bristol Widowmaker" and that it was not popular with the troops or with the crews flying it.

With Christmas over, Max and I begin to ask if we could go out to the operational Squadron (No. 66) in Singapore. Eventually our request is granted, and we are to be sent out essentially untrained on the machine. I am sent out at the beginning of February 1966, reporting to No. 66 Squadron at RAF Seletar, and meet the CO, Squadron Leader "Bunny" Austin. He takes me to a tailor in Seletar village to get fitted with two items in khaki – bush jacket and shorts – as well as a pair of desert boots. He also hands out two green Australian Air Force flying suits, thin cotton and ideal for the hot, humid climate. He explains that his pilots have an average of three tours on helicopters, the average age is 45, and the Squadron has many Master Pilots who had previously served in Aden with No. 26 Squadron. I am age 24, on my first operational tour on helicopters, and have 100 hours of helicopter flying to my name, mostly dual. I and the other first tour helicopter pilots that are to follow me are to be trained up within the Squadron, and for our first few months we will be closely supervised. We are sorely needed as replacements for the many pilots that have completed their tours and are now due to return to the UK. I meet Wing Commander (Helicopters) John Dowling, who is in charge of No. 66 (Belvederes) and 103 and 110 SQNs (Whirlwinds) based at RAF Seletar. He has gained fame some years previously by lowering the spire on to the roof of the new Coventry Cathedral using the Belvedere. My first flight, on 9th February, in the Belvedere is with Flt Lt John Charlesworth, and we cross over the Straits into Malaya, with its neat palm oil and rubber plantations. After a few weeks of learning to fly the Belvedere around Seletar, it is decided to continue my training in Borneo, where the Squadron had an operational detachment at RAF Kuching in the Western sector. Their role is to support the Commonwealth Army battalions in their ongoing military campaign with Indonesia, "Confrontation". I fly with Gordon Camell, who flew Lancasters during the war and jets afterwards. I am his replacement, and when I am qualified he returns to UK and eventually California, where he sets up a successful business.

Alongside the Belvedere,
RAF Seletar Singapore – 10 FEB 1966.

I meet my Flight Commander, Flt Lt "Dinger" Bell, and he explains some recent events that had resulted in some essential modifications. A recent major accident in Borneo, caused by failure of the yaw control cable control system, had resulted in great concern in all quarters. Newly promoted to Squadron Leader, and Squadron CO, Sqn Ldr "Bunny" Austin had ordered his Belvederes to be grounded until the MOD sent out teams from Westland to fix the yaw cable failures and from Rolls Royce to fix the engine starting problems, which had caused difficulties when operating in remote areas. Both teams arrived, professing that this was the first time that they had been made aware of the problems. The yaw cable problem is solved by drastically reducing the flying time between inspections of the system and replacing the cable at every inspection. The starting problem is solved by locking the starter gas turbine into the flow of gases from the combustion chamber fuelled by AVPIN. This results in a quick spin up to 10,000 rpm for the Gazelle engine, which then lights up and then winds up to idling. There had been a number of single-engine, single-pilot flights out of remote insecure areas back to Kuching, when one engine would not start. Both of these long-term problems are now solved, thankfully before I arrive on the scene.

The Belvedere was designed to have a nose up attitude on the ground – to meet a Naval requirement to be able to load a torpedo from the front. After trials, it was rejected by the Navy and the 26 machines that had been ordered by the MOD were offered to the RAF for troop transport. It had a manual throttle controlling the R rpm between 240-260 in flight, AVPIN engine starter system, ladder to get into the cockpits and cabin, no stabilisation or autopilot, and an armour plate behind right hand pilot's seat. This, incidentally, gives protection from the starter motor on the No. 1 (front) engine, which when spinning up to 10,000 rpm could shed its small turbine blades on occasion. The pilots are hidden from sight for the crewman by the front engine and are linked only by intercom. There is a narrow passage from the cabin to the cockpit around the engine on the port side. Use in flight would be very noisy and very hot. The cockpit is noisy, with a high level of vibration coming mainly from the intermeshing rotors, front engine and gearbox. Flying in the hot moist climate is normally done with the right-hand cockpit door slid back; cool, but draughty, and you need to hang on to the maps and flight board. The performance at sea level is good – 120 knots at maximum all-up weight with an internal load. With a big boxy shaped external load like a Land Rover, with its high drag, the maximum achievable speed is 80 knots. The CO makes me SQN Flight Safety Officer, with a brief to prevent accidents, particularly helicopter pilot error accidents, as in the Vietnam War – which is in full swing – these are causing most of the losses, running into hundreds, if not thousands, rather than direct enemy action. If I am to pontificate to crews on safety matters it requires me to set an example and to be safe, efficient, and professional at all times. This turns out to be a good move long-term.

I am briefed that the overall policy from the Defence Secretary Dennis Healy is for the containment of any fighting to be within Borneo and the use of minimum force to achieve that aim. So, no bombing over the border in Borneo, no bombing of Indonesia, and no shooting down of aircraft transgressing across the border, although they are being tracked on radar. Military operations can only be conducted to catch raiding parties coming across the 1,200-mile-long Borneo border (this is not to be crossed by Belvederes, though some Whirlwinds are tasked to do so on special missions). This is done by flying troops out to the nearest border fort following an incident and setting up ambushes, hopefully catching the raiders on their return journey. There are a number of successful engagements and casualties are taken on both sides. The media, based in Singapore, are not interested in these little skirmishes, as Vietnam is taking their attention, and they leave us alone to get on with the job; much to everyone's relief.

Ann's flight out to join me at the end of March is an Indulgence Flight, for which she has to pay £46. She gets up to Heathrow, is put aboard an Eagle Airways Britannia with lots of families, and sets off on her first ever flight. An hour later, over Rome, the Captain announces that one engine's oil pressure is low and the aircraft is returning to Heathrow. After waiting several hours back on the ground, all the passengers are taken to nearby accommodation. Ann is equipped with a frilly night dress, ready for the tropical heat, but she is in a room with no central heating and snowflakes at the window. Next day they climb aboard another aircraft and set off again, some 22 hours late. In aviation language, "time to spare – go by air." Routing via Kuwait and RAF Gan in the Indian Ocean, she eventually arrives at RAF

Changi in Singapore in the evening. We meet up and stay with Paul Deakin and his wife. Next morning, I have to get up early and set off with other helicopter pilots for a week's jungle survival course up in Malaya! We learn to find food, water, make shelter and move, as well as coping with leeches and creepy crawlies. If we ever end up in the jungle on our own, we know how to cope. Ann and I rent a bungalow just round the corner from the Deakins, but with an Amah helping out there is little for Ann to do. She has been busy teaching Geography for the last five months at a high school in Swindon, so a big change.

Having arrived at out our detachment in Borneo, Kuching Airfield, I am briefed by the CO that there are to be no heroics; as only two machines out of four are likely to be serviceable on any one day, it was important to bring the machine back intact at the end of each day's flying, ready for the next day's tasking. The standard operational procedure is to fly two captains up, i.e. no co-pilots as such; the pilot in the right-hand seat is the aircraft commander at the time. I am issued with the famous white maps of Borneo, made up from aerial photos. These show the coastline, rivers, latitude/longitude, and grid, but no contours, settlements, or roads. Over the first few detachments I make up my own set of maps, using other pilots' maps for locations of riverside settlements, mountains, airfields, border forts, ground features and clearings for helicopter use. On flying days crews are issued with a STEN gun and a full magazine in case we come down somewhere, though there is nowhere in the cockpit to stow it. Also issued is a flak jacket, which is too cumbersome to wear so is hung up somewhere in the cockpit. The pilots are mainly Master Pilots of many years' experience, on their second or third operational tour. As a first tour pilot with 30 hours solo helicopter flying to my name and the first of a stream of replacements, I am happy to be looked after. The daily weather forecasts are vague: winds – light and variable – and in the afternoon heavy showers dying out at dusk. First thing in the morning a mist rises from the jungle, requiring a reduced forward speed and obscuring the horizon, making navigation more difficult. It is important not to fly over the ill-defined border, as the "Indonesians" have anti-aircraft gun emplacements and had used one of them just before I arrived to shoot down a Whirlwind piloted by a new boy flying solo. It is also important not to fly in a direct line to a border fort, but to change direction every five minutes or so while flying 100 feet above the treetops so as not to give away the flight's destination. This hopefully prevents mortar rounds being targeted on the respective border fort as you arrive! The destinations are referred to on the radio by a colour code – Red 3, Green 7, Blue 5, etc. The Belvedere, at 120 knots cruising speed, takes a lot of stopping because of its momentum, so a straight in approach to a helipad starts a mile away, or a 90 degree turn closer in is required. This technique is not advisable with an underslung load, for which a slow plodding approach is necessary to prevent a swing developing, especially if the load was being carried on the end of an eighty-foot strop.

It is not all serious work, and the 6th of June provides an opportunity for everyone to let their hair down. The Squadron detachment of aircrew and groundcrew have a big party at Kuching Airfield. Besides being the 6th of the 6th in 1966 for No 66 SQN, we are celebrating the continuing serviceability of the machines, the influx of new young pilots, and the leadership and positive attitude of the new Squadron Commander. We feel the future looks good. To build up my experience, I volunteer for every possible flight and soon acquire the nickname "Dauntless Dave". Morale is improving, as the Army are using us more to move the troops around and involving us with the deployment of the SAS from their island base direct to the border forts. Also, we are being deployed on short detachments into the 2nd and 3rd Divisions of Borneo, an area where the Navy are operating with their Wessex.

The night before carrying out a task, the Army tasking officers come up to the airfield and present their requirements for the next day. The pilots taking on these "Trans Tasks" quickly work out the most efficient way of transporting the troops, netted loads and, sometimes, 105mm field guns. A new concept for me, the disposable load (the total weight of fuel and payload not to exceed 5500 lbs) clearly limited what could be carried at the start of a flight, as the full fuel load was up to 4000 lbs. The sequence of the task is agreed and written down on scraps of paper and the next day the flight is carried out, usually without a hitch.

We are briefed from time to time that clashes had taken place in the jungle along the border and over the following days we bring back to Kuching our wounded and Indonesian prisoners of war. When we bring back the SAS troops, each man wears different style military kit and carries a bulging rucksack, a machine gun, and bands of ammunition. A normal soldier and kit is listed at 250lbs per man, but we list the SAS at 300lbs. They are clearly professional killers, looked the part, and I am just glad that we were on their side!

Sqn Ldr "Bunny" Austin is keen on get-togethers for the aircrew, to boost morale. Typically, when he is in Kuching, there is a run into Kuching town for a Chinese meal in the marketplace. An old vehicle with a failing gearbox takes us all in. Having put some tables together, cans of Tiger beer are stacked around us, and a mountain of egg fried rice appears in the middle of the table, with numerous delicious side dishes all around. In the background are the squawks of chickens, noisy families, and the bustle of traffic around the square. The atmosphere is welcoming, and I learn how things are run on detachment from our main base in Singapore. At our base at Seletar, being on the coast, the Boss has organised a speed boat called the "Rattler" for everyone on the Squadron to learn how to water ski, and most weekends the Squadron turns out to participate or simply watch and socialise at Seletar's Sailing Club. I learn on two skis and eventually make it to one, which is surprisingly manoeuvrable. Seletar has a great outdoor swimming pool, 50 metres long and a good temperature. Just to see if it was possible, I swim half a mile using the breaststroke, learn some lifesaving, and teach Ann to swim; this after she failed to learn after seven years of trying to use cold outside pool in the grounds of a big house, with mosquito larvae floating in it. Not inspiring at all.

As my experience builds up, I am tasked to go further away from Kuching, into the area to the east, where there are almost continuous hills, primary jungle, and wide rivers. We use the rivers for navigation, with the convention of keeping to the right if following its course. One day I am tasked to Sibu airfield, 100 miles east of Kuching and meet up with a civilian liaison team who need to be flown around various locations for talks with local tribal headmen. The only problem is that the amicable talks drag on, with no awareness that we need to be back at Sibu by nightfall. Eventually I have to start the Belvedere, making a lot of noise, at the agreed departure times, to give the team the excuse to leave and pick up their schedule. Another time I am tasked into the Navy forward base at Nanga Gatt, causing a problem, as we need a landing pad much larger than that required by their Wessex. I am briefed that recently two Wessex had collided in mid-air, crashed into the river and all on board were lost, so I keep a sharp look out and make my intentions known over the radio. I am given a number of two-to-five-day detachments and it falls to me to make the appropriate decisions and work with various people en route. One of these is a Malaysian entertainment team that we fly around from base to base, returning to our hotel in Sibu for overnight. Their favourite song is "Fly Me to the Moon", and as we fly from base we are all singing this over the intercom system to keep our spirits up as we fly over mile after mile of primary jungle to our various destinations.

One day I am tasked to land near a native tribal village "longhouse," and we are there for three hours as our Army passengers go off on their mission. Our crew sit down on the floor, converse with the elders of the longhouse using sign language, give them our sweets and show them our maps. We are white-faced men descending from the sky, so we are treated as honoured guests. On the walls are pictures of the British Royal Family taken from magazines from about the 1930s to the 1950s. They proudly show us the knives and sharpening stones that the Army has given them as part of the "Hearts and Minds Initiative". The tribe, in turn, has provided trackers to help our soldiers follow the Indonesian raiding parties as they return to the border. As we leave, our Army passengers say that over the years the natives had accepted helicopters, but would be startled by motor vehicles if they ever appeared. They add that the natives in this part of Borneo had been head-hunters until recently. Hopefully, they are favourably impressed with the noise and powerful rotor downwash of the Belvedere as we depart. We keep well clear of the palm leaf roof of the longhouse on departure, leaving it intact!

In October 1966 our CO, Sqn Ldr "Bunny" Austin comes to the end of his tour and is replaced by Sqn Ldr Paul Gray. He is different, more studied and thoughtful, as he takes over the responsibility for a Squadron spread out over a wide area, conducting military operations in Borneo, training in Singapore, and week-long exercises with the Army in the Malay Peninsula up to Penang in the West and Mersing in the east. Fortunately, he carries on in the same spirit of supporting his men and is keen that everyone can relax when they came back from a detachment in Borneo or an exercise upcountry. He supports the use of our "Rattler" water ski boat and becomes a mean boat driver – you need to hang on tight as he sweeps round corners with you on the outside of the bend.

On the Flight Safety side of things, he is keen on a new theme poster every month, with a view to preventing pilot error accidents. The themes encompass: dehydration; look-out; eating properly – hard work burns fuel fast; good preparation before a flight; assume nothing – check everything; and taking everything you might need in the air with you. There are a number of challenging situations faced by his pilots, and by his engineers over his tour; thankfully, all resolved without one fatal accident or Belvedere being lost.

The start of 1967 signals the end of the confrontation in Borneo, and in March the four Belvederes are flown to Kuching docks and loaded aboard a ship as deck cargo and ferried to Singapore. At the start of the confrontation they had been flown to Kuching from Changi, Singapore, some 400 miles, fitted with ferry tanks and grossly overweight, the vibration being such that the pilots could not read the instruments for the first hour. The military campaign in Borneo comes to an end and is declared a success, with the cross-border raids being contained and the war not escalating as in Vietnam. The political situation in Indonesia changes after a military coup, when President Sukarno is deposed and is replaced by General Suharto. After the regime change, one million communists and sympathisers in Indonesia are rounded up and the confrontation with Malaysia comes to an end after a Peace Conference. Most British and Commonwealth troops move back to Singapore, to a life in barracks, which the soldiers hate. I am told that we lose more soldiers in barrack room fights and deaths on the roads in Singapore than we did in operations in the jungles of Borneo.

*Two Belvederes flying over the Malay
Peninsula on exercise.*

In July 1968, out of the blue, I am detached for two weeks to
Hong Kong. I am going to be one of the officers manning the
"Riot Control Cell" in the basement of the HK Police HQ. My
duty, should riots occur, is to liaise with the available helicopter units so that their helicopters can monitor the movements of
the rioters. I naturally contact the units and arrange for flights
over Hong Kong, the New Territories, and the islands to fully understand the area in which I am operating. These flights
are in single engine Whirlwinds, and I do feel exposed when
flying over densely packed urban areas, but the engine keeps
going and I enjoy the view. Having seen the scenery, I invite
Ann to fly up from Singapore with their airline and stay for
my last week of duty. After enjoying her silver service flight

in one of their latest jets, we meet up and head for her hotel. On my time off, most days we are exploring, using ferries and buses to get about. Feeling intrepid, one day we board a bus to the last stop in the New Territories. As we travel out into the countryside, we are eyed with amazement by the local women in their native black dresses, often looking after baskets carrying live chickens, but we are respected with head bows as they pass us. Perhaps white-skinned people don't venture out this far too often.

In the evening we have a good choice of restaurants, the first being the "Normandie", with delicious French food and wonderful service. Later we dine at the Hilton, with its gently rotating restaurant giving panoramic views of the harbour and the anchored ships. For a complete change we get out to Aberdeen, where the accommodation and restaurants are all afloat. What do I have to do to get a tour out here?

After the successful operational flying in Borneo, "the powers that be" decide that our Squadron, now based in Singapore, will remain very much on a war footing, with no let-up in activity. Flights to familiarise crews with Navy ships with flight decks are laid on, and to give experience to ships' crews of a helicopter that was much larger than the Navy Wessex. HMS Intrepid, anchored in Singapore Harbour, receives many flights. Out in the South China Sea, the carrier HMS Bulwark accepts a number of movements. On the first flight to it, the landing on board the aircraft carrier is no problem, except the Belvedere, being 92 feet long overall, takes up the space of two helicopter pads. Fuel is offered with a pressure refuel nozzle, but the Belvedere is gravity refuel only, with filler holes high on the fuselage. Eventually an adapter is found, but the fuel being offered is not the standard Avtur but Avtag – not on the cleared fuel list in the ops manual for the aircraft. So, a decision is taken to put the fuel into just one tank, start the engines on normal fuel and then switch to Avtag in flight for just one engine. There are no problems with the engines on the flight back, and the engineers are happy with the fuel situation when we land back at Seletar.

During 1967 a new era starts, with the training up of New Zealand and Australian soldiers in jungle warfare prior to their deployment to Vietnam. They are initially based at the Jungle Warfare School at Ulla Tiram, Malaya, and need us to train them for massed heli-copter assaults against dug-in enemy positions, with Gurkhas act-ing as the enemy. With the return of the Belvederes from Borneo, there are continuous exercises in Malaya throughout 1967 and '68, with a permanent detachment of two Belvederes to RAF Butterworth, near Penang. The Army base is at Terendak, near Malacca, on the west coast. Big exercises take place every month in Malaya, with up to 4 Belvederes and 10 Whirlwinds from the RAF plus two Sikorsky S 61Ns from the Royal Malaysian Air Force based at Kuanton on the east coast, and also some Wessex from the Royal Navy.

One of jobs given to me is taking convoys of lorries from Singapore and setting up and running tented base camps in Malaya to support various exercises. The requirement is to provide 4 Belvedere-sized landing pads and a spare pad for visitors. 50 yards away from the dispersal area a domestic camp is set up to meet the requirements for engineering support, accommodation, cooking, messing, and an operations room. This complex is all put together with easy to assemble frame tents. Though conditions are basic, the atmos-phere and humour is similar to that portrayed in the M★A★S★H series of films. During the day, food and refreshment are pro-vided dawn to dusk at the cookhouse for returning flight crews and the hard-working groundcrew. Every evening, cans of cold Tiger beer are available, cooled in a chest filled with ice mixed with salt to make it melt, and drop the temperature. We sleep well on our camp beds under mosquito nets until a welcome cup of tea at dawn heralds another long flying day. On the last night of each exercise there is a big bonfire to dispose of items not going back to Singapore, and the collective spirit is good. Our guests, the officers of the units we have trained up for duty in Vietnam, are happy with the experience they have gained working with us, using a range of helicopters. A few months later they will be using that experience for real in Vietnam ...

During one of the big exercises at the Army base of Terrendak, near Malacca, Ann flies up in a Dakota to join me, sharing a house with Army friends. As she enters the aircraft cabin, she spies a British Army Medic and promptly sits down alongside him. After all, you never know when you are going to need help on these aeroplane things! On another occasion we swap houses with our Army friends for a week. Driving up through Malaya in our little white Mini, we see signs for "Utara," but there is no such place on the map. Later we find out it means "north." We also drive up to Penang, a beautiful island with wonderful, palm-fringed, sandy beaches. We are invited to a local wedding for part of the first day — they go on for days, apparently.

For the mass helicopter assaults, the CO often choses me as the lead navigator, with himself as aircraft Captain and Formation leader, with up to three Belvederes and ten other helicopters spaced out behind in loose formation. There is a need to keep the formation speed at no more than 90 knots airspeed so that the Whirlwinds from 110 and 103 SQNs can keep up. The navigation to the Drop Zone over the mainly primary jungle involves getting to a clearly recognisable Initial Point, such as river junction, and then flying on a steady heading and at 90 knots airspeed for the appropriate time, hoping that the cleared area for the assault is where you expected it to be. Touchdown is to be within 30 seconds of planned arrival time. With the landing area secure, the onboard troops roping down, the Belvederes return within two hours with underslung guns and ammunition trailers, putting the guns down on the ground markers. The 105mm guns and trailers are clipped onto the load hook under the belly, and as the touchdown area is approached the cockpit load switch is set to automatic. As the underslung load touches the ground and the weight comes off the hook, it opens automatically and releases the load. We then clear the area immediately. The guns would have been used to soften up the enemy positions before the ground assault went in.

To support the increase in flying, all Belvedere spare parts within the RAF are sent to the Squadron at RAF Seletar, with surplus items being stored at the adjacent Maintenance Unit. The squadron has 16 machines, with a large number of pilots, crewmen and engineers, and new air-conditioned facilities for the aircrew and ground crew are built. The block built for the aircrew has briefing rooms, a big crew room, a locker room, and showers. Fortunately for everyone, a local café sets up shop on the end of the hangar, providing filled rolls and liquid refreshments on demand. Most aircrew and groundcrew need to drink a gallon of water a day, working hard in the hot and humid atmosphere. I get used to putting the lifting straps on Land Rovers, prior to them being lifted as underslung loads. One day an Army unit turns up in a large truck instead of a Land Rover for a joint exercise, so I have to borrow the CO's personal Land Rover for half an hour as we put on the straps, fly it round the local area, and then give it back to him undamaged. Possible brownie points?

Another day there is an incident when a blade of grass is seen stuck through the strong "D" section of a main rotor blade on a pre-flight inspection. It is stuck in a crack in the blade emanating from the leading edge. When the protective covering is peeled back to expose bare metal, it is noticed that the crack had started from a straight- line scratch in line with the edge of a trailing edge blade pocket. When the rest of the blade is examined, other straight-line scratches are revealed, also in line with the edges of trailing edge pockets. The aircraft are grounded and reps from Westland are summoned. All blades are checked and a significant batch that had been manufactured between two dates all show these scratch lines, which clearly would lead to cracks growing over time, and would have led to the failure of the blade under load. The scratch marks, it transpires, had been made by a keen young chap in the factory who, instead of using a HB pencil to mark the blade where the pockets were to be glued on, had decided to use a metal scribe, because the lines would be thinner. We are fortunate that this error is picked up.

Another three let-offs occur to the same two pilots. The first occurs during a roping down demonstration. At 80 feet in the hover, whilst some Gurkha soldiers are using a rope positioned at the door to descend to the ground, there is a big bang. The control of the Belvedere becomes sloppy, so the captain decides to descend and land, much to the surprise of the soldiers underneath on the ground. The captain lands alongside them and then lowers the lever. There is another bang and bits of rotor blade are flung in all directions. It transpires that the synch shaft had failed, allowing the rotors powered by their own engine to run at different rpm. Whilst in the hover the rotors do not intermesh, but as soon as the Belvedere lands and pitch is taken off, the rotors clash and the blades break up, scattering debris far and wide. Fortunately, the soldiers on the ground are close to the machine and the debris goes out above their heads. Had this failure taken place in forward flight, the Belvedere would have been lost.

Some months later the same two pilots are carrying out a radar calibration exercise on the east coast of Malaya, some 80 miles from Singapore. The requirement is to hold a hover over the same ground position at 8,000 feet. As they come to the hover, needing full power to do so, there is a loud bang. Immediately the captain puts the Belvedere into full autorotation descent at the same time as putting out a mayday call. Fortunately, there is a large open space in the jungle next to the coast, and a normal landing is made. As the captain lowers the lever on touchdown and closes the throttles, the rotors quickly came to a stop, even with the engines running. On inspection afterwards, the front gearbox, which was behind the pilots' heads, is found to be too hot to touch and has seized up completely. Had the failure occurred in the rear gearbox, the pilots would not have had any warning until the gearbox failed completely, and the Belvedere would have broken up in mid-air.

A few months later the same two pilots are flying in rain over a populated area of Malaya. A flock of large birds appears in front, and to avoid them the captain decides to descend and pass beneath them. As he does so, there is a loud bang, so he lands on a football pitch. Around the front undercarriage legs are the remains of high-tension electrical cables, which neither pilot had seen. Fortunately, they did not end up in the rotor system, as the Belvedere would have been lost. After this accident the two pilots never fly together again, and to the end of their tours neither one is involved in a serious incident.

About mid-1968, the MOD contracts to buy the first batch of Chinook helicopters as a replacement for the Belvedere. Our Squadron pilots are asked if they would like to volunteer to go to Philadelphia for a six-week training course and then continue with the first Chinook Squadron, wherever it was going to be based. I volunteer, along with many others, and we are disappointed when some months later, in a MOD economy drive, the Chinook order is cancelled. However, it is also decided No 66 Squadron would remain in Singapore until end of March 1969, then to be disbanded. This was the first helicopter Squadron to disband as part of the "Withdrawal of British Forces from the Far East." The other RAF Squadrons would disband in turn. All serving personnel are asked to extend their tours until that date, so another nine months of jungle flying on top of all those overseas allowances for me! I can now pay for a civil fixed wing instructor's course at Singapore's airport and fly light fixed-wing over Singapore and Malaya most weekends. I am checked out as a parachute dropping pilot, and some weekends I am dropping sports parachutists from the door of the aircraft at 2,000 feet. On my first trip a young man freezes on his first jump, and I have to land with him half in, half out of the aircraft. After a talking to by the instructor, he goes up again and makes his first jump. At the flying club I complete my instructor's course with Hercules pilot, Flt Lt Herrington, in record time and take on my first student, Army Warrant Officer Bates. We train at weekends at the International Airport, flying the Chipmunk and the Cessna 172, Skyhawk. He completes his course and gets his private pilot's licence. He hopes to become a commercial pilot eventually. I continue flying sightseeing passengers around Singapore Harbour, which they enjoy immensely. Ann does not like the idea and will not fly with me – an opportunity missed. One day in the Flying Club's bar, an American is buying all the drinks and talking in a loud voice. He is recruiting for Air America (code for CIA) and wants fixed wing pilots to operate in Cambodia. Pilots can state their salary expectations, nominate what currency they wished to be paid and to which foreign bank they wish it to be paid into. I speak to my chief engineer for his view.

"It's all about gun running and/or drugs. You are likely to have a short and exciting life, but unlikely to live long enough to enjoy retirement." Thank you, but no thanks. I make a quick exit.

The big exercises upcountry afford the opportunity to fly at night in very dark conditions, mainly from airstrips in the jungle. The idea is to gain experience in making approaches to a basic landing "T" without using the aircraft's landing lights. After a few circuits are completed, a netted load is attached to the hook, and after making an approach to the T the aircraft is marshalled sideways to the drop point for the load. It works out better than we expect. Having used the basic T for judging the approach angle, we try various other light systems for judging the approach angle, sometimes steep, around 10 degrees, sometimes shallow, around 3 degrees. We also try splitting the controls so the co-pilot operates the lever and manual throttle and the captain operates the cyclic stick and yaw pedals. The captain judges if an adjustment in the approach angle is required and calls for appropriate power changes. This system works until approaching the hover, when we find that power changes cannot be made fast enough and the captain has to take over full control.

Training begins in January for the demonstration in March, prior to the disbandment. The final exercise upcountry is from 3rd–12th March and Exercise Crowning Glory is the largest to date. It is based at Mersing Airstrip towards the northeast corner of Malaya, involving day-flying only. I find myself flying mainly with the CO. All of us find some of the Land Rovers we are picking up are heavier than listed when being picked up as underslung loads. They must be equipped with extra batteries, extra radios and have the spare fuel tank full. We cope, using full power and dropping the rotor from 260 to 240 Rrpm as we transition into forward flight. Once we gain 35 knots we climb away nicely and by the time we fly to the drop off point and need to come to the hover, we have used a lot of fuel and hence have spare power.

Back at Seletar, formation flying training begins, mainly echelon port, with turns being announced beforehand and limited to 10 degrees of bank with a slow roll out onto the required heading. It is important when flying astern to stay above the downwash of the Belvedere ahead. Eventually we got the spacing down to about 1.5 rotor diameters.

Training for the BIG DAY, 8 Belvederes in formation, a rare sight, practicing for the big display prior to Disbandment, 20 MAR 1969

No 66 Squadron prior to Disbandment, Belvederes in background.

In a diamond-shaped formation, some nine Belvederes carrying guns, Land Rover trailers, and soldiers sweep over the place where everyone is watching – the big slipway near the Seletar Sailing Club. Having overflown the display area, the machines carrying the gunners peel off and in turn hover over the display area as the gunners abseil and rope down to secure the area. Next the guns arrive at five-minute intervals to be lowered onto the marked spots. With the guns in place the ammunition trailers are flown in, and the guns loaded with blanks. As the last machine disappears off to shut down in dispersal, the gunners fire a salvo of shots. This was a demonstration of how quickly the gunners can be deployed and made operational. As we land our XG 474, we were aware that the other helicopters are being dismantled already. Max Sceats and I, as the high time pilots, and Warrant Officer Tex Ward, Crewmen Leader, are rushed by Squadron Land Rover to where the AOC and the CO are reviewing the display, surrounded by hundreds of people. We are presented to him as representing the Squadron's efforts over the years. The AOC says the Squadron has finished on a high note and had demonstrated the capability of the 66 SQN's Belvederes in supporting Army Operations in Borneo and training in Malaya and that we should all be proud of our achievements. All of the aircrew have a last party together before we are sent on our separate ways. Our CO, Sqn Ldr Gray rises to the rank of Group Captain over his next few appointments, and I am posted to RAF Ternhill in Shropshire for a Helicopter Instructor's Course flying the single engine Whirlwind Mk 10.

Within the next few weeks, we have our farewell parties and Ann and I are booked to fly home in a VC 10, together this time. For our party in the garden of our bungalow, I get hold of a parachute that will not be going back to the UK and spread it across a tree in our garden for decoration. We have a big tub full of cans of Tiger beer in iced water. Music is playing on our new tape recorder. Early in the morning, Dennis Southern climbs in to the tub to cool off! A few days later and the professional packers arrive with wooden crates. Our stuff will go by sea to the UK; we will be kept informed as to where it is, and it will be delivered to the address we specify. With the UK withdrawal from the Far East now happening, it is an end of an era. My tour has been exciting, well paid and, fortunately, without a scratch. I have gotten used to flying a big and powerful twin-rotor helicopter and working with the Army. We all wonder how Singapore will cope with the UK military gone. We need not have worried, it seems. However, for Ann and me, heading off to RAF Ternhill again, with married quarters booked already, a new adventure looms!

The Army in the Far East are concerned at the loss of the tactical lift capacity of the RAF Belvedere. The Navy Wessex could not carry 5,000lbs underslung or 18 troops internally. The tandem rotor Belvedere helicopter, with its ability to operate at a max. all up weight of 18 troops/5,000lbs, even when the load was underslung, from the deepest of clearings on hot and humid days with zero winds was impressive, even though that might involve dropping the Rotor RPM from 260 to 240 at max. allowable torque during the transition to forward flight.

During the three years of operations and training in which I was involved, no aircraft or crews were lost. With the backing of proper maintenance and professional crews, more than 10,000 hours were flown across Borneo, Singapore, and Malaya. The only machine to be returned intact to the UK is now in the RAF Museum – XG 474. Another machine, XG 452, the 5th prototype that never saw RAF service, is at the Helicopter Museum at Weston-super-Mare. My personal flying total was 935 hours, being achieved between 9th Feb 1966 and 20th March 1969, gaining me a High Average Rating. Subsequently to the scrapping of the Belvederes in Singapore, the RAF came back to tandem rotors with an order for 50 Chinooks to be based at RAF Odiham, as its standard heavy tactical lift helicopter for use by the Army. Used now by many armed forces throughout the World, some 1,000 Chinooks have been produced in various Marks and it is still in production. It has a very good underslung load capability, good internal space – allowing 44 troops – and a good rear ramp, enabling rapid loading and unloading and a position for a tail gunner with a GPMG. Now, every day, the Tandem Rotor Concept is proving it's worth in military operations around the world, especially at altitude.

Chapter 9: Search and Rescue – RAF Leconfield, Yorkshire

(April 1969 – August 1972)

On returning to the UK in March 1969 I find I am scheduled for a Helicopter Instructor Course, which I had requested, and a Junior Command and Staff Studies Course (JC&SS), which I had not, both at RAF Ternhill near Market Drayton, Shropshire. A very senior officer decrees that for administrative reasons the two-month JC&SS course will take precedence and would impinge on the instructor course. In spite of strong protests all round, the decision stands. So, I start the instructor's course on the Whirlwind Mk 10 three weeks behind the others, and it proves impossible to catch up. I am taken off the course after 60 hours for insufficient progress. After the rest of the course graduates, I am given a Search and Rescue Course based at RAF Valley, Anglesey, on the Whirlwind, which I enjoy immensely, and on completion I am posted to B Flight, 202 Squadron, RAF Leconfield, near Beverley in Yorkshire. On leaving RAF Ternhill, I am informed that all future instructor course students would always start together on the same day or not at all, a lesson learnt, hopefully. I am told by one seasoned instructor that I was a lucky fellow. Is this because I am leaving the regimented training regime, or that I was going to Search and Rescue, where everyone appreciated the freedom of action that was part of the job during call-outs? Having experienced this freedom of action, I never go back. However, I am aware that failing an expensive Helicopter Instructor's Course, for whatever reason, is not good for your career.

Leaving Ann at her parents, I go ahead to Leconfield and find a lovely semidetached house to buy in Molescroft, Beverley, quite close to the base and shopping, and just a 10-minute walk to the marketplace. It belongs to OC Ordnance Disposal at the base, is fairly new, and in a very good condition. Having bought it, I drive Ann up from Berkshire with the cat in a box on the back seat and in our new car, a Ford Escort. Through snow showers, we just manage to make it up a long snow-laden hill a few miles from our new home. Welcome to Yorkshire.

I join B Flight and meet the Flight Commander, Peter Pascoe, a navigator. Our unit is in a hangar just 50 yards from the Squadron HQ with all the supervisors, CO, QHI and Nav. Leader. Sometimes, they will drop into our unit unannounced when we are on 15-minute SAR standby, ready to scramble. We are trained to make use of our flying skills and use our common sense, not deal with paperwork or directives from Group, worried about complying with them. I think they wanted to be reacquainted with the real world, people using their skills, knowledge, and experience to rescue people whenever and wherever needed. However, we could do with some notice of their arrival, if only to get the coffee cups and kettle ready.

What is clearly crucial in this job is good crew cooperation. In the hover in a rescue situation, as the pilot I cannot see what is happening underneath the helicopter. I need to trust the instructions given to me by the winch operator and fly smoothly and accurately so that the winchman on the end of the cable has a stable approach towards the survivor. Clearly, members of the Flight have years of experience and I need to respect them, whatever their rank, to get the maximum performance from all the crew members when it matters.

At RAF Leconfield, our mission is to come to the rescue of any aircraft in our area, military or civil, which is having problems. We are controlled by the Rescue Control Centre (RCC), which is located near Edinburgh. Historically, many RAF aircrew have ejected from their jets over the North Sea. However, our main work now is rescuing injured trawlermen somewhere in the North Sea and flying them to the nearest hospital, which is usually Hull or Scarborough. These are tasks coming in from HM Coastguard. Our flying averages out as 20 hours a month, mostly training. That includes 12 engine-off landings (no more than 6 at a session) and 12 practice forced landings (one a flight, initiated by a crew member). We are flying a single-engine helicopter, so we need to be able to cope if the engine fails at any stage of flight. One of my colleagues experiences an engine failure while flying at low level. He gets the Whirlwind down on a rough field and it is recovered to base by road. Although everything looks normal, a crack is found in the airframe, and it requires a Category 3 repair (serious) at a Maintenance Unit. The engine had lost power due to a well-known failure, the closing of the inlet guide vanes on the compressor. Although we are on call at night, our rescue training is only carried out in daylight. Night flying is also confined to circuits around the airfield only. My initial training with trawlers is with a group anchored off Grimsby waiting for high tide to dock, swinging on their anchors. Lots of masts, rigging and deck equipment to avoid with the winchman. It is clearly easy to tangle the winch cable around a mast or rigging, resulting in a long hover as the winch operator unravels the cable. The winch operator can cut the cable if all else fails. The trawlermen give us baskets of cod for our efforts and as a thank you for the rescues we have carried out for them over the years.

A lot of training is carried out in Bridlington Bay, in the company of an RAF Marine Craft Unit (MCU) launch acting as rescue standby. We practice hovering over water using a wooden lattice cross strung together (drum) as the target. The pilot has to fly accurately for the winch operator to pick up the drum using the hook on the end of the winch cable. Sometimes we have a live survivor who we winch down to the surface with a dinghy, which they inflate and climb into. Then we fly a low-level circuit and on the final approach lower the winchman so his feet trail in the sea on his way to reaching the dinghy and securing the survivor. With several of these exercises complete, we practice "Decks," hovering over our rescue launch, transferring people to and from the well in the stern. Sometimes we ask the launch to make way at 10 knots at a 30-degree angle to the wind, so the pilot has a good view of the front end of the launch. Sometimes we ask it to drift, simulating engine failure. When we come overhead in the hover the pilot cannot see the launch, which will gently spin underneath and drift erratically. He relies completely on the instructions of the winch operator for clearance underneath and correct position over the launch. Practice makes perfect and we practice every week.

A typical day in the life of a SAR crew:

12.45: Our new crew assemble and change into flight kit, including immersion suit, with lifesaving jacket and bone dome ready to don on a scramble.

12.55: We begin our handover with the off-going crew. We note the weather forecast, the radius of action (how far we can go out to sea, do a rescue, and have fuel to return to base) and which helicopter is on first standby, if a second helicopter is available. I look at the tech log, checking the helicopters have been serviced and noting any deferred defects and the fuel state, normally full.

13.00: Come on watch, our crew look over the helicopters, checking that all the normal kit in the cabin is there. I check over the cockpit and set the switches ready for a quick start up. Everything satisfactory, we make coffee for everyone involved, using our own personal mugs, and discuss our training trip. What do we individually need to complete our monthly training requirements? We agree what to do, where to do it, route out and back, passengers, survivors, drum, smoke floats and MCU involvement. I brief the crew and passengers and sign the authorisation form with all the exercise numbers, crew names, and names of extra people. I ring Air Traffic with details of our flight, alert the ground crew, walk out with everyone, walk round, climb in, switch the engine fuel computer on, and then commence the start-up checks from memory. Our navigator can travel in the cockpit, or in the cabin, if the flight is local. He can change easily from one location to another in flight. We lift off on tower frequency and change to approach on leaving the circuit. As normal, I climb to 1,000 feet – good height if the engine fails, as we have plenty of forced landing options flying over the open countryside of East Yorkshire. I check in with Coastguard, as we are heading for Bridlington Bay, where we find the MCU launch already at sea, and on this frequency ready to watch over us. We launch a smoke float and carry out a low-level circuit, coming to the hover at 30 feet, noting the wind direction and strength. We drop a drum into the water and then fly round in a circuit and, under instruction from the winch operator (either our navigator or winchman), come to the 30-foot hover and hold it until the drum is caught. Then, on the instruction "Up gently," I lift the lever so the helicopter rises slowly. After several of these drums, we exercise with the launch (decks), transferring people to and from, so we all get training. After that we lower a survivor and dinghy into the water, and we complete a circuit as the survivor climbs into the dinghy. When he is ready, we approach into wind and lower the winchman with a NATO strop, which will go over the shoulders and under the arms of our survivor. When the survivor is secure, our winchman checks that the survivor is disconnected from the dinghy and gives a thumbs up, showing he is ready for the lift. Normally, the instruction to me will be "Up gently," but might be "Hold your height – winching in," a more controlled lifting procedure. As the winchman and survivor together come up to the cabin door, the winchman ensures the survivor's back is facing the cabin so that the winch operator can pull on the back of the strop to pull him into the cabin. Once both are inside and well away from the door, the survivor can be released from the strop and directed towards a seat. In the real situation the door would be closed, and the survivor would be strapped in and checked over for injuries and given any necessary first aid or pain killers as the helicopter headed towards the nearest hospital. The cabin floor and sides are covered in a waterproof layer to protect the structure from saltwater corrosion. Once the "wets" are over we head to base where, on landing, the rear crew hose down their kit to wash off the salt and change into dry kit. Over a coffee, we hold a debrief including everyone involved while the helicopter is turned round by the ground crew and refuelled. Once that is done, I need to reset the cockpit switches, ready for the next scramble.

Next, what to have for the evening meal? Who is to cook it and who is to wash up? What's on the Box for the evening? As night falls, the helicopters are checked over, put in the hangar and our readiness state changes from 15 minutes to 1 hour. Our aircraft state, 2 serviceable, is logged with RCC near Edinburgh. We fix dinner and then settle down in our crew room or our bedrooms, usually aiming for lights-out around 10 p.m. Next to my bed is the telephone, with a direct line to RCC. I hope for a quiet night, as I set the alarm clock for 7 a.m. and start reading SOPs (standard operating procedures) – so soon asleep.

It's morning already, hoorah, so I get up, wash, shave, flight kit on, and then fix breakfast. By then both helicopters are outside, ready for their ground runs, checking out all systems and leaving switches ready for a scramble. The new weather forecast is available, so our navigator recalculates our radius of action. All being well, I phone our RCC and report two helicopters serviceable. At 9 a.m. our crew begin planning the day's training. Then the phone rings, and our navigator picks it up and starts writing on the scramble pad, with a carbon copy underneath. The call is from the Coastguard Rescue Centre, concerning a trawler 80 miles NE of base. They have a seaman with an injured arm, having had an accident with a deck winch. Details are recorded of the trawler: registration, name (Christabel), hull colour (black), proceeding in a SE direction towards Hull. It is within our radius of action, so we can go. I nod my understanding and run towards the helicopter as our navigator sets off the loud scramble bell. I climb in and switch on the engine fuel system computer, which takes 20 seconds to warm up, and then start strapping in and plugging my bone dome into the intercom system. Checks completed, I get the thumbs up from the ground crew manning the fire extinguisher and push the engine start button, watching the jet pipe temperature as the engine accelerates, to ground idle. When ready to start the rotor, I get clearance from outside and slowly accelerate the rotor up to 100% normal rotor rpm. Pre-take-off checks, and checking all satisfactory in the cabin, I lift to the hover, carry out more checks, then begin moving off, calling the tower for take-off. All clear, no other traffic and we are on our way. Our navigator comes up with the first course to steer – 045 degrees NE. I turn onto that and check that the main and standby compasses agree. As we approach the coast, I call the Coastguard and outline our mission. He copies our information and will come back if anything changes. As we coast out, I check that everyone is wearing a lifejacket. Our navigator works out that we have 20 minutes to go before we intercept the vessel, so it is worthwhile calling on the standard maritime frequency, "Christabel, Christabel, this is Rescue Helicopter zero one do you read? Over."

"Read you loud and clear, my position is Latitude… Longitude.. steering 200 degrees, proceeding at 12 knots for Hull, over."

"Thank you, heading towards you with our lights on, let me know when you see us, over."

"Certainly will. One of our crew has wrecked his arm in our deck winch and needs hospital to fix it, over."

"OK, copy that. We plan to take him to Scarborough Hospital. Our winchman will come down with a stretcher and will lift him in that. Has he been given any pain killers? Over."

"Yes, one shot of morphine, and I can see your lights on the horizon, you need to turn right a little to find us, over."

"Thank you, doing that. When we arrive, I will ask you to turn into the wind so we can put our winchman down more easily, over."

"That's understood, over."

We see the trawler at five miles, making a good speed. Our nav. leaves the cockpit by lifting his seat and going down a fixed ladder into the cabin. At a mile to go, a smoke float is dropped, and we circle and note the wind speed and direction – 200 degrees and 15 knots.

"Christabel, can you make your course 230 degrees and speed 5 knots? We will lower our winchman with a stretcher. After pick up we confirm we will go to Scarborough Hospital, over."

"Copied."

With everything ready in the cabin, we close with the trawler and assess that the best spot to lower our winchman is the small open deck area at the stern. He has 20 minutes available on deck, because of fuel considerations, before we need to lift him off or leave him behind. We lower him into the open space, and he unhooks from the cable. We circle, keeping an eye on what's happening on deck. After 10 minutes, we see all is ready for the lift off and close with the trawler. The winchman takes the winch hook lowered to him and attaches himself and the stretcher and gives a thumbs up.

"Up gently," instructs the winch operator, "he is clear of the vessel, move left, descend gently as I winch in. At the door, bringing them onboard, closing the door, you are clear above and behind, clear climb."

As I turn on course to west, our navigator reappears in the cockpit and straps in. "Make the course 275 degrees, ETA the school sports ground 15 minutes."

As we arrive, we see the ambulance waiting in the middle, and note the surface wind from chimney smoke from nearby houses. We land, the ambulance crew bring out a trolley, we load our injured seaman onto it, and he is transferred to the ambulance. We wave goodbye, and lift off, heading for base, avoiding the houses surrounding the playing field. 25 minutes later we land in dispersal and the fuel bowser is already there. I shut down, sign in on the tech log and flight authorisation sheet, and write a signal for the RCC, stating what we have done and the name of the survivor. The helicopter is refuelled and turned round by the ground crew, ready for the next flight. It is too late to have a training trip before handover to the next crew, so coffees all round, short debrief, mark up 2 Decks for the training record, and make the place clean and tidy for the oncoming crew at 13.00.

Something completely different happens at the end of February 1970. Our QHI (qualified helicopter instructor), Flt. Lt. Brenden Spikins is getting married in Anglesey at the end of the month and we are authorised to take a helicopter across with some passengers, and I am to be the pilot. On Friday 27th we take off and head west across the Pennines to RAF Valley in Anglesey, in good weather with lovely views of the hills. We land at our sister SAR Squadron (22 Sqn) and get transport to the Officers' Mess. Next day, a big Welsh wedding with lots of family and guests. Ourselves, in our best Number One uniforms, are heavily outnumbered. A good day, and one to remember.

The next morning, a Sunday, suitably late, we climb aboard our Whirlwind, having seen the weather forecast for the route – westerly wind, cloud base 2000 feet above sea level, icing level 6000 feet. We plan our route along the coast, clear of the North Wales Mountains, past Chester and then northeast towards Yorkshire. As we approach the high ground of the Pennines, it is clear that we will not get through flying in visual contact with the ground, so I turn away from the hills and begin climbing up into cloud to safety height (4,500 feet) before turning back on track. As we climb through 3,500 feet, we emerge into sunshine above an extensive white cloud layer below. Our Decca navigator shows us our position, but we can't use it to let down through cloud, so I call the nearest Master Diversion Station (always open 24/7), RAF Waddington, near Lincoln. We give our position in terms of range and bearing from them. We show up on their approach radar, become identified and check their weather – no cloud below 2,000 feet, so we can descend in their immediate area if needed. We press on, heading northeast, and as we clear the Pennines the cloud thins, and we can see the ground clearly. We thank Waddington for their flight watch service and change frequency to Leconfield Approach. Their weather is good, so two hours after take-off we touch down in dispersal, shut down, check in, then head for home; a long and successful weekend.

Our "Decks" training with the MCU is put to good use on 13th July 1970 when picking up the two-man crew of a USAF Phantom, who ejected over the North Sea near Whitby after the flying controls had locked up. Their parachutes are seen by a passing Hull trawler, MV Brinda, who picks them up. When we arrive on the scene, we have to persuade our two-man crew to put down their brandies and be ready to be winched up into our helicopter! 30 minutes later had land at base and an ambulance takes them to the Medical Centre for overnight observation. A few scrambles involve the Lightnings based at the nearby RAF Binbrook. One accident occurs at night, when a Lightning disappears while carrying out a low-level ident exercise on a slow moving Shackleton. A search of the area for the pilot proves fruitless. The aircraft is discovered months later on the seabed and is recovered to the surface intact. The wheels and flaps are down, the cockpit canopy was hinged open, the ejection seat still there, but no sign of the American exchange pilot …

Another scramble occurs when a Lightning has an engine fire at night over the North Sea and the pilot ejects. His rescue from the sea at night is successful, but something we do not train for, causing some controversy. RAF Binbrook, however, were happy to have him back safe and well. RAF Leconfield itself is a Maintenance Unit for Lightnings, and occasionally on post maintenance air tests problems crop up and we are scrambled to be ready if the pilot ejects.

After driving the new car, a Ford Escort, for a year, Ann and I found that it was not good in side-winds, so we buy a new Citroen GS, which had just come out. We like its steering, its good brakes, its soft suspension, and its large, unobstructed boot. We kept buying this car over the next 15 years, three in all, until they changed the design.

On a bad weather day, 20th November 1970, one of our crews is doing a cross-country in West Yorkshire. A mayday call is transmitted and, being duty crew, we are scrambled to investigate. En route to the area, we are informed that the helicopter has crashed and that we were to call in at RAF Finningley, near Doncaster, to pick up a photographer. In pouring rain, we find the wreckage in a field, surrounded by Police. It is clearly evident that our services are not required and, after the photographs are taken for the Board of Enquiry, we return to Finningley to drop off the photographer. Landing back at base we have to give the bad news to everyone. We have lost a crew of three, a passenger, and one of our two helicopters. The pilot was a Canadian on an exchange tour. The passenger was a WRAF admin officer from Scotland. Four pilots, including our CO, are invited to attend her family funeral near Edinburgh. We travel up by train and are made most welcome on this most sombre occasion.

Mid December 1970, my logbook shows I have clocked up 2,000 hours flying across many types of military aircraft and helicopters, so an excuse to have a celebration with off-duty aircrew at our house in Beverley. It goes well, especially in the small kitchen, where the wine is being handed out. There is a lot of interest in my new car with its special soft suspension and power assisted brakes and steering, which make it a delight to drive. Later that year another Citroen GS appears in our Sqn car park, and as Ann and I drive around Yorkshire we wave at these new Citroen GSs whenever we spot them.

On 31ˢᵗ May 1971, a call from the Coastguard. Could we try and rescue a boy who is stranded on a cliff face at Huntcliffe near Saltburn? The local Cliff Rescue Team is being mobilised, but we might be quicker. I consult with my navigator and winchman and we are all prepared to have a go, so the scramble bell is actioned and we are soon on our way. It takes 25 minutes to arrive on scene and we get an update from the Coastguard Mobile, positioned in a Land Rover at the top of the cliff, just above the teenage boy we can see about halfway up the cliff, standing on a ledge and clinging on to the rock face with both hands above his head. Before we move in, we discuss our options. Firstly, the winch cable, at 65 feet, will not allow me to place the helicopter in a hover above the top of the cliff face, so I will need to hover alongside the cliff face as close as I dare and hope that that is close enough for the winchman to reach. If not, then we will have to swing him in to grab the boy with both hands and pull him off the cliff as he swings away (physical lift). The boy has been there for an hour, so is getting tired and will eventually fall off, so we make the decision to try and rescue him. I tell the Coastguard what our plans are and that I will go off frequency during the rescue attempt so that I can concentrate on the instructions of my winch operator.

After the pick-up we will move away from the cliff face, descending slowly, and once over the sea in a 30-foot hover bring the winchman and the boy up to the cabin door, with the winch operator helping to pull them both into the cabin. Because we have discussed the plan and understand each of our responsibilities it goes quickly and easily, and within minutes we are landing on the cliff top, close to the Coastguard Land Rover. My winchman, F. Sgt Hart takes the boy forward and hands him over for safekeeping. Job done, crowds gathering and fuel looking low, it's time to return to base. In the post-flight signal to RCC we mention the necessity for a physical lift, expecting some reaction, but there is no comment.

Because of my previous experience of being Flight Safety Officer I am asked to carry out the same accident prevention publicity work. I get flight safety posters and accident summaries from Group. As on my previous squadron, pilot error features in most accidents, and reading about other people's experiences helps me not to repeat them. I also get to read the confidential anonymous reports of helicopter pilots in all three services. Lack of awareness causing near accidents seems to feature highly, especially during display flying, whether authorised or not.

On the morning of 16th June 1972, we are returning to base from the North with 10 miles to go when the big red ENGINE FIRE WARNING lights up. Immediately I start descending and transmit a mayday call to base, then alert my crew, who are both in the cabin.

"We see no signs of fire down the back," comes the response. The engine instrument readings are all normal, so probably yet another false warning from our simple fire detection system. I keep the engine going and use it to make a normal controlled touch down in a wheat field. I do a rapid shut down as my navigator, Ian Booth, takes a fire extinguisher round to the nose, ready to put out any fire. All is normal, so yet another false warning is confirmed.

Then a voice over the radio, "Copied your mayday – with you in 5 minutes." It is our new CO, Sqn Ldr Reekie, relieved to find us in one piece as he lands alongside. After discussion it is agreed that I would fly it back to base on my own, with him in escort watching my port side. No problems. Investigations show bent wires producing a false fire warning, so the entire wiring system is replaced. A month later my report is returned to me with the comment "Captain took correct action." Nice to get some official support from on high for my actions.

We do extensive training with the local lifeboats, and their inflatable Inshore Rescue Boats (IRBs), especially around Bridlington and Flamborough Head. We also take part in occasional displays on Community Lifeboat Days, with both the Lifeboats and IRBs. Sometimes the crowds would number hundreds. On 2nd March 1971 we participate in a big exercise at Flamborough Head. This time the 5-year-old son of the Flamborough Head Coastguard cliff rescue team leader, Ron Drysdale, runs around in delight in his new red wellingtons. 30 years later, with a balding head, he is commanding an Attack Submarine for the Royal Navy.

On 17th March, as we are carrying out winching offshore, the winch stops working. As I glance down at its power source, the primary hydraulic system, the pressure is jumping around. I select primary system off, which means the secondary system is now powering the flying controls. I make a landing on level ground at the top of the cliff and inform the Coastguard that we are making a precautionary landing due to hydraulic problems and to inform our base. 20 minutes later, a helicopter lands alongside with spare parts, four ground crew, and spare hydraulic fluid. With the "A-team" at work, the leak is soon found and repaired, and we are on our way. In future, most winches are electric, so do not affect the flying controls if there is a problem.

Operation Golden Eagle:

During training flights by Prince Charles at RAF Cranwell, a helicopter from our Flight is positioned on SAR standby at nearby RAF Waddington, in case he has to eject. My first flight is on 20th April 1971 and over the months of his training I complete 20 flights. Fortunately, our crews are not required. After his training is over, he asks to visit our SAR Flight at Leconfield. It so transpires that this is the same day that Ann goes into labour with our first baby, and I am hopping from one foot to another as he goes round our crew room, shaking hands and saying how much he appreciated our looking after him during his training. Eventually his entourage moves on and I am released to go home and take her to Beverley Hospital. No problems, having eventually made it home, she wanted a drive around the Beverley Common, the Westwood, before she was taken in! I am not wanted by the nursing staff, and by the evening I am sent home to await a telephone call. Christopher was born in the morning of 14th July. For breakfast, Ann is offered black pudding or scrambled egg on toast; this is Yorkshire after all.

Shortly after I arrive on the Flight, the Squadron becomes involved in an International SAR Competition, hosted in Belgium, but being new I am not involved. The first year the crew from our Flight won; the following year we come second but beat the Royal Navy, who had put in a lot of time and effort into their preparations. It transpires that the Royal Navy are bidding to take over UK SAR from the RAF, so the result is significant. During the competition it becomes clear that half the points awarded are for the results of the flying and half are awarded after post-flight disputes are resolved. Our CO, Sqn Ldr Taylor is adept in these circumstances and gains many points for our team. Many European SAR Agencies take part, using techniques, equipment and helicopters that differ from the ones we use. The competitions are artificial in content, so little is learnt for future use in operational rescues. The mingling with other crews and sharing experiences show we all had common problems, such as weather, communications, and equipment reliability.

My secondary duties include working with the local press to gain publicity for the RAF. Every call-out in which I am not involved, I am called in from home to tell the local papers about ongoing rescue missions and when the helicopters might land at hospitals with those we had rescued. B Flight is also requested to give presentations about SAR to local organisations, mainly the Women's Institute. A winchman and I drive out to the village hall with a film, a winchman's safety harness, a NATO strop, and a single-seat dinghy, which we get one of the audience to inflate by pulling on a cord and subsequently sit in, ready to be rescued. Because we are visitors, we are often asked to judge their cake-making competitions or crafts. A lot of reputations appear to be hanging on our decisions! One day we receive an invitation to give a presentation to the nearby College of Agriculture before their annual formal dinner. As usual, we show the film about RAF helicopter SAR, followed by a demonstration by our winchman using the NATO strop to secure a survivor (a volunteer from the audience) in a dinghy which they inflate by pulling on a cord. Our CO, Sqn Ldr Taylor, comes along to see that all goes well, which it does. We are all invited to the dinner afterwards, very cheerful. At Christmas time, B Flight receives letters, gifts of drink, and Christmas cakes from friends and relatives of those we had rescued during the year. One lady reassures us that "her Jim" was now fully recovered and has got a new sailing dinghy following his rescue by us from the River Humber in August. From time to time we are reminded by our superiors that if we judge that people are in imminent danger we should, if necessary, rescue them against their will and leave their equipment behind. The RAF will back up our actions if there is any complaint. One lady who lives close to Scarborough Hospital and sees our helicopter come in from time to time with casualties sends the Flight a big homemade cake every Christmas for many years. Eventually, we are invited to give a presentation and display at Scarborough Grammar School for the benefit of the pupils. It goes down very well; so much so that our new Flight Commander, Brian Gill, ends up marrying the Headmistress!

6th June 1972; a scramble call from the Coastguard. An inflatable dinghy with six boys on board is seen drifting out to sea off Withernsea, driven by the wind. On arrival at the scene the local mobile Coastguard suggests that we fly out to sea for a minute and then turn back towards the coast. With his binoculars, he can see both the dinghy and my landing lights, so can direct me so that my inbound course is in line with the dinghy. With six to pick up, I dump some fuel so I can pick them all up and regret that decision immediately afterwards; I haven't seen them yet! Suddenly, there they are, 50 yards ahead, all waving. Lucky boys! My winchman goes down and sends them up two at a time, coming up on his own and leaving the inflatable dinghy to drift off across the North Sea. We land on the beach near the Coastguard Land Rover, our young lads head off towards their grateful parents, and we depart for base, landing back with sensible fuel. Lucky all round, I would say.

So, after 43 rescue missions, getting my Master Green Instrument Rating and an "Above the Average" rating in my log-book, I am posted at the end of August 1972. My next tour is on the ground at RAF Coningsby a jet fighter station) near Woodhall Spa in Lincolnshire. My new job is to take over as the Station Community Relations Officer (CRO) from Sqn Ldr Watson. Clearly, I had fitted in well with helicopter SAR, a very big change from flying troops or underslung loads around the jungle. I had seized every chance to gain experience and work with the many talented and experienced crew members. Every successful rescue mission is down to good teamwork by the crew, underpinned by reliable helicopters, produced by our hard-working ground crew. As Ann and I were preparing to go, the Government announces that the construction of the Humber Bridge will go ahead. Instead of putting our house for sale through Estate Agents, we decide to sell it ourselves on a rapidly rising property market. We put a big notice in the front window: "FOR SALE – APPLY WITHIN." Pretty soon we have lots of people coming around, some looking like Estate Agents. Eventually we sell to a young couple at a good profit and set off to Woodhall Spa, near RAF Coningsby, to buy a house for our next tour of duty. We choose a large house with a lawn and small orchard – "Green Ridges" had won a design award in the 1930s at the Ideal Home Exhibition. It is indeed an ideal house for Christopher to grow up in: sandpit for his Tonka toys, a big lawn for his pedal car, and an orchard for cooking apples. Also, it is just 100 yards from his first playschool. Another adventure begins – this time on the ground at an RAF Station, where there are 50 noisy Phantoms using reheat on take-off, day and night, seven days a week ...

Chapter 10: Community Relations Officer (CRO) RAF Coningsby – Lincs

(1972 – 1975)

After looking around the area, Ann and I buy a big house on the edge of Woodhall Spa some five miles away from the base, an easy commute on quiet roads. Reporting for duty in the RAF Station HQ, I find that the CRO has a big office with lots of aircraft photos on the walls and close to the Station Commander at the end of the corridor. I am to report directly to him and clear all my activities on and off the RAF Station. I meet Sqn Ldr Watson, and we have a week to conduct a handover. At this time RAF Coningsby is a very big, active, and noisy operational base. The Phantom jets based there need to use noisy engine "Reheat" for take-off, as they are very heavy and need extra thrust until reaching 1,000 feet, when less noisy "Cold Power" could be selected. The Phantom is a multi-role fighter and Coningsby has a squadron specialising in each role: Air Defence, Ground Attack, and Photo Reconnaissance (day and night). There is also an Operational Conversion Unit (No 228 OCU) for training. Some 50+ aircraft are based at Coningsby, supported by 2,500 active young people, with money, sports cars, and confidence, with all that that entails. The airfield has been there since the war, in a variety of roles. The aircraft carry out noisy low-level flights over the UK and Europe, as well as practising air-to-air combat over the North Sea. Crashes do occur, both at the airfield and elsewhere. From time to time the airfield has visitors from other NATO Sqns in Europe, and is used as a "target" in various NATO Exercises. The airfield operates on a 24/7 basis and the high perimeter fence is patrolled by policemen and guard dogs. There is only one entrance to the base, with a barrier and a guard room. There is only one standard dress for CROs, best uniform, all the time. Coffee must be provided for press conferences and visitors. The local reporters come from newspapers based in Horncastle and Boston. I am to look after a press conference with these reporters every Monday morning at 10 a.m. They come with notebooks and cameras and bring copies of their papers for the Station Commander, Group Captain David RK Blucke to read. I am to work with his PA (a Sgt Secretarial branch). For administrative reasons he buys a one-page-per-day diary, using it as the Station Master Diary – logging all planned events in one document – to avoid overlap. Only he makes the entries, in green ink, with his initials and date. He buys a Who's Who, to update ourselves on visitors, and an Oxford English Dictionary to check our spelling. Often, like me, he works into the evening, especially if the Station Commander is also working late on paperwork.

One day I receive a full briefing from Sqn Ldr Watson: "Your job, David, is to keep the local population and local authorities on side via weekly press conferences and evening visits from local organisations. These visits are authorised by a Station Administration Order, signed by the Station Commander himself, so that everyone is aware of the purpose of a group of civilians being escorted around the Station. Also, you are editor of the "Phantom", the Station Monthly magazine – what the Squadrons have done and where they had been. You are the initial point of contact for the local community representing the Station on a 24-hour basis, for which you get a free BT phone in your house and half your calls paid for. Everything you handle and distribute has to be unclassified. Make it clear when talking to the flying units that you have no security clearance for this job. Fortunately, having a background of flying helicopters, you know nothing about modern jet fighters and how they operate, so there is nothing you have to forget. There are a few perks with the job. I took two reporters to Singapore for a week to cover a SQN detachment, arranged through Head of PR at Strike Command. They had both produced special editions of their papers covering their trips. Very useful publicity. After a year in the job, you might bear it in mind. Also, you should arrange to go the Strike Command

HQ near High Wycombe for a briefing about your job. A few months later you should go down to London and meet the RAF PR Branch at the MOD and make contact with the people there and see how they can help you with publicity material. This is the outline programme in your desk diary involving you for the next six months. I don't know how much public speaking you have done, but when I am facing an audience, I select someone towards the back and talk to them personally. Everyone else feels they are being addressed in the same way. Make the talk short, in general terms, and with no aviation or RAF language. In recent years we have built a "Hush House", so we can run a Phantom on an engine ground run inside with full reheat power selected and still hold a conversation outside; useful, especially on a Sunday. The noise and jet efflux are directed straight up, so no sideways noise affecting the nearby village of Coningsby. Some 80% of our media reports are positive to the RAF, and currently RAF Coningsby provides 50% of the RAF's recruiting material. Our Station Commander is keen on his Station, his Squadrons, and on promoting the multi-role Phantom. People realise that any task you have as CRO has come down from him, so you will find most sections will fully cooperate with you. Let's get out of this office and have a tour on foot of the establishment."

He takes me around the station to meet the heads of departments. The first one is the Ground Photographic Unit, with their photographers, studio, and developing and printing facilities. As CRO I will be working with them a lot (eventually half their workload). When we want to visit the Operational Squadrons, we need to phone ahead to the Adjutant to fix a meeting with the CO. They are busy people, so we try not to bother them, but as CRO we can help them with publicity, photographs, and information if needed. The Squadrons operate independently and are capable of being deployed overseas at short notice using aerial refuelling (during my tour, a Sqn detachment is sent to Cyprus following the Turkish invasion starting on 20th July 1974. No shots are fired, but several transport aircraft carrying Turkish troops are escorted away from overflying the UK Sovereign Base areas by our fully armed aircraft).

No. 228 OCU is also a shadow squadron (No 64 R), capable of mobilising in the event of war. During our evening visits with groups, we look into their maintenance hangar, seeing aircraft in various stages of being dismantled, with hatches open, wires and tubes everywhere, and hydraulic fluid dripping into puddles on the concrete floor. The aircraft look big and the wings look small, and you wonder how they get airborne.

One day I receive a letter from the leader of the Dogdyke Village Orchestra, offering to give a free concert of classical music at RAF Coningsby. Their village is within three miles of the airfield, so affected by our aircraft noise. The Station Commander is very keen and instructs me to fix a date and time, suitable location and put an entry in Station Routine Orders. They turn up in a coach, and I climb aboard and take them round to the station cinema, where we sort out their chairs, music stands, and a dais for the conductor. With the Station Commander, OC Admin, and several other officers in the front row, the rest of the seats fill up to a total of around 250 altogether. The orchestra's manager introduces them and each piece before it is played. The programme runs for 45 minutes and, fortunately, is not interrupted by aircraft taking off. The concert goes down well – nothing like modern pop music. They finish to long applause. The Station Commander and OC Admin are pleased with this local involvement. Perhaps it will happen again?

MOD Air send a film team down to produce a "filler," a two-minute slot for TV companies to use to fill in gaps in their schedules as and when necessary. It is about aircraft noise and the steps being taken by the RAF to mitigate it. We go onto the airfield alongside the runway and film our Phantoms taking off – plenty of noise there, as well as 40-foot flames coming out of the back of the aircraft. Very impressive – what you get when burning fuel at three gallons a second! Then we go to the Hush House, where the engineers run an engine at full power inside and a normal conversation can be held outside. Just to emphasise the point, the film crew want a scene of a child blissfully asleep. I know just the child, one who is asleep at 7 p.m. every night, so my Christopher makes a short appearance without any effort at all.

Christopher at play with Ann on the lawn
of our house in Woodhall Spa

Today, a recruiting officer from the MOD arrives with a photographic team from a London agency. Their requirement is to get photos of airmen and airwomen doing their normal job and, later, in a social environment, and with their agreement use the photos in recruiting material. The photographs of the airman climbing into the insides of aircraft are no problem, complete with oily overalls (looks authentic); similarly for the airwomen in Air Traffic Control, assisting the controllers, complete with clip boards and coffee cups. Several are taken so that MOD will have a stock to choose from. Fortuitously, there is a "Coningsby Festival" event happening next evening, involving the nearby Tattershall Castle. This is an informal gathering for a "Cheese and Wine" party for everyone in an interesting environment – a medieval castle, but with modern music from a portable tape recorder. I suggest that the recruiting team pay the five-pound costs of the people they want to photograph plus several of their friends to make up a party. The castle managers have let it be known that special wine glasses with an image of the castle etched on will be on sale, to commemorate the occasion.

Once the wine is flowing, people relax and look natural. Lots of photographs are taken and lots of wine glasses bought (currently, I use mine most days at home, and they still work well). Later, having got all the photographs they need, the team invite Ann and me to a meal at a restaurant in Coningsby village. We hear all about the machinations that happen at the MOD (nothing that I would volunteer for). They are pleased to come to RAF Coningsby, they always get what they need, and as a result at least half of the recruiting material produced features the Station.

From time to time the Station receives requests to host an AGM for an organisation, and to visit the Station. The first comes from the Cooperative Movement and goes well, and I address an audience of several hundred before the film about RAF Low Flying. The next visit is from the Country Landowners Association, requesting facilities for an AGM, a formal lunch with off-duty officers, and a quick tour of the Station. The request is reviewed by the Sta Cdr, OC Admin and me, covering what costs would be met by the RAF and what costs would be borne by them. This is all accepted by both sides, and we are sent a list of attendees, which included many Lords of the Realm. We propose a top table for the lunch for the Committee members and senior RAF officers. The non-committee members, including several Lords, are to be sprinkled among the ranks of junior officers. The weather that day is good, and as the many chauffeur-driven Rolls and Bentleys turn up they are directed to a temporary grass car park. The visitors board a fleet of RAF buses before going to the main Station Briefing Room, where I have a short presentation and film about Low Flying ready. We split the group into parties of 30 and tour the Station as it is working. Going into lunch, there is a table plan, so everyone finds their seat. The many tables are decorated with Squadron Silver. I stay outside ready to field any problems. I can hear the noise of conversation down the corridor. After the lunch we all board the buses for the station cinema and with the Committee in charge, the AGM goes through in 45 minutes. Back to the waiting buses and back to the cars and drivers. Eventually they are gone, and we go back to our offices. Next morning, the Station Commander calls me into his office. He is very pleased to have rubbed shoulders with members of the House of Lords, and to have "showcased" the station as it was working. Some of the Lords had served in the war and are impressed with the young officers that they met at the lunch and saw flying the Phantoms. The whole station was involved with the visit and it went smoothly. Thank goodness for the good weather though, the sunshine makes everything look better.

Out of the blue, Wg Cdr Lavender, CO No. 6 Sqn, calls me with the news that King Hussein of Jordon has accepted his invitation for a private visit to No. 6 Sqn to celebrate an anniversary event. Wg Cdr. Lavender had trained him to fly jets many years ago and had thought it appropriate to invite the King. The reply accepting was immediate, and the RAF has to inform the Foreign Office of the King's private visit to the country! They do not stop it, but send a representative along to see what transpires. Having arrived, the King flies in a two-seat Jaguar fighter bomber, with an instructor in the back (having flown in from

Lossiemouth, Scotland). The King flies on a two-hour low-level route up to Scotland and back, carrying out mock attacks on targets en-route. There is consideration that the Jaguar might replace some current operational jets being flown by various countries in the Middle East. The King's ADC flies in a Phantom, carrying out interceptions over the North Sea. The private visit to the UK is witnessed by Sqn members and families and a contingent of national and local media. At least 20 members of the press and two TV crews cover the King's inspection of the Guard of Honour in a hangar, as well as the flying and the display in another hangar of the range of armaments and fuel tanks that the Phantom could carry in the Ground Attack role. The weather is good, and there are no incidents to mar the day. A formal dinner in the Officers' Mess, involving No 6 Sqn Officers and wives, is laid on, followed by short speeches about the history of No. 6 Sqn, which had spent a lot of time in the Middle East. Finally, the King presents a solid silver model of a Phantom to OC No. 6 Sqn, destined for the trophy cabinet. Unusually, the Sqn had been presented with a second Royal Standard – by King Abdullah of Jordon on 15th October 1950, for long service in the Middle East. No. 6 Sqn spent all of WWII in the Mediterranean Theatre. In 1942 it was equipped with the Hurricane 11D, with two 40mm "S" guns for use against tanks in the Western Desert, acquiring the sobriquet of the "Flying Tin Opener".

One day, I am called into the CO's office. "Sit down David. You will be glad to know that your name is not on this long list of redundancies." He is holding a signal several feet long. "I am very upset, many fine men that I know with Fighter experience are being thrown out mid-career, including one who is a Staff College Instructor. This list involves mainly fixed wing fighter pilots but no helicopter pilots, as we are short. That's why you are OK. Lots of Chief Technicians as well. I will have to give at least two presentations to those affected, running over the options that are available. This is a bad day; the Air Force is losing valuable expertise. How are we to encourage skilled people to stay in the Air Force long term? This is all confidential for the moment. That is all."

I have never seen him so disconsolate, and there is nothing I can say that could be helpful. I make a mental note; we are in the hands of the politicians. Even holding a Permanent Commission, I can be made redundant at 3 months' notice should there be a change of policy at the top. I need to be aware.

After a liaison trip to Strike Command PR, it is agreed that on the next Sqn detachment to Singapore I will be able to escort two local reporters out for five days to cover the event. I raise this situation with my normal reporters, and they are all for it.

When the situation firms up with dates a few weeks ahead, my Boston newspaper wants to send a lady reporter instead of my regular contact. I check with Strike Command PR, and they are happy as long as she has a passport and is an accredited reporter. So it's all OK; arrangements are finalised and we head down to RAF Brize Norton, near Oxford, and present ourselves to "Departures". There we learn that the reporters are classed as VIPs and will sit in the front end of the VC10, while as escorting officer I will be in the main section with the families. No problem, we will meet up when we land at RAF Gan in the Indian Ocean. I quite enjoy the rear facing seat, the view from 30,000 feet and having meals served at regular intervals. Amazingly, the children are quiet and well behaved.

We land at RAF Gan, at nightfall. As we leave the aircraft, I manage to team up with my charges as they are met by the Station Commander in his No. 1 uniform, there to greet the senior civil servants and other VIPs. We all climb into a coach and are whisked to an air-conditioned room with fresh coffee and cakes before being taken to our air-conditioned accommodation. I plead that I remain with my charges, and we all settle down for the night. In the morning we wake to tropical sunshine, palm trees, and access to a coral sand beach. We can't resist paddling in the sea and getting a passing airman to take a photograph of our little group sitting on a wall. Then it is off to breakfast, followed by the Departure lounge and up the stairway into the aircraft with a smiling new crew who will take us on to Singapore.

We land at RAF Changi, on the east side of Singapore and are met by a dozen people holding cards with names on them. I spy my name, and we meet a young Flight Lieutenant who will look after us and shepherd us around in a Land Rover during our stay. 20 minutes later we check into a three-star hotel, where we will stay for three nights, full board, paid for by HM Government. Over coffee we discuss an outline plan to meet the Squadron at RAF Tengah and spend some time socialising, swimming, and looking at the highlights that Singapore could offer. The three days pass in a blur of meetings and photo opportunities, with meals and drinks outside. My young lady reporter is having the time of her life, and I feel I need to keep our little group together and focussed on our mission. On our last evening there, a group from the Squadron and ourselves team up to tour Chinatown and have a meal in the marketplace, where all the transvestites parade around in their long dresses and deep voices. We all are having a good time celebrating our good fortune; life is a beach, currently, and we all lap it up. Tomorrow is another day and will look after itself ...

Sure enough, the return to the UK goes without a hitch and we disembark from the RAF VC10 into grey skies and a blustery wind. We agree the date for our next meeting at Coningsby and how their newspapers will present the story. They bring out special pull-out sections covering the deployment of the Sqn, its purpose (to demonstrate the rapid reinforcement that air to air refuelling can achieve), and photos of aircrew and ground crew around their aircraft in the tropical sunshine. It is good publicity for the RAF and might help recruiting. For me, going back to Singapore some five years after I left in March 1969, there are big changes. New roads, new buildings, and new docks, coupled with big plans for land reclamation from the sea. To think I had been worried how they would cope when the British Forces left!

I get a telephone call mid-morning from the wife of one of our Squadron's pilots. She is aware that I will looking after a visit to the Station by the local Probus Club tonight. Can she and two other wives join the group for the visit?

"Our husbands tell us nothing about what goes on at the base, and we would like to learn something, however general."

"Yes, fine, I agree, be at the Guard Room by 7 p.m. with some ID."

With my group arriving by coach, we all transfer to an RAF bus, and I hand out the visitor passes to wear on outside clothing. In the impressive Main Briefing Room, I welcome everybody to RAF Coningsby and outline the programme: a film about RAF low flying and then visits to the OCU hangar, the flight simulator, and Air Traffic Control, followed by refreshment in a Public House in Coningsby village. The film outlines the requirement for low flying training – not appearing on radar screens – and the need to confine this to certain parts of the country (designated Low Flying Areas). We walk together to the back of the OCU hangar and are welcomed by the engineering officer. The hangar is brightly lit, and we can see several aircraft in various starts of disassembly, engines out, hatches open, wires and tubes everywhere, and red hydraulic fluid dripping into drip trays on the floor. Men are working in their overalls under some aircraft, which are on jacks, warning notices everywhere, so we stay well clear; the work goes on and we are cheerfully ignored. Times up, and it's a short walk to the flight simulator. In the flight simulator we stand behind the instructor's chair as he gives problems to the crew in the "box," causing them to declare an emergency and request assistance. Leaving them to recover to an airfield on one engine and an electrical failure, we walk a short distance to Air Traffic Control. There we split our group, with half going upstairs to "Local", with controllers looking after all aircraft movements visually within five miles. We watch aircraft take off using reheat; clearly visible is the 40 feet of flame coming out of the back. Even inside triple glazing we hear the thunder of the engines as they thrust the aircraft up into the sky. The other half go into a dark room where radar screens show aircraft movements up to 100 miles away. Calmly, the controllers are separating the aircraft taking off and those landing and others transiting through the area, handing over as necessary to RAF Surveillance Radars for long distance flights. At the scheduled time on the programme, I gather up my group, check numbers, and head to the Guard Room for them to board their coach. The officer's wives zoom off without a word. Surprised, stunned or shocked at what their husbands are getting up to flying these aircraft, I never learn, but there again, no complaints.

Having bought a house in Woodhall Spa, Ann and I need to integrate with the various activities in the Village. I join Rotary and attend their meetings in a local hostelry and discuss fundraising events. I am able to give useful publicity for the events by displaying posters in the various Messes at the base. I learn that quite a few officers have bought houses in Woodhall Spa, famous for its golf course and the home of the Dambusters, No 617 Squadron. At the base, I am prevailed upon to give a talk about "Buying a House" to the Wives Club. Most of them have followed their husbands from base to base, living in Married Quarters, and are missing out on the steep rise in property prices that is taking place throughout the UK. I outline the various types of mortgages and some legal aspects of buying property. I explain that I was on my third house, moving round the UK on posting. Judging by the in-depth questioning, it was clear that several wives were giving the idea a lot of thought and were going to talk to their husbands! Certainly three Wg. Cdrs. buy luxury bungalows in a new estate, a few yards from our traditional home with its orchard producing cooking apples by the box-load. At an important social occasion Ann and I meet the MP for Horncastle and Louth, Sir Peter Tapsell, who becomes the "Father of the House" (2010 – 2015). Also at the gathering is the American harmonica player Larry Adler. He makes it look so easy as he gives a quick demonstration of his talent. As our Christopher is growing up, he is eventually old enough, at two, to attend a play group. There is one just 100 yards away, but down a main road, so he is put into a harness and walked securely there and back. As an only child, he now gets used to playing with other children and sharing toys. Ann gets to meet other mums, and more friendships start.

I am called into the CO's office on the morning of 9th August '74. The Parish Council of my village of Woodhall Spa have requested a visit.

"You can do this one, David. Fix a suitable date and draw up the Admin Order. All yours." He passes me the letter, marked "CRO – Fix", with his initials and date. As I leave his office, I notice his very full in-tray. As I pass through his PA's office, I mention that fact to him.

"He will leave half of it until he returns from his trip with 41 Squadron this afternoon. I can see another long day coming on."

Later, in the afternoon, I hear the Public Address booming out, "CRO to ring OC Operations now."

I dart into the nearest building find a phone and dial his extension. "OC Ops here. Right, David, come to my office straight away. I can't discuss it over the phone." Click.

Five minutes later I knock on his door. "Come in," booms his voice, "sit down, David, and take some notes. Firstly, the Station Commander has been killed along with his Navigator Flt Lt Kirkland of 41 Sqn, in a flying accident near Downham Market,

189

Norfolk. There has been a collision with a low-flying light aircraft. As OC. Ops I take over responsibility as Station Commander from now on. I am going to be very busy these next few weeks. I want you to handle the press and work under OC Admin, agreeing what can be said and done in the circumstances. That is all."

I hurry back to the office and book a Priority call to Strike Command and I am put through in seconds to the Head of PR. He is very calm about my news. "David, you may not be aware that, on average, the RAF loses 25 aircraft a year around the world through accidents. I will help you with this one. I will put in the post today the CVs of the crew, ready for your next press conference on Monday with your local newspapers. If there is going to be a funeral locally, then invite the local press. Any questions you may get over the phone, direct them to the MOD RAF Press office. Inquiries will be handled day and night. I will just confirm the number. Keep in touch with me on a daily basis. You are going to have a busy time this next two weeks. Good luck."

I make suitable notes and knock on the door of my new boss, OC. Admin. It is mid-afternoon and already a very smoky atmosphere in his office (five years later, he dies of lung cancer). I run over what Strike Command has said and what action I propose to take. He nods his acquiescence.

"Just let me know what you are doing, and when the funeral arrangements are firmed up, I will brief you. You need to know that anyone close to David Blucke, like his PA and many senior officers, will be distraught. He was a Flyer, never happier than flying with one of our Squadrons. A Group Captain at 42, he led from the front. His hands-on leadership was inspiring. However, we all need to carry on. The station is continuing with training flights. Don't approach 41 Sqn, they will have their hands full for the next two weeks. Check in with me first thing in the morning and before you go home every day. I assume you will have your normal press conference on Monday. I may have some photos for you. Things will be strained as we all readjust. A new Station Commander will be drafted in within weeks. That's enough for today. Try and get some sleep tonight. I will see you when you check in tomorrow."

Eventually there is a full military funeral for the Station Commander, and the service is held at Coningsby Village Church. The Church is packed, with many standing at the back and outside. My job is to look after the local press and acknowledge local council leaders as they arrive. The station is quiet for a few hours during the service. It is moving to see the RAF station and the local community coming together in this moment of grief.

Three weeks later, the new Station Commander arrives: Group Captain Dennis Allison (later AVM). However, I continue to report to OC. Admin and put up with his smoky office. There is talk that the Battle of Britain Memorial Flight will be coming to Coningsby and the public will have access. That will need some planning. It will have its own publicity arrangements, so I will not be involved as CRO. In Feb '75 the new Station Commander calls me into his office, saying my posting to Cyprus (what posting?) was cancelled, but I will be going overseas to Anglesey at the end of March and returning to Search and Rescue, joining 22 Sqn at RAF Valley. I like RAF Valley, as it is close to Snowdonia with its lakes and mountains, and I will be paid to fly over it in a helicopter! My successor, Flight Lieutenant Porter, ex-Canberras, will be posted in early to give a two-week handover. Clearly this job, CRO, is considered important at MOD level. I learn that CROs are being established at all major RAF Stations, and not just those with Fighters and Bombers.

During the handover to my successor, on 3rd March 1975, a Phantom crashes near the home of our main local noise complainer, who lives two miles out along the runway centreline. The pilot is faced with an engine exploding and catching fire while he is flying over the airfield at 400 feet. He and his navigator successfully eject. We visit the house, get through Police Guard eventually, and the owner, a lady, is hysterical.

"You did this deliberately, just to spite me for complaining!" She is clearly traumatised and in no mood for conversation. She drags us round to a corner of her farmhouse, where a wing tip has taken out about 20 bricks. She was lucky, as she was inside at the time. The aircraft debris has mainly ended up in the big drainage ditch (River Witham) at the end of her garden. I understand she moved eventually, quite understandably.

As part of the handover, we prevail on our local reporters to run an article about the change of face of the CRO, with appropriate mugshots and background information. Flt Lt Porter and I go round the local area speaking to Council officials and introducing my successor. We both receive the same message from all sources:

"We put up with the aircraft noise, the influx of young people, and all that that entails, but please stay open, as you pump a lot of money into the local economy and drag us all into the 20th Century!"

I am on my way, at the end of March 1975, to RAF Ternhill for a SAR Refresher course before going to C Flight, 22 SQN at RAF Valley, Anglesey. Once there, we put our house at Woodhall Spa up for sale. The housing market is still affected by the "Oil Embargo" following the Yom Kippur War in the Middle East, so there might be a delay with the sale. I get an unfurnished Married Quarters on the "Patch" at RAF Valley, so we move across. Christopher starts primary school on the base in September, age 4, and loves it.

Chapter 11: Anglesey Search and Rescue

(1975 – 1979)

In early April I go across on my own to RAF Ternhill and start my refresher course on the Whirlwind MK 10, my first flight being on 7th April. All the old flying skills come back, and I remember all the checks. On 16th April I regain my Master Green Instrument Rating, very pleasing. With the basics completed, its off to the Search and Rescue Training Unit at RAF Valley Anglesey to train in Holyhead Harbour for "Wets and Decks" and in Snowdonia for "Mountain Flying." I am briefed on the psychological effects of flying in mountains and the need to continuously scan the flight instruments for attitude and airspeed, as just looking outside at the mountains gives false clues to these vital parameters. All training is completed by 30th April.

On 1st May I report to "C" Flight 22 Squadron at RAF Valley, which is just a few hundred yards away, with its own hangar for the helicopters, a wooden hut containing offices, and a combined Ops room and Crew room. I meet the CO. Flight Lieutenant John Garnons-Williams, whose previous tour had been in Cyprus, lucky fellow. During the first week I am shown around Anglesey and the low-level routes to get to and from our base in bad weather for both training and operations. Often, we fly in weather in which the station's fixed wing Gnat training aircraft are grounded due to poor visibility or low cloud base. Within a week I am on-shift and responsible for my actions on training and Search and Rescue missions. Training continues, with up to three flights a day, making use of the good weather. My first rescue mission is on 10th May, a search for a yacht reported missing. We did not find it in the area we were told to search.

I apply for and get a married quarters (MQ) on the "Patch" and I bring the family across from Woodhall Spa. We leave our house there in the hands of an Estate Agent and say goodbye to our friends. We enjoyed our tour in Lincolnshire, but Anglesey now offers sandy beaches and, half an hour's drive from our MQ, the mountains of Snowdonia. Our MQ is at the top of a road and close to the medical centre, plenty of open space for us to play outdoors with Christopher. We are living next door to my helicopter instructor, Bob King, through whose hands I had passed during training. I make enquiries and it is agreed that Christopher can start in September in the Reception class of the primary school at age 4. Being on the base, it is for children of RAF families, so teaching is in English. Christopher likes it and is happy to walk there, rain or shine, with Ann in escort. After dropping him off she can pop into the NAAFI shop close by for groceries.

Flying with "C" Flight continues at about 20 hours a month, usually with two training flights during a 24-hour duty shift, sleeping overnight at the unit. During daylight hours we are at 15 minutes notice to scramble in the event of a call-out by the RCC, the Coastguard Operations Centre, or the Police HQ in Llandudno (for mountain rescues). In the crew room we listen to the emergency radio frequency, 243mcs, and if we hear a mayday call in our area we can scramble at our own in-itiative. Although we are based at a Master Diversion Airfield, ready for aircraft emergencies 24/7, most of our scrambles in-volve civilians in trouble on the coast, at sea, or in the near-by mountains.

On 11th May I fly the Station Commander, Group Captain Edwards, to the Outward Bound School, "Plas y Brenin", near Capel-Curig for a Liaison visit. I land the Whirlwind on a patch of grass at the end of a lake, adjacent to a footbridge to the Centre. As a crew, we all go in together, taking a NATO strop, and have the opportunity of addressing their Mountain

Rescue Team. My winchman, Ian Brunton, shows them how to secure the strop around their shoulders, before they would be lifted up to the helicopter by the winch. We brief how to approach and leave the helicopter on the ground when the rotor is turning, using the safe zone. Helicopters can carry rescue teams from an assembly point, many miles forward and possibly thousands of feet upwards, towards the site of an incident, saving them a lot of effort. Similarly, when survivors are found they can be put aboard or be winched up into a helicopter and then flown direct to a hospital, giving them the best chance of recovery. After a question-and-answer session, four members of the team volunteer for a flight up to the nearby Glyder Fawr, with its flat mountain top, where we can practice winching in an open area. With them all strapped in, I start the Whirlwind and, keeping the cabin door open on take-off, they can see the wonderful countryside from an aerial view. Within 30 minutes the exercise is completed, and we return to drop off the team members and pick up the Station Commander. Once airborne on our way back to base, he asks to take control as we fly down Llanberis Pass, usually a route clear of low-flying training jets. He flies all the way back to RAF Valley, including the landing, an experience a lot different to the Gnat jet trainers he normally flies. Our visit to the Outward Bound School has gone down well, and I am invited to visit them and be taught how to paddle a canoe. On arrival for my treat, I change into a wet suit and plimsolls and, with their chief instructor, head out into their lake. I am taught to paddle and to recover if I ever end up capsized in the future. I can see why people enjoy canoeing on lakes, and down quiet rivers, though white-water work is clearly beyond me.

On Christmas Eve I am tasked to deliver a special Hamper from RAF Valley to the crew of the Skerries Lighthouse. On board is Padre Knight and the Station Commander. Being a remote spot, I don't shut down, and it takes just a few minutes for the handover and a few greetings. Being new to C Flight, I am on duty for the morning of Christmas Day but home in time for a splendid lunch, prepared by Ann, with all the trimmings.

1976

The year kicks off on 23rd January, with a search for four missing walkers in Snowdonia. In our helicopter we can cover a lot of ground quickly, but they are found by the Ogwen Valley Mountain Rescue team and are reported to be in good shape. Back at base, on the 27th we launch for a "precautionary" scramble for a Gnat jet trainer reporting difficulties. He lands safely and we log just five minutes flying. The year continues with a mix of scrambles, with problems in the mountains of Snowdonia and along the Anglesey coast. Training continues every day to keep our skill level high and to develop crew co-operation.

On 1st April we are tasked by the MOD to work with the Blue Peter team from the BBC, who are producing a programme about the Beaumaris Lifeboat, which operates in the Menai Straits. The team report to C Flight, and with our crew and some curious groundcrew, we learn what is required from us. Apparently, the team want to film from our helicopter and capture shots of the Lifeboat travelling at speed, filmed from alongside and also passing underneath the helicopter hovering at 50 feet. A number of "takes" would be necessary and later on they would select the best shots for the programme. The team and our crew go out together to the helicopter to discuss where people needed to sit, what harnesses they would need and what intercom requirements are necessary. That sorted, we fill up the crew room and I brief the flight and their director briefs the film shoot. We all know what is going to happen and we ring up the Beaumaris Lifeboat Unit and agree timings. The weather is good, with the usual westerly wind of 20 knots. With a good radio link on the Coastguard radio frequency, we are able to co-ordinate our requirements and the film shoot goes well.

Back at base we are promised that we will be informed when the programme goes out.

When the programme is broadcast there is about five minutes of coverage, clearly shot from above, but no mention of the use of our helicopter. However, it was fascinating working with the Blue Peter team. They certainly earn their money.

On 24th April we are scrambled by Air Traffic Control. The pilot of a single-seat Hunter reports that his port wing is on fire. He is turning the aircraft towards the sea and is ejecting. Sure enough, as we select "Homing" on the emergency frequency we can hear the characteristic bleeping sound of a SARBE beacon, and the needle responds on our direction-finding instrument. We coast out near Maltreath, on the south coast of Anglesey and soon spot an orange single seat dinghy. As we approach, the pilot opens his protective canopy and switches off his SARBE beacon. Our winch operator, Peter Pitcher drops a smoke float to check the wind direction and strength; southerly at 10 knots. No need to hurry, we have practiced this situation many times before, and we need not rush to get it right. Our winchman, Dick Amor, is lowered as we make our approach to the dinghy. He secures the pilot in the strop, checks the dinghy is not attached, and signals that they are ready to be lifted.

On the instruction, "Up gently," I apply a little more power, and both are lifted clear of the dinghy. In seconds they are being brought in through the cabin door. The rescued pilot is checked for injuries – thankfully there are none – and we head back to base. As we head towards the shore, we see the ejector seat on a sandy beach, so we land alongside and load it into the cabin. It will be useful for the investigation, and it might be a hazard to the public. We are cleared by Air Traffic Control to fly direct to our medical centre, where we land, and our pilot is taken in for a check-up. It is good to use our training for a rescue involving aircrew. It is why we are based at RAF Valley in Anglesey, a Master Diversion Airfield and a busy jet training base.

Not a week later we are scrambled for an accident near Dolgellau. Two Gnat training aircraft flying at low level have collided and crashed, killing four instructors. We land near the crash site and my winchman and navigator get out to see if they can do anything. Already the local police are there, guarding the area. All they need is more manpower. I pass the message on through a radio link and within an hour, members of the RAF Mountain Rescue Team are flown in by helicopter, equipped to remain on site 24/7, as needed. A week later the Station Commander flies with me on a recce of the Anglesey coast, looking its best on a blue-sky day. He flies the Whirlwind around the lovely scenery, then back to base for a normal landing in our dispersal. I feel he appreciated a break from the confines of his office.

May brings holiday makers flocking to the Anglesey coast, some taking to the water for the first time in kayaks. On 30th May the Coastguard scramble us to an incident near Trearddur Bay. A group of seven kayakers from a training school are reported in difficulties at the bottom of a cliff face in rough water, driven there by a strong onshore wind. As we arrive at the spot, the Coastguard Land Rover is there monitoring the situation, but they cannot effect a cliff rescue, so we have been called in. The situation is not ideal; the strong southerly wind means I have to point the helicopter into wind, thus having the cliffs out of sight behind me. Our winch cable is just 65 feet long, so to carry out a rescue I need to lower the helicopter into a wide cleft and hold my position accurately as my winch operator Terry Hannaby lowers our winchman Dick Amor down towards the group, some of whom are already in water, holding on to their companion's craft. It takes 15 minutes to get them all up and squeeze them all into our small cabin. I know that we are overloaded, but the strong wind means I do not need to use excessive power to hover. As the last survivor is brought aboard, I am instructed to fly away from the cliffs as the kayaks get smashed up on the rocks below. A minute later we land alongside the Land Rover and Terry leads them out. We will get their names later for the record, but we head back to base for a well-earned coffee. That down, and the helicopter refuelled, the Coastguard scramble us again. A climber has fallen down a cliff near Penrhyn Mawr on the mainland and is injured. Luckily, this time we can lower Dick with a stretcher down to the incident site easily, and a few minutes later we move in for the pickup. With that completed its off to the nearby Bangor Hospital, where an ambulance is waiting to take our casualty directly into their A&E department.

As the year rolls by, Ann and I are increasingly bored with our MQ existence. I spend a lot of time at home on "Second Standby," confined to the house or garden, ready to be called in for duty if the "First Standby" crew are scrambled. There is nothing we can do to the MQ and the garden looks neat and tidy. So, Ann and I consider buying a house locally, ensuring that Christopher can remain at the same school. We settle on an old farmhouse, "Gwynfryn", in the district of Rhoscolyn, near Holyhead. It had been used for B&B for some years and there is large caravan on site, plumbed into the services and ready to be rented out. To bring the farmhouse and caravan up to scratch there is a lot of work that I can do while I am confined to the house on call. Any job that I undertake must be such that I can leave it at short notice. I am a dab hand at painting and decorating, so I can see myself being productively employed over the coming months. Gwynfryn is to be our new residence, and I can't wait to start work and explore the local countryside and coastline on foot. Because we need to get our Christopher to school when I am on duty with the car, we need to buy another one. Ann spots a bargain on the NAAFI noticeboard and I get another, somewhat old, set of wheels for £65, an Austin A30. It gets me to and from work, and that's all it is needed for, so will suffice. Over the next two years Ann and I improve the house and extensive garden, as well as building a sand pit for Christopher's Tonka toys. While the work is being done, we experiment with taking in some paying guests as well as renting out the caravan. It keeps us occupied, and we gain valuable experience. On days off, we head up to Snowdonia to explore. One day, as a family, we set off on the Miner's track from the Pen y Pass Café on the Llanberis Pass, up towards the Snowdon summit. Christopher marches off and, as a five-year-old, sets a cracking pace. We follow the track around Lyn Llydaw, then the path steepens going up to Glaslyn. Having arrived, he is all for tackling the steep, stony zig-zag path up to the summit. Ann and I have to gently talk him out of it, and we all wash our hot feet in the cold lake waters. We promise him a soft drink at the café when we return (we have forgotten to bring any boiled sweets or water, not expecting to venture so far). We return wearily at days end to our former farmhouse in Rhoscolyn. Over the years we follow the improvements to the house that subsequent enterprising owners make, using Google Maps and estate agents' websites. With more and more development on site, the valuation increases rapidly. The latest owners are making a go of it, providing a lot of holiday accommodation. One day we must go back and see for ourselves. By contrast, we find out from our friends in Woodhall Spa that our lovely old house there has been knocked down and a new modern building is going up on site. Ouch!

The promised introduction of the twin engine Wessex as a replacement for the single engine Whirlwind begins to take place in the Autumn. One by one, our pilots go off to RAF Odiham near Basingstoke for the conversion course. My course starts on 10th September and, over 43 hours' flying, covers every aspect of its operation, mainly in support of the Army. So, a week of the course is on Salisbury Plain under canvas, and the flying involves carrying underslung loads and operating into forest clearings by day and by night. We also practice instrument flying under the hood, carrying out various procedures for descending safely through cloud towards airfields. My final handling check is conducted by Master Pilot Walker on 15th October. That completed, I head for home after a month away, my little Austin A30 working hard to get to 50 mph and reminding me to get the heater fixed! Back at base, I am checked out on flying the Wessex in the mountains, on coastal cliffs, and Decks and Wets in Holyhead Harbour. In every way, the Wessex is a big step up from the Whirlwind, not least in having two powerful engines (2500 hp total) to counter strong downdrafts and turbulence when mountain flying. The cabin is a lot bigger, so we can pick up more survivors at one go and carry large mountain rescue teams with their stretchers and rucksacks. Coupled with the provision of a 300-foot winch cable powered by an electric motor and auto stabilisation on the flying controls, this is just the sort of helicopter that is needed for the jobs we are called upon to do. More and more I look forward to going to work and gaining experience of flying over and operating in the mountains of Snowdonia, whatever the weather.

*Approaching a RAF Marine Craft Launch,
Holyhead Harbour*

Search & Rescue Wessex in Dispersal, RAF Valley Anglesey

At the end of 1976 the first BAE Hawks arrive at Valley to take over the advanced jet training role from the Folland Gnat, which had entered service in 1963. From a helicopter pilot's point of view, one jet is the same as another as they fly around North Wales at low level and high speed. To help prevent collisions we put on our bright landing lights as well as our anti-collision lights, and of course we are painted yellow all over. We know that the jets exit the Low Flying Area by flying along the A5, past Capel Curig, over Lyn Ogwen and climbing up over Bethesda, so we avoid that area for training. If we are called out to a rescue in that area, we keep a good lookout along the route that the low flying jets are likely to travel.

From time to time the Police Control Centre in Llandudno brief us about people reported missing somewhere on Snowdon. They usually have a description of the group – numbers, ages, clothing – and the planned destination. Can we do a quick look at some of the many routes that lead from the Snowdon summit down to local car parks? They will also call out the Snowdon

Mountain Rescue Team, who will follow various routes up to the summit – if necessary, into cloud. On training flights, we fly up these tracks, pathways, and Snowdon Railway, in good weather and at slow speed so we remember the twists and turns, obstructions, and location of any refuges. People must wonder what we are up to, but we receive no complaints. Some routes in, like the Watkin Path, are almost level tracks initially, with plenty of space to land if required. Then, after a while, the path becomes very steep, with no chance of landing; picking anyone up will involve winching. Around the top of Snowdon there are just a few places where you can land a helicopter and, if clear of people, we practice landing on, so we know in future what can be done if the summit is clear of cloud. Some mountain summits, like the Glyders, are smooth and can be searched even if covered in cloud, with the helicopter pointing into wind and moving sideways to the right, with about 10 feet wheel clearance from the ground, with all 3 crew members looking out in the direction of travel.

1976 will be remembered as the year of the Great Drought across most of the UK. In North Wales the forests are tinder dry, and on 27th August we are called out to help with a large forest fire near Llyn Crafnant. We land to pick up the Fire Chief so that he can see the extent of the fire and where it is spreading. We keep our distance from the pall of smoke and turn down a request to fly over the top of the biggest blaze; we are in a single-engine helicopter, and it might be pushing our luck to attempt this. After an hour he has seen enough, and we reunite him with his team. The fire burns for many days across forests and moorland, and there is little that can be done.

A few weeks later we get a request from the police to fly past a remote house with a high wall around the back garden. They suspect that stolen cars are being stored there, away from public view. We agree to fly past just once at 500 feet, with the cabin door open so photographs can be taken as evidence. Sure enough, as we fly by I can see from the cockpit the vehicles packed together. We understand the police conduct a raid a few days later; another case solved.

Operating in the Snowdonia National Park we get requests from time to time to help with restoring paths that the thousands of visitors have worn out. Our part in the task is to carry loads of stone in a net as an underslung load, from the car park at Pen y Pass up a thousand feet or more to where the restoration team are working. It is good training for us and makes us familiar with that popular path, should we need to search along it for missing walkers in the future.

On 23rd November our crew are tasked with carrying out some dry winching with a group of 10 fast jet trainees on a week's survival course near Capel Curig. We fly in to the Plas y Brenin Outdoor Centre, land by the lakeshore, and shutdown. It gives us a chance to brief the trainees in what to expect if they are rescued over land. They will be offered a NATO strop at the end of the winch cable, which they need to put over their shoulders and secure the toggle. When ready to be lifted they should give a thumbs up and they will be gently lifted up to the door of the helicopter. On arrival they will be turned round to face outside, and the winch operator will pull them into the cabin and after removing the strop, point them to a seat for them to strap in. While we are briefing, some instructors and students of the Centre are listening, and continue to watch as we bring in the helicopter a few minutes later and start winching. Having loaded up with 10 trainee pilots, we take them for a quick flight around the nearby Snowdon Peak, leaving the main cabin door open so they can see the magnificent scenery.

Winchman with survivor, double lift

1977

The year opens quietly in regard to SAR ops, so every shift it's training, training, training, keeping those crew co-operation skills up to the mark. Something different on 23rd January: we look after the Liverpool Echo, give them a demonstration of dry winching and take them up for a local flight, and back on the ground discuss the rescues we have done over the years. They plan to produce a special article about the "Boys in Blue on Standby to Rescue You" for their newspaper, which will be good publicity for the RAF.

A similar requirement for a visit comes from the BBC for 12th and 13th February. They wish to film in Snowdonia, which is covered in snow and looking very bleak. We use up four hours of flying time in the area, and we hope they have got the footage they want.

As spring arrives, more people come to Snowdonia and start making their way along the Snowdon Horseshoe, a classic scrambling route along ridges, which includes the summit. On 12th March we get a call to rescue a girl who has hurt her leg on a knife edge section of the famous Crib Goch. She can't move and she can't be carried off, so it needs to be a helicopter that comes to her rescue. As we circle overhead, we are all aware, as a crew, of the updrafts, downdrafts, and turbulence that we might encounter as the westerly wind passes over the sharp ridge. I discuss with the crew my proposed oblique approach path to where she is with a group of people around her. Our escape route will be to the right, where we have thousands of feet of space to drop into if needed. As we come to the hover overhead the group, we need very little power, so the wind must be updrafting at that point. My winchman F. Sgt Berry secures her in a strop, and they both come up together. I hold my position until they are on board and the cabin door closed. Ten minutes later we land at Bangor Hospital, and she is helped out and assisted in her walk to the waiting ambulance. She is the first of many casualties that we expect to pick up in Snowdonia as the year progresses.

A special formation fly-past is planned for 26th March for the town of Bangor, and our job in our helicopter is to carry a jet pilot who will communicate with the formation leader and a contact on the ground and brief the contact on the progress of the formation – either a few seconds late or early on arrival. The plan is that the formation will pass over the visiting VIP as he is greeted by the Lord Mayor at exactly 3 p.m. We have a rehearsal three days before the event, which goes well. On the actual day our crew are invited to the briefing, where the formation leader runs through the action and possible contingencies. The formation cannot change speed or route during the last mile, so the contact on the ground needs to communicate any need to speed up or slow down the greeting with the Mayor. With all the preparations made, the flypast goes over as hands are shaken, so smiles all round.

On the 8th April we receive a call from Police HQ to pick up three children who are with their uncle on a small boat currently on a mudflat near Widnes. Apparently, their Mum is concerned for their safety for some reason and wants them brought home now! We respond to the request and within 15 minutes find the craft at the position stated. As we circle, we can see the children waving happily, along with Uncle. We are tasked with their rescue, and we can see a police car stationed nearby, so I have no alternative but to bring them up to the helicopter and put them ashore by the police car. I brief my winchman that they are to be rescued, against their will if necessary. Within minutes they are on board, no doubt wondering what all the fuss is about, and we are landing alongside the police car. The children are handed over and are on their way back home to Mum. We hear no more and we don't enquire.

Out of the blue, on 8th May, I receive a signal authorising me to carry Very Important Persons in accordance with Queen's Regulations. A few days later my crew are tasked with flying an Air Vice Marshall from Warton Airfield near Liverpool to a destination near Lancaster. On the way back home to Valley with just our crew on board, and crossing the Irish Sea, I put out a "Practice Pan" message on the emergency frequency, to see how alert the Emergency system is. Drayton Centre come straight back with my position, 45 miles NE of Valley, and will hand me over to RAF Valley for my recovery. It's reassuring to know that the system works well 24/7.

On 20th May I am appointed a display pilot, which means I will be tasked by the MOD with carrying out flying displays at various events in North Wales. I need to drive to each event site in advance to look at the display area and see how close any crowds, tents, stalls, balloons, and aerials might be. Usually, a discussion with the event organiser ensures there is sufficient separation between the helicopter and any potential problems. On the day, my crews are pleased to demonstrate their rescue techniques, and we close the display with a wingover manoeuvre, which looks impressive and makes a lot of noise. Shortly after the first display I get a call from an instructor on the Gnat trainer jets. He is interested in flying helicopters, and can he come along for a flight as an introduction on how we fly? The next display flight, he comes along, we fit him with a helmet, conduct a crew briefing and put him in the front seat so he gets a good view as we head for Portmadog and a school sports field.

He sits there, arms folded, feet away from the yaw pedals as we carry out our display.

Only when we clear the coast and have climbed to 1,000 feet do I invite him to handle the controls, of which the Collective Lever will be a new one. After five minutes he learns how small the control movements are required to be to make a turn or change speed or height.

After 10 minutes he hands back control, saying, "There is a lot to learn, and it's a completely different way of flying."

"Well, if you get on the RAF basic helicopter course it will be 100 hours flying over several months. After that you will retrain on an operational helicopter and never stop training thereafter."

I descend towards the southeast corner of Anglesey at our top speed of 120 knots, well below his training jet's stalling speed. I am showing him our bad weather, low level route from operating in Snowdonia to getting back to our base at RAF Valley. Essentially it is following the coastline, which is low profile, without obstacles, and with features that identify where you are along the route. I start by flying along the deserted beach, at 100 feet and 120 knots. I imply that the forward visibility is reducing and to be able to stop with the distance we can see I reduce speed to 70 knots and height to 50 feet. We are using minimum power and making good progress along the shoreline. I point out features such as rocks, wooden posts, and logs stranded above the high-water mark, which I tick off from my memory of the route as we progress. Assuming again that visibility deteriorates further, I reduce my speed, so my airspeed is below minimum indication, and the clearance with the ground beneath my wheels is around 10 feet. It feels like driving a bus at 30mph, and we can easily go round any obstacle or stop completely. As we near the town of Rhosneigr we climb to 200 feet so Air Traffic Control can see our lights, and we are cleared low level direct to our dispersal with the jets flying around above. As we shut down in dispersal our marshaller indicates that the droop stops in the rotor head are in and we can safely stop the rotor. Over a coffee and debrief we answer a few of our young pilot's questions. Clearly it is a completely different way of flying from fixed wing jets. What happens to him in the future, however, we never learn.

C Flight gets requests to deliver a talk about SAR to local organisations such as WIs, Probus Clubs and Round Table. Because of my previous experience, it falls to me to deliver. These talks, with a film and a demonstration of a rescue from a single-seat dinghy, go down well, and my fame spreads. Eventually I am asked to deliver a presentation to the Royal Aeronautical Society at Chester. As an Associate Member, I feel honoured to be asked. It is agreed that I will go across with Ann, and after the event we will have a dinner with members in a hotel where we will be staying the night. Where Ann is useful to me is that she sits at the back of the audience, and I talk to her personally. She can indicate to me if I am talking too quietly by holding her ear, and if talking too quickly, by holding he fingers across her mouth. It goes well, and the questions show that they are astonished that for the responsibility that SAR pilots take on, they are so young! I have to point out that SAR helicopter crews are often the first professional rescue service to arrive at the scene of an incident and are effectively the "On the Scene Commander." From what the crew can see, they can make an assessment of what they can do and what further levels of support is required. For shipping accidents, there may be a requirement for one or more lifeboats to be launched to stay near the ship for days. There may be a requirement for an airborne radio link to be maintained to ensure ship to shore communication. The helicopter can only pick up so many people, depending on cabin size, and it might be necessary to set up a continuous stream of helicopters to bring in needed help such as firefighters and equipment, engineers, and deck officers to replace injured crewmembers. Having offloaded, the helicopters can load up with survivors for transit to the shore. Sometimes, it is found that the winchman, having spoken to the captain, wishes to remain with the vessel after he supervises the lift of survivors up to the helicopter. The ship's crew and passengers know that the helicopter will come back for him, boosting their morale. Also, as the next helicopter arrives, he can give a briefing of the situation using his radio and organise the appropriate number of survivors. Even yachts have benefitted from having a qualified "helmsman" drop in and take over as de facto captain of a crew laid low by seasickness. Every rescue situation is different, and the crew as a whole take time to assess each situation and work through their individual involvement. A plan is agreed and followed and if the situation changes, the plan changes. Every successful helicopter rescue is a crew effort, and sometimes a rescue situation will involve multiple agencies operating together by day and by night and in rough weather. At a later date I am invited to give the same presentation to the RAeS Branch at Cheltenham. It gives Ann and me a chance to look at the shops there and visit her home in Shrivenham (near Swindon).

At the end of July, a review of the RAF is planned at RAF Finingley, near Doncaster, to celebrate the 25th Anniversary of the Queen's accession to the Throne. There will be a parade, a static display of aircraft and a flying display. I, with my crew, am tasked with being part of the static display with one of our yellow SAR Wessex, being part of a line of helicopters and small aircraft. The parade is held in a large hangar, as showers are forecast, and right on cue, as she inspects the parade, hail patters down on the roof. Later, our crew are all smartly at attention as the Queen and entourage are driven past the static display; our trusty Wessex has never been so clean. Afterwards, we all move so we can see the flying display, especially the new Harrier Jump Jets. Hovering in the air and turning round on the spot is most impressive, as is their ability to operate without runways, which could be useful in any future war. One person clearly not watching, as the BBC Television News shows that night, is the Defence Secretary, Fred Mulley, who is seated next to the Queen and is clearly having trouble staying awake after the big lunch. The relationship of the Labour Party and the Armed Forces is not good, with rumours of a possible run down as currently we are at peace with the world.

Static display of aircraft and helicopters, RAF Finningley

Approaching school summer holidays means young air-minded cadets are coming to RAF Valley for their summer camp. There is a need for pilots to fly the two-seater Chipmunk aircraft to provide air experience flying for them. Being already qualified, I volunteer and get checked out by Sqn Ldr Merry. I get a thorough briefing about the fixed wing aspects of the airfield and the need to be aware of the jet trainers flying around doing circuits at RAF Valley and the nearby satellite airfield, RAF Mona. A good lookout is essential, and we need to fly well clear of cloud and switch on our landing lamp so that we can be more easily seen. However, once we get to the Menai Straits area we can demonstrate aerobatics, loops, rolls, stalling, and spinning, as well as allowing the cadets to take control. It is a completely different way of flying from helicopters, not least on landing, when we need to maintain a good airspeed until touchdown, and, being confined to runways, the landings are sometimes cross wind.

One good weather day I fly into the mountains of Snowdonia to make a comparison with flying the Wessex helicopter. My young cadet is not happy with his first experience of turbulence, so we turn round and go back to the Menai Straits. Certainly, I feel happier flying in the mountains in a Wessex helicopter, rather than a light fixed wing aircraft. Over the summer camps I fly 10 hours on the Chipmunk, and it inspires me to get my Private Pilot's Licence back. I make contact with the Flying Instructor at the Mona Flying Club, Mr McKenzie-Blyth, and begin my training on the Cessna 150, a type I am familiar with from my time in Singapore, so no problems. After 10 hours flying, I pass my final handling check on 28th September and get my Licence, my first step into the World of Commercial Aviation in the UK.

One night, when I am on shift, a storm blows up. Our helicopters are put in the hangar, as the rotor blades are flexing up and down with the wind. At home, Ann looks outside and sees our wooden framed garage leaning under the strain, but there is a car inside, our little Austin A 30, in danger of being damaged if the garage collapses. She pops outside in the rain and wind, starts the car, and with the garage creaking all around her, reverses it out and parks it well clear. During the night the garage collapses and is a sorry sight. Next day I ring the insurance company and I am told to submit my claim, one of thousands, and enclose some photographs. My claim for the repair is agreed and a local builder not only makes a good repair, but it looks a lot stronger than it was originally. Christopher, meanwhile, has been concentrating on constructing buildings in LEGO in his large playroom, possibly training to become an architect? His other project seems to be designing motorways, judging by his large drawing book full of plans for towns and villages with associated linking roads, bridges over rivers, and flyover junctions. In his new sandpit, his Tonka toy bulldozer is put to good work clearing a way for a new road to be constructed. When the weather is good and he is not at school, Ann takes him to Treaddur Bay beach. With her comfortable, seated against the sea wall, Christopher heads off to the edge of the sea with his bucket and spade. An hour later he has constructed an impressive sandcastle with a deep surrounding moat. As the tide comes in, it fills the moat and everything is very satisfactory, for a while. The castle then begins to slide into the moat as wavelets wash over the scene. Never mind; there will be another chance on the next fine day. It's time to go back to Mum, perhaps she could do with an ice cream as well, before heading back to prepare an evening meal for the paying guests. Ann keeps busy as we let out the large static caravan for short holiday lets and long lets over the winter. Over the forthcoming years Rhoscolyn becomes a popular holiday area, with its own small sandy beach and access to the rocky coast.

Watching television, he becomes keen on the weather, with its highs, lows, air masses, fronts, and precipitation. Perhaps he has a future as a weather forecaster on the television; job for life there. Later still he is avidly following the rugby as Wales fields an all-conquering Rugby squad to take on the World, with key players like Gareth Edwards, JPR Williams, and Phil Bennett, the captain.

The weekends and holidays afford the chance of exploring Snowdonia on foot. Ann and I head out to Beddgelert, noting the Welsh and English road signs, and begin an exploration along a disused railway line near the river. Being intrepid, we are undaunted by a long tunnel with a little daylight showing at the end. Very many years later we are to travel along this route by train, as the railway is restored as a tourist line. The walk is a great success and leads to many more, helped by my frequent helicopter flights in the area and being able to note down tracks which are not shown on the Ordnance Survey maps. The countryside and the lakes away from the high ground are just wonderful to explore on our own, and very much away from the crowded tourist hot spots.

As holidaymakers flock to North Wales, C Flight is busy rescuing them from dangerous situations. In addition, the presence of a helicopter in North Wales means we can be tasked by MOD with extra jobs which we are happy to undertake. On 11th August we are tasked to take several VIP passengers out to a giant crude oil tanker, MV Bellamya, moored off the north coast of Anglesey, near Amlwch. There is no need to search for it, as we can see it from 15 miles away; the only problem is where to land on it. We will have to circle around looking for a large letter "H" on some part of its expansive deck. Sure enough, about midships, we see the landing area and two men with fire extinguishers at the ready. We make a slow approach, noting all the pipes, masts, and other obstacles around, and make a soft touchdown on the inch-thick steel deck plating. The VIPs are escorted out in a safe direction from our Wessex and the ship's crew take them the 100 yards to the bridge. Cleared for take-off, we back out until well clear of the ship, and only then accelerate into forward flight alongside the huge ship.

Out of the blue, a call from Postings at MOD: how would I fancy 5 years at the MOD as a junior Staff Officer, now my tour is due to finish shortly? "Good for your career prospects," says Wg. Cdr. "Bugs" Bendell. My immediate reaction is negative; I enjoy flying helicopters and I am good at doing that. I have only flown the Wessex for a year, and with its powerful engines it is just the sort of helicopter that you need in the mountains.

"Well, the only alternative to turning down this posting is leaving the Air Force at 38. We need 200 General Duties Branch officers to come to the MOD every year. Think about it and give me a call within seven days, this is my extension ..."

I have been considering it for some time, and Ann is keen for a more stable lifestyle, not moving every two to three years. The North Sea offshore oil industry is currently booming, needing experienced helicopter pilots, and is based mainly in Aberdeen and along the northeast coast of England. Also, leaving at 38 means receiving an immediate pension and a tax-free lump sum to help you settle down somewhere, and no worry about being made redundant mid-career by politically inspired changes in Defence policy. I need to speak to the base Education Officer about how to land a civilian career in aviation. I also need to talk to the Accounts Officer about getting the RAF Pension, tax-free lump sum, and possibly commuting the pension to get a further tax-free lump sum. Much to my surprise, they are both very enthusiastic about my leaving the security of a career in the RAF for a career in new offshore oil industry. The Education Officer helps me draw up a CV, with training on one side of the A4 size paper and tour-by-tour flying experience on the other. The CV will be the basis of questions at a job interview. Within days it is produced, and 10 copies run off for good measure. Similarly, the Accounts Officer counsels me to leave at 38, accept an immediate pension, tax-free gratuity, and commutation of the maximum 50% of my pension to secure a further tax-free lump sum. With my experience, I should secure a permanent position in a helicopter company with an increase in salary and a final salary related pension at the end of my career.

"Basically, you don't have a choice, David. This is a good opportunity which will not be here forever. You must take it. I will guide you through the process. Now lets us look at Queen's Regulations about the latest payments being authorised." He produces a thick tome, finds the appropriate pages, and starts to write down a column of figures. "These are today's figures; any increase in pay for the RAF before you leave will increase these figures by the same amount. Now, if I were you, I would start the process right away by writing to all the helicopter companies. When you give your decision to the MOD, suggest to them that you stay at RAF Valley until the end of your service, an extra 18 months in post. They have problems getting people to Anglesey because it is remote from the South of England. I feel sure they will accept your request. And, by the way, when you are on pension you will also be on the Reserve list, in your case Juliet. If they need to call you back to the Colours, the country will be in a bad state indeed. Good luck with this. Keep in touch until it is all settled."

A week later I am on the phone to the MOD, and request to retire at age 38 and stay in post until that time. It is all agreed quickly; I need to put my request down on paper with the appropriate form supplied by our Administration Officer. After that, all I need do now is fly professionally to the end of my tour and get an Airline Transport Pilot's Licence (Helicopters and Gyroplanes) before I set off for any interviews. Life is going to get busier, I feel, as Ann and I consider the transition to civilian life.

Having made my decision, I speak to our Squadron Commander, Sqn Ldr Alex Sneddon. It transpires that he, too, is leaving at 38, along with one in four pilots on the Squadron, including Peter Beglan, from our own C flight. When I speak with our new Flight Commander, John Stirling, just posted in from Scotland, he is very supportive. For years he has watched the major oil companies coming into Scotland and setting up large bases around Aberdeen. To carry people out to the exploration rigs and production platforms, they require big helicopters that can operate in all weathers, day and night, and of course skilled and experienced helicopter pilots and engineers. Currently, there is a shortage of both. Whilst he is happy to stay with the RAF (he goes on to fly Chinook helicopters from Odiham), he completely supports my move to become a civilian helicopter pilot.

On October 31st we scramble for an American F-111, which is diverting into RAF Valley on one engine. For some reason the other engine exploded, but the crew were able to maintain control and get it down in one piece. It is tucked away in a hangar for weeks while a working party from RAF Lakenheath in Norfolk sort out all the problems. Later, on 2nd November, one of our two-seat Hunters has engine failure and makes a successful landing at RAF Llanbedr, on the coast above Aberystwyth. We are tasked with bringing the two pilots back to RAF Valley. I hope they enjoyed the lift in a slow, vibrating machine with not much of a look out. However, we drop them alongside their unit, so convenient for them for signing in, and explaining that their machine is 50 miles away. This sortie notches up rescue mission 108 so far on this tour; that must mean a few lives saved, at least.

Two weeks later C Flight has a week-long visit from the Group Standardisation Unit (GSU). An experienced pilot, navigator, and winchman fly with us and watch as we carry out our planning, briefing, training, and debrief. At the end of each flight, we individually get a debrief on how we performed and our crew co-operation. I note down the remarks, everyone can improve after all, and note the standard that I achieve. When we go into the mountains, being thrown around by turbulence, I see my "checker" is hanging on grimly as we pass over sharp edges and sudden drops. Coming from behind a desk most of the time, it is a rude awakening to the real world of rescue in the mountains. However, I get a good write up, yes there is room for improvement, but the basics are clearly there. "Keep up the good work," is the message. At the end, C Flight gets a written report on what is satisfactory and what can be improved. I ask if I can volunteer to fly with them on their next visit, as I have learnt a lot this time.

"Probably not, we like your attitude and you don't need as much supervision as some others." I take that as a compliment. OK. I just need to carry on producing the goods day after day until the end of the tour.

1978

There is lot of snow falling over the hills and mountains as the year progresses. This does not deter walkers and climbers from going into the mountains of the Lake District and Snowdonia. Many are ill prepared for the bad weather, and it becomes one of the worst periods in recent years of them getting into trouble. In both areas, RAF SAR helicopters are busy with callouts for a variety of situations. For C Flight, we notch up our first 2,000 operational missions since the unit was formed, 22 years previous. The weather is often atrocious, and often all we can do is fly in civilian and RAF Mountain Rescue Teams to an area, where they can continue on foot into the falling snow. In an article in the Times of 13th February, there is praise for the RAF and the rescue teams and criticism for climbers setting out without out without ice axes, crampons, or helmets. The work being undertaken by the RAF crews, often in bad weather, is vindicating the decision to replace the old single engine Whirlwinds with a mix of twin-engine Wessex and long-range Sea Kings, now coming into service.

The snow blankets the country, and drifting snow is blocking many roads in Devon. On 19th February we get a call from RCC to deploy to RAF Chivenor in North Devon to assist in casualty evacuation and emergency food drops. I ring our Mountain Rescue Section and request two members who would assist us in our task for as long as we are needed. With my crew, navigator Chris Gibbons and winchman Steve Lynch, we hold a briefing with our engineers, who will lose a machine for an unknown number of days. We sort out paperwork, technical log, and spare items, as well as some clothes, blankets, and some refreshment. Then we are off, heading across Cardigan Bay and staying clear of the hills, routing round snow showers. On arrival at RAF Chivenor, I find their helicopter dispersal and the waiting marshaller. We land, shut down, and all troop into the Ops room for a briefing. We are needed to go to a remote farmhouse, pick up an injured man and take him to Barnstable Hospital. We are issued with the local maps, and are soon on our way. We find the farm and circle around it, trying to find somewhere level to land. The road is the best option, and soon my two crew members plus two mountain rescue chaps are heading to the farmhouse with a stretcher. We need the four of them to carry the loaded stretcher back and we have to forego the offer of tea and homemade cakes that the farmer's wife had prepared. Back towards Barnstable, find the hospital, land alongside the police car, and transfer our patient into the waiting ambulance. Flying back to our new base and surprise, there is camouflaged Wessex outside the hangar, obviously from RAF Odiham near Basingstoke. The hangar door is wide open, and I am worried about shutting down the rotor in the open in this gusting strong wind. Time to try out taxying into the hangar and shutting down inside where the air is calm. Chris Gibbons marshals me forward checking my rotor tips are well clear of the roof. No problems. Then another surprise, a burley Chief Technician comes forward and offers his team to service our machine and refuel it ready for the next morning's tasking. I accept with grateful thanks, its been a long day already and we all need to get some food and sleep. A third surprise back in the Ops room. The Squadron wives have prepared huge plates of sandwiches and cakes as well as tea and coffee ready to be poured. While availing ourselves, the duty Ops officer briefs us all on tomorrow's tasking. The pick up at our Hotel will be 8am, Met briefing for all crews at 8.30 looking to get the first flights away by 9 am. We can expect to be flying all day with shut-downs for refuelling only. Transport is leaving in 15 minutes, the Hotel will accept us in Flying kit and outdoor mountaineering kit and boots. The rooms, breakfast and dinner have been paid for. Any drinks down to our own account. At the Hotel in central Barnstable, I have a quick shower and shave and all five of us stream into the bar resplendent in our outdoor kit. We need not have worried about having enough cash for drinks, as the locals insisted we sat at the best table, took our orders for refreshing beers and quizzed as to what was happening around them. OK, we will have to cope as best we can! Into dinner with a set hot meal, the snow having curtailed some supplies and the Hotel is full as the snow drifts have disrupted travel. By 9 pm we tumble into our beds having booked early calls for 7am. That loud knock on the door can't be morning surely?

Another day, another 4 missions, flying from dawn to dusk. The weather is poor with low cloud and snow flurries so we can only fly slowly if we need to keep contact with the ground. The only way to be sure of where we are is to follow line features, such as roads, railway lines, power cables and rivers keeping them to the left. Sometimes, at road junctions in remote areas we stop and hover alongside and read the sign-posts especially if we are getting close to our destination. Once we have the casualty on board we can climb up into the cloud to safety height, then head towards the Bristol Channel and let down over the water, turning back towards Barnstable Hospital once we are visual with the surface. It is all a very time-consuming process, clocking up 8 hours flying, sustained by the coffee and sandwiches laid on by the Squadron wives.

With such a big operation going on, the Media have made it to Chivenor to report what is happening to the public. Fortunately, they are confined to the Ops room leaving the Planning room free for the crews to work unmolested. Another Wessex from Odiham has made it through along with additional transport, spares and a Detachment Commander. I thank him for the technical support that his groundcrew have provided, which enables me to concentrate on the flying. Just as well as at the end of the day on 20th February as we are preparing to head for the Hotel, an emergency request to get baby food to a remote farmhouse cut off by snow drifts.

My navigator, Chris Gibbons and I plan out a route how to get there using roads for guidance. We have two powerful aircraft landing lights plus two hand- held lights that can be shone from the cabin door in any direction. If we lose contact with the ground in any whiteout conditions, we will climb quickly to safety height and then let down over the Bristol Channel to return to Chivenor. As normal, we brief everyone together including the Ops officer, outlining the changes from our day operation. The flight proceeds slowly as we follow the minor roads towards high ground. What people on the ground must have thought about these lights in the sky moving slowly along the roads, pausing only for sign-posts to be read, I can't imagine, but we get no complaints. It takes over an hour to get to the farmhouse just 45 miles away from Chivenor, and we hand over a large quantity of baby milk. I figure that our best recovery route is to climb up into the cloud, up to safety height and proceed at 100 knots towards the Bristol Channel, let down over the water and recover low level to Chivenor. It works as planned and as we touch down in dispersal we are surrounded by ground crew with the refuelling bowser in the back ground. As I log two hours night flying I am aware of a journalist from the Daily Telegraph talking to our Ops officer. The five of us cram into the transport and head for the Hotel, where we are met at the door and guided into the dining room where a special table is ready for us. As we sit down a tureen of soup arrives, along with five cold beers, followed in due course by the rest of the hot meal. We need this and there is no conversation as we concentrate on replacing the calories we have used up over the day. We are needed next day so it will be the 7am knock on the door as usual. Never mind, we will sleep well …

Next day, the weather is improving at last and a BBC TV crew have arrived to record the snowbound countryside so on our second flight to a remote farmhouse, where a young man needs to get to Barnstable Railway Station so he can get to his Prep School, they film the bleak countryside and the snowploughs making slow progress along some narrow lanes. The Wessex from Odiham are being used more and more and we learn that we will be released tomorrow to go back to our base in Anglesey. A quieter day, just three flights and four hours flying. The weather forecast for tomorrow looks good for a direct flight back with a tail wind. For a change we finish early, head back to the hotel for our final night, and get to bed not exhausted.

Our last day, 22nd February, the weather continues to improve, and we go to four locations to pick up casualties as well as dropping off food, mainly bread and vegetables, to a few others. With our involvement finished we gather up all our kit, including our technical log, and at midday we are on our way, no time for long good byes. We understand the Media have been impressed with the RAF involvement in this emergency, which thanks to the introduction of the Wessex has been very effective. Flying home, we can see Wales clearly from 2000 feet above, still covered in snow. As we reach Anglesey, I route along the shore-line with the cabin door open so our mountain rescue chaps can see the shoreline rushing by at 120 knots. As we approach the airfield and change to Tower frequency, I can't resist mentioning that we are returning from Devon having left 4 days previously. "Welcome back, runway in use 15, QFE 1022, you cleared direct to dispersal low level." Good, now to proceed slowly into dispersal, land softly and shut down remembering every switch. As we troop into "C" Flight we are met by our CO, John Stirling. "Right, good to see you back. Once you have checked in you can stand down until 1pm tomorrow when we will have a debrief on how it all turned out. The engineers will sort out the machine. I understand you have had an exciting time. You can tell me all about it tomorrow"

The rapid development of the Offshore Oil Industry and the insatiable demand for qualified helicopter pilots and engineers is leading to demands for Union recognition and industrial unrest. In my discussion with my peers it would seem that the RAF would have me back from early retirement for up to 3 years from the date of retirement as long as any payments made were returned. So still feeling secure about leaving. Not only myself and some colleagues are planning to leave but unknown to all of us at least 100 helicopter pilots across all 3 Armed Services are leaving, mainly to fly over the North Sea. What the Helicopter Companies want is experience of flying twin engine helicopters, on instruments, at night and over the sea. I fit the requirement exactly. All I need to do is gain as much experience as I can before early retirement from the RAF, and get my civil licence as soon as practical.

Out of the blue in June, while briefing my crew for a training trip, there is a knock on the door and an airman comes in and announces "There is a lady in the corridor holding a baby and she wants to see you Sir, as you are responsible"! "She better come in and take a seat "She is ushered in and I don't recognise her face or the baby wrapped in a blue blanket". "I thought you would like to see Gareth now that is 2 months old and fully fit. My puzzled face makes her continue. You may remember taking me to Bangor Hospital from the Medical Centre on the 4th April. I was visiting there for a routine pregnancy check when I suddenly went into labour, my waters broke and the Doctor called you to fly me to Bangor Maternity Unit straightaway as an ambulance journey might take too long. Your helicopter turned up a few minutes later and with a nurse and your two crew to look after me I was there in 10 minutes and rushed into the unit where Gareth was born prematurely. He is now fully fit and putting on weight day by day, thanks to your quick reaction and the care of your crew". It is not often I get to meet the casualties that we look after and I am lost for words. I remember the event, recalling that I had self authorised a scramble, not having time to clear the decision with RCC. In our post flight signal to RCC and our HQ this situation was explained and no comment came back. I assumed that by this tacit acquiescence, my decision was endorsed. The young lady declined a cup of coffee saying she had to give young Gareth a feed and she was off, leaving me just a little unsettled !

25th August and an unusual request from Air Traffic Control. A twin-engine Beech Travel Air, under their control routing towards the airfield with an engine problem has disappeared off their radar screen and communication has been lost. I press the scramble bell and within minutes we are heading low level towards the North West. As we look at the area of the Holyhead Harbour we can see the aircraft on the surface of the water and as we get closer we can see people standing in the water alongside it. It appears to be intact so a gentle ditching then. All we need to do is land on the beach 100 yards away and check that there are no casualties needing hospital treatment. I can see a Police Car making its way to the area along the beach so if we are not needed it will be their responsibility. Having landed facing the scene, my two crew members in the cabin wade out into the harbour in their immersion suits to meet the pilot and passengers. The report comes back that all 5 occupants are all OK, shaken yes but no injuries. Having consulted with the Police, it was agreed there was nothing we could do and they would take charge of the incident. We report to Air Traffic that we are returning to dispersal and that we would have a phone conversation to update them. Many months later I receive a copy of the accident report, apparently there was a fuel problem that affected both engines. Because of salt-water contamination the aircraft could not be repaired and was scrapped.

13th October. We have just come on shift, myself with Frank Haggerty (Navigator) and Terry Freeman (Winchman) when a call from RCC for a VIP flight. Proceed soonest to RAF Brawdy in South West Wales, refuel, go to Port Talbot, pick up the Undersecretary of State for Wales, find damaged Oil Tanker, circle, return him and come back via RAF Brawdy. We note down all the details, including the weather in the search area, low cloud and mist and the weather at RAF Brawdy is the same. Right, it will be a ground controlled approach (GCA), using radar to get down, we practice those so no problems there. With all the maps needed plus the technical log we set off, the weather deteriorating as we head South across Cardington Bay. Calling up RAF Brawdy they have no aircraft flying and they can offer us a GCA on their active runway. Their weather is poor, cloud base 200 feet and visibility 400 yards. They will provide a "Follow Me" truck on the runway so if I follow that it will take me to where we will be refuelled. Luckily, flying a helicopter I can slow right down on the final approach, and we see in sequence the approach lights, threshold lights, runway edge lights and the flashing light from the "Follow Me" vehicle. We line up behind him with 10 feet wheel clearance and follow him in the fog to the dispersal with the awaiting refuelling bowser. 20 minutes later we are ready to start up. With no other aircraft flying, we can take off from where we are straight into the low cloud, and set off for Port Talbot and a large grass area on the sea front. We find Port Talbot, and see the group of cars. After picking up Mr John Morrison and 2 others, we set off to look for the damaged oil tanker 50 miles to the West. We are soon in radio contact on the Marine Distress frequency and ask for his weather and his position in Lat and Long. The visibility is estimated at 400 yards and the cloud base 200 feet. We note his position and plot it on our maps and on our Decca Rolling map. If his position is accurate, we should find him. He confirms there are no other aircraft in the area. We reach the reported position but no oil tanker or trace of oil in the sea. Because we have no direction finding on Coastguard frequencies we have little option but to start an expanding square search. After 30 minutes we have not found the oil tanker, so our fuel requirements dictate that we return to Port Talbot, mission not accomplished. Our passengers have seen the misty conditions and understand the need to return, so 30 minutes later we drop off the party at the awaiting cars and head back to RAF Brawdy to the West. Their weather is poor as is the weather at our base in Anglesey. Our orders now are to shut down at RAF Brawdy and stay overnight and look to recover to base mid-morning. Because we are all wearing immersion suits we all are dressed alike so we can keep together as a crew as accommodation and food is fixed for us as we are classed as a "Diversionary Crew "Suitably refreshed, we recover to RAF Valley without difficulty. Post flight we feel we need to point out that the lack of direction-finding capability led to failure of the mission. It is well known problem that has been cheerfully ignored for a long time. Our CO, John Stirling, agrees that we should highlight this problem yet again in our report to the RCC. As expected, there is no feed-back, (it would require a modification and some expense,) so we carry on as we are. This flight took 5 hours 20 minutes for no result. We need to keep asking even though our requests for improvements are rebuffed. One modification that we need is a radio so we can talk to our own RAF Mountain Rescue Teams both during training and on actual operations. Having put in a request for this facility, the reply comes back with "If you need to communicate with a unit why don't you land alongside and hand over a written message at the end of a Forked Stick" Was this Staff Officer being facetious or is he completely out of touch with SAR operations in the mountains?

Because we are leaving the RAF and moving it would be more convenient to move from a MQ than trying to arrange to sell Gwynfryn and buy elsewhere at the same time. So the house goes up for sale, is sold, and we move back in an MQ for the final months of my service. A different address to the previous MQ, but still quite convenient. Christopher has moved up to a Junior school which has an "English" stream for the children of RAF parents at Valley. He still likes school so that is good.

Something very different crops up in November. I am required to help out at another Wessex Unit, at RAF Manston in Kent. I will be despatched for 10 days. Their area of operation covers the Straits of Dover and the Thames Estuary, so a lot of potential maritime incidents. On 12th November I am given a local area recce; the white cliffs of Dover are very impressive and, being both high and vertical, any rescues would need to be confined to the rocks at the bottom. Out at sea, the unit is frequently called to take firefighters and their equipment out to passing ships that have caught fire or been involved in collisions. They regularly practice with local crews, so actual call-outs proceed well both day and night. The Coastguard Rescue Centre monitors the Channel day and night with both a radar and visual watch, and all vessels should be listening out on the Coastguard frequency. With standard training across the Squadron, I am quickly checked out and placed on shift.

Decks training with a RAF Marine Craft launch

A week later, an unusual scramble – a cross channel hovercraft, which has been struck by a freak wave, is damaged and making its way towards the nearest beach. Within minutes of getting airborne, we spy the hovercraft halfway up a beach near Ramsgate. The passengers are offloading onto the beach and the propellers are stationary. We land at the top of the beach, and my two crewmembers walk down to talk to the captain to see if anyone needs hospital treatment. The answer is no, and our help is not required, but thank you for responding to our call for assistance. Later that day I take a call from the General Manager of Hoverlloyd, based in Ramsgate, thanking me for responding to their emergency. Because I know nothing about hovercraft and their operation, we agree to a meeting tomorrow, over lunch in one of the best Hotels in Ramsgate, and he is paying. Right. So, for me, my best suit, shirt and tie, notebook and pen, and my copy of the Wessex Emergency Check List, in a handy flip card design. We meet up, and I judge by the deference of the head waiter that my manager is well known there. We talk about yesterday's accident and the difficulty the "pilot" had in controlling the direction of travel with the damage caused to the hovercraft. He managed to beach it some miles from the normal ramp near Ramsgate, where it will be repaired before going back out to sea. The manager was not aware that hovercraft could be involved in any accident, and yesterday's situation has come as a shock. By contrast, I show him my Emergency Check List flip cards, which fit into a large trouser leg pocket. As a handy reference, the notes detail the immediate actions for all known Wessex major emergencies involving engines, controls, electrics, and instruments. Having taken immediate actions necessary to contain an emergency, there are listed some considerations about future actions that could be relevant. The manager flips through the check list and is amazed at how useful such a document might be for his hovercraft operation. He will talk to his Chief Pilot about what might be appropriate. We talk on about hovercraft operations, on sea and on land, and how well they can travel at speed over any flat surfaces, be they water, sand, mud, or low vegetation. Little did we realise that the RNLI would eventually establish hovercraft to rescue people on several tidal estuaries in the UK, including London. We carry on talking about what considerations would be relevant to a rescue helicopter crew coming out to one of his hovercraft. Clearly, we could not put down a winchman with any propeller rotating. He tells me that, in his machines, they can brake to a stop. Also, the large top surface of his machine will bear the weight of people, and there is easy access to the roof if people need to be rescued.

A few days later I get some experience of operating in the busy shipping lanes, picking up a seaman designated for Dover Hospital, from the P&O oil tanker "Pass of Glenclunie" as she steamed down channel. Just looking around I can see six ships all using the one-way shipping lanes. Looks good in daylight with good visibility, perhaps not so good at night or in fog. Not for me to worry about, as I pack up and return to Anglesey on 22nd November.

Meanwhile the "Winter of Discontent" carries on, with public sector strikes coupled with one of the coldest winters for 16 years. Rubbish accumulates in the streets and burials are delayed. The Labour Government loses a Vote of Confidence in the House of Commons and as a result of the General Election on 3rd May 1979, Margaret Thatcher and the Conservatives sweep into power with a majority of 43 seats. Shortly afterwards, the Armed Forces get a very substantial pay rise backdated to 1st April, which boosts my prospective RAF pension and gratuity. The Accounts Officer's advice was right after all.

1979

Now, to get my Civilian Flying Licence, I need to apply to the Civil Aviation Authority (CAA) and see what they require. Back comes their letter. They need me to get a pass in exams on Aviation Law and Weight and Balance. They suggest a correspondence course and exam in London. Owing to my extensive helicopter flying by day, by night, and in cloud, they only require someone to assess me for General Handling and my Unit Commander, John Stirling, is authorised to conduct the flying test on behalf of CAA. During the test and on approach to the final landing he fails an engine fuel computer, which results in that engine maintaining a high power setting until finally switched off. I handle that emergency in a satisfactory way, and he writes "Passed" in every section of the form. Eventually, after passing written exams in Air Law and aircraft weight and balance, I get my Air Transport Pilot's Licence, (ATPL (H)). With a white cover and complete with photograph and medical certificate, it serves as a passport, so is to be taken with me whenever and wherever I am a crew member on a commercial flight. I promise to keep John posted as to job opportunities, it's a small world we all operate in after all. He advises me to sell myself dear – get written job offers from companies, which you can use to get the job you want in the company with which you have your last interview. As a family we head up to Perth, Scotland, for my first interview – with Gleneagles Helicopters. They ask me what I know about Sqn. Ldr. Sneddon, my current Sqn Cdr (he has applied for a position, which he secures, but after a year in post he returns to the RAF). Good to know that procedure works if required. After just a 30-minute interview a contract for employment is pushed across the desk for signing. I say that my wife and my solicitor will want to read it before I accept it. Job done, contract in hand, we head up to Peterhead, some 30 miles north of Aberdeen, and I find the HQ of North Scottish (later Bond Helicopters). I am interviewed by Captain Harry Joy, with whom I trained in 1965 on the basic helicopter course. Again, a contract is soon pushed across the desk. They need helicopter pilots who will work offshore for two weeks at a time. I say that I will have to consider it and shake hands. Aberdeen looks dreary in the rain and mist. Christopher, for some reason, is not well, which is unusual, and so far, he is not impressed with Scotland. Later on, I go to Gatwick to be interviewed by British Airways Helicopters (BAH). They like my near 1,000 hours flying on tandem rotor helicopters, as they plan to buy the Civil Chinook helicopter to operate with the Shell Oil Company from their base at Sumburgh, in the Shetland Islands. Because they work with the Pilots' Union (BALPA), all new pilots recruited start as co-pilots and typically spend three years in that role before being considered for captaincy. If I am prepared to move to Shetland, promotion might be quicker. They will write me a letter saying I meet their entry qualifications. Finally, an interview with Bristow Helicopters at their HQ at Redhill airfield near Reigate, Surrey. My interviewer is George Puddy, who I met during my time at RAF Ternhill in 1969. It's a small world, indeed. Having spent five minutes describing the company and its worldwide operations, he offers to show me around the Redhill unit. I choose this moment to state that I am looking at two positions within the company, if they are available – Redhill or at Great Yarmouth in Norfolk, where I know that Bristows operate the civil twin engine Wessex 60, thereon which I have 700 hours flying experience in the SAR role. I hand over the three offers of employment that I have received so far, one of which I will take if Bristows can't offer me one of these positions. He looks at me for a few seconds and then says he needs to consult with the Operations Director.

He comes back 10 minutes later with the letters and two cups of coffee. Yes, the company will offer me a post at Great Yarmouth, even though they are currently overmanned. "We like your seven years SAR experience, your experience of operating twin-engine helicopters, and your Master Green Instrument Rating. We can make use of all that experience in due course." He then outlines the job offer, "You would start as a Captain, with 2 increments on the salary scale, with extra payments when you achieve your Civil Instrument Rating and for flying a twin-engine helicopter. The annual incremental date for the company is 1ˢᵗ July. You will start training at Great Yarmouth on 1ˢᵗ June, during your resettlement leave, but as we can't pay you (as you are still being paid by the RAF) we might be able to refund some of your expenses in moving from Anglesey. We will write to you today confirming this offer of employment and if you confirm acceptance in writing, the position will be held open for you."

All that advice I had received over this last year, coming to fruition. I enjoy a celebration dinner at the nearby Chequers Hotel that night – another career beckons, and I am flying helicopters long term with a worldwide company and starting on my favourite, the twin-engine Wessex.

However, events across the world, in Iran, begin to cast a shadow. Revolution takes place and the Shah is deposed. Bristow Helicopters has large operations there, which, because of its links with the former regime, feel under threat. Eventually, on 9th March, in a carefully planned operation, all the helicopters and staff are flown out in broad daylight to adjacent countries (This is the basis of James Clavell's novel "Whirlwind"). About this time, I am negotiating buying a house in Great Yarmouth for my new job. I write to Bristow to state my situation. They come back with confirmation that my job would be kept open for me and look forward to my starting on 1st June at the Great Yarmouth Operation. Notwithstanding the surplus they have of pilots and machines currently worldwide, the company will continue to expand. This support at a crucial time is appreciated, and noted by my fellow RAF pilots, many of whom are thinking of changing careers. Some of them follow my example and others stay on, becoming "Specialist Aircrew" and receiving extra pay.

The final months on C Flight are very busy. When not flying, I concentrate on the paperwork involved in leaving, claiming a pension and gratuity (I can have some in advance to help moving). I write a three-page submission, "How to improve the Wessex in the SAR Role", for a Flight Safety Competition. The joy of this entry is that the judgement will be at MOD level and that the submission should pass through the chain of command for comments at every level. I sit down with my fellow pilots and compose a wish list of improvements that are needed in equipment, training, communication, and standard operating procedures. Many of these grumps have been cheerfully ignored for years. Perhaps, with so many pilots leaving, it might stir up some action at the appropriate level. I get it typed out in Station HQ and Classified for limited circulation. I get a phone call from the Station Commander, Group Captain Edwards, for a pre-retirement interview and to discuss my submission. He goes through the items, expressing disbelief that we can't communicate by radio with our own RAF Mountain Rescue Teams or with the civil teams with whom we do a lot of work. Also, he did not realise that at dusk the SAR helicopters are put into the hangar and locked in, and the unit reverts to one hour's readiness to fly, even when the Station is night flying. I have to explain that in the event that any pilot has to eject over the Irish sea, requiring a night pick up from his dinghy, it would be likely that the rescue helicopter would come from RAF Lakenheath in Norfolk. The helicopter involved would belong to the USAF, who have equipment and crews trained for this task, as currently, on C Flight we do not carry out any night rescue training, on land or sea.

I hear subsequently that things change substantially and many of the communication items are incorporated in the RAF Sea King Mid Life Update.

However, at the end of the interview he offers me a flight in a Hawk training jet as a "thank you" for my 20 years' RAF Service. I was not expecting that, but accept cheerfully. A phone call to the CO of the unit and a date and time is fixed, and as I have flown jets before, I will not need any pretraining. On the appointed day, I report to the unit and meet a young Flying Officer who finds a "G suit" and protective helmet for me, complete with oxygen mask, and a combined lead for all the essentials I will need during the flight, which I will plug into my ejection seat. Things have moved on considerably since I last flew jets. He briefs me on the use of the Ejector Seat. If I hear him shouting "Eject, eject!" I pull up hard on the black and yellow ring between my legs. The canopy will shatter, my helmet visor will drop automatically, and my ejector seat will fire. The next thing I will realise is that I am swinging underneath a parachute.

"Don't wait, or you will be on your own." He briefs me on the weather we might expect, popping up to Scotland to look at the Great Glen and some side valleys and then returning via the Lake District. We walk out and I climb into the back seat, where the ground crew strap me in and plug me into the intercom, oxygen and G suit connector. Canopy closed, he starts up and we taxi out to the runway and are soon airborne, climbing rapidly towards the clouds. He checks in with a Ground Radar and is cleared up to Flight Level 300 (30,000 feet) as we head north. Now straight and level, he hands over control and I note how quickly we can put on bank, pull G, and climb rapidly. The altimeter has numbers for the thousands of feet, rather than just a pointer that can be misread on an old style three-pointer altimeter. Soon we catch up with a jumbo jet with four condensation trails, and we stay five miles behind so as not to be seen by the airliners captain. Approaching Scotland, we are cleared for descent to Safety Height and, with airbrakes out, descend rapidly towards the clouds. We emerge over the islands of southwest Scotland; I can clearly see the Island of Mull. We turn right up Loch Linnhe towards the Great Glen, descending to 500 feet at 360 knots airspeed. Even from the back seat I can clearly see the shape of the Great Glen ahead and the bulk of Ben Nevis rushing towards us. As Fort William passes underneath, my pilot tells me he is turning left into Loch Arkaig and pulling "G" to get round the corner.

The Loch flashes by and my pilot says he can see high ground ahead covered in cloud; time for a quick exit. I feel the push in my back as he selects full power, and the G force as he pulls up the nose into a steep climb. Seconds later, we emerge from cloud with clear blue sky above. He calls the Ground Radar, we are identified, and we turn onto south and head towards the Lake District. As we approach, we are cleared to descend towards the Solway Firth, which comes up on cue as we emerge from cloud. I can see the mountains of the Lake District looming ahead, but no obvious way through. I am told to look out for other low flying aircraft; there are frequent near misses here. He knows the way, and soon the town of Keswick flashes by under the left wing and Derwent Water under the right. We lift up over rising ground and he puts Windermere running down the port side. Seconds later we are climbing up over Morecambe Bay and calling Radar with our planned route to RAF Valley in Anglesey. With 50 miles to run, we are handed over to "Valley Approach", are identified and cleared for descent over the sea to 2,000 feet where we are clear of cloud. We are given details of the runway in use, and the QFE and altimeter setting, and we can join visually. As we slow down, I am asked to look out for other aircraft in the circuit. Joining downwind, I hear the undercarriage going down and see the three green lights in the cockpit. We turn onto finals for the 9,000-foot-long runway and the wing flaps go fully down, the airspeed slowly reducing as we approach the threshold.

I feel the runway coming up around my ears and feel the wheels impact the runway. We don't brake but roll quickly to the end and turn off for the big dispersal. We slow to walking pace as we are marshalled into place. The engine is shut down, the canopy opens, and the ground crew help me undo all my straps and help me out of the cockpit.

We debrief over a coffee in the crew room. Clearly, flying modern jets is a young man's game; you have got to be physically fit and mentally sharp. My young pilot is going onto Harriers and will be spending a lot of time flying low level, probably in Germany. I will also be flying low level, but only over the grey North Sea going out to oil rigs. Not quite so exciting.

Finally, on 15th April, after four years on site, I complete my last scramble (No 173 at C Flight 22 Sqn RAF Valley Anglesey.) Time to "clear" the Station, hand in kit, and pay any dues. The Clothing Store only want back my aircrew watch, my Nav Bag, and my white protective helmet. All my flying suits and clothing I can keep; very useful over the next few years. At most locations where I say goodbye and thanks, there is disbelief that I am leaving the RAF for a more secure career – I must be brave!

As I check out with the Education and Accounts Officers, I thank them for their help and guidance, absolutely invaluable. Finally, I hand in my RAF ID Card, Form 1250, and am on my way to Norfolk with the family, to a new house, job, and school for Christopher. As one door closes, another one is opening. Another challenge awaits …

Chapter 12: Great Yarmouth Norfolk

(1979–1981)

May 1979, We move into our house in Blake Road, Great Yarmouth. It is a semi-detached three-bedroom house, with a drive and single garage. It is situated two roads in from the beach, in a quiet neighbourhood, and just 100 yards from the Grammar School. Junior school is fifteen minutes' walk away and Christopher joins a class of his own age group, even though his education is more advanced. The long beach is steep shingle, ideal for the numerous fishermen, but no good for making sandcastles. Further down the beach, towards the town centre, are the pleasure gardens, with little boats and an amusement arcade, fascinating to young boys. There is a town pier, and further into town an indoor swimming pool; we can all make use of that. The town centre reflects its maritime history, and further on are the docks and quays, supporting the numerous ships servicing the offshore platforms. In summer, the town is crowded with holiday makers, and in winter, with the cold east wind, it is deserted. Having arrived in the area, we buy our third Citroen GS in a row. We like the soft suspension, the powerful brakes, the roomy boot, and the precise handling. They don't make them like that anymore. As we plan to be here for some time, Ann and I make plans for improving the house and gardens. As we don't know this part of Norfolk, we feel we need to explore the Broads, the beaches, and the seaside towns, as well as Norwich; we should get some time off work to do this once I have become qualified.

I check into the operation at North Denes aerodrome and meet the Chief Pilot, Captain Gordon Lucas. I am not required on duty until 1st June, but he shows me the hangar, the Operations room, and the dispersal, with its numerous landing pads. The airfield is grass, but the runways are marked out in white. At the corner of the hangar is a low power Non-Directional Beacon (NDB) which we can use for homings and let-downs to the airfield in bad weather. He has seen my RAF Flying Logbook and likes my 700 hours Wessex experience, and my Master Green Instrument Rating. He would like me to get a Civilian Instrument Rating as soon as practicable; they have a small unit on site which will provide the training. As the training is expensive, I would need to sign a training agreement, so that if I leave the Company within seven years I would need to pay back a proportion of the initial cost. As I intend to stay with the company long term, I am happy to make that commitment, even though I will never see the bill.

The operation at North Denes is a small unit supporting the daily commute of maintenance workers to nearby Amoco gas platforms. The Wessex is flown by a single pilot, with a crewman in the cabin to look after passengers, freight, baggage, and manifests. The nearest platforms are in the Leman field, just 15 minutes flying. We use a Decca Navigator, complete with dials and a roller map with the platform locations printed on it. The next main group of platforms is the Indefatigable (Inde) Field, 30 minutes' flying from the shore.

The first month of flying training starts with a bang on 1st June. Captain Ben Breach, head of Line training, starts with a handling check, then I fly with other pilots out to platforms, and he gives me a final line check 15th June. Now I can fly out to the rigs on my own with a crewman. On 17th June there is special underslung load task at Basildon; our task is to lift an air conditioning unit to the roof of a new building. Captain Pearson carries out the task, and I help out on the ground as needed. On 22nd June my formal I/F training begins on the single engine Bell Jet Ranger, using the ILS at Norwich Airport. On 6th July my Instrument Flying (I/F) training is switched to the Wessex, flown by Captain Ben Breach. Eventually I am put forward for an Instrument Rating flight on 15th July. I fly out to the rigs in the morning, quick sandwich lunch, then a briefing by Don Sissons,

CAA Examiner. I fly the trip as briefed; there are no surprises and I pass all sections. Very satisfying.

Over coffee I listen to a comprehensive debrief, the main point: "Flying over the sea, especially at night, looking at the surface can give you the wrong impression. Only the flight instruments can tell you your airspeed, height above the sea and attitude in relation to the horizon, all crucial parameters for safe flying." I am now cleared to fly in cloud and at night and am to be paid extra money for getting my Instrument Rating. Some pilots do not have Instrument Ratings – they are not required by the oil company, as flying is mainly in daylight and clear of cloud. For some pilots without ratings, it means less money but no chance of being posted to Aberdeen, where ratings are required. Some pilots have businesses locally and wish to remain at the North Denes Operation. On 2nd August I am checked out for night rig landings by Ben Breach. With all the necessary training, June, July, and August are very busy months, with up to three flights a day. The pilots who are not instrument rated fly only in daylight. From the Inde Field we can see platforms in the Dutch sector, and with a strong SW wind it can be quicker to fly to Den Helder airfield in Holland than battle against a headwind returning to base. Some platforms can supply fuel. Other smaller fields are serviced by a small Bond Helicopter operation, also from the same airfield. Bristow controls the airfield, providing an ATC service giving runway in use, pressure settings, and airfield weather. Our bad weather diversion is Norwich Airport, with an ILS let-down to 200 feet. Just 10 minutes flying north is the North Sea Gas Terminal at Bacton, where the pipelines come ashore from the various production platforms and where gas can be pumped to and from the continent. Gas was first found off the east coast of England, the first gas field to come on stream was the West Sole Field in 1967; later Leman in 1968, Indefatigable in 1971, and the Rough Field in 1975. The finding of offshore gas led to the creation of the National Gas Grid, with imports from the Middle East, Norway, and Europe, as well as UK gas from onshore and offshore wells. The 1970s and 80s are a time of rapid exploration of the North Sea for oil and gas reserves, and the rapid building of production platforms. The aim is to achieve self-sufficiency for the UK in oil and gas consumption as soon as practicable. Oil and gas revenues accruing to the UK government go to the Treasury for general expenditure. By contrast, Norway invests its oil and gas revenues into a Sovereign Wealth Fund, with expenditure mainly on infrastructure for its five-million population. As the UK Treasury receives this windfall tax from the Offshore Oil and Gas Industry, the pound, now being a "Petro currency," increases in value, making imports cheaper and exports dearer. UK industry cannot compete, and unemployment rapidly increases to over three million by 1985.

On 4th November, to use up two hours' flying, I choose to carry out two ILS & NDB approaches at Norwich Airport to gain valuable experience. I fly with Captain Paul Bently, who will eventually be in charge of the SAR unit at Sumburgh in the Shetland Islands. On 2nd December I am sent to Paul airfield near Hull to help out for 10 days. My work is to fly passengers out to the BP West Sole Field, shut down, and return late afternoon every day. On return to North Denes, I find myself on duty on Christmas Eve and Boxing Day; one of the perks of being the "New Boy."

1980

On 17th January I file an incident report. As I land on a platform a large tarpaulin blows up into the air and flops to the helideck just outside the rotor disc. As a loose article, it should not have been anywhere near the helideck, and I was lucky to have got away without any damage to the helicopter. Two months later, on 19th February, the Chief Pilot's Wessex goes unserviceable (u/s), so I am tasked with taking over his shuttle flight on top of my own. In all, it involves 22 offshore landings and 4 hours 25 minutes' flying total, a very long day. In March I am sent to on a two-week detachment to Broadford, Skye to assist our operation supporting the Navy. They are conducting trials of various torpedoes and need to move observers around the underwater range in Broadford Sound. I carry out a special flight to RAF Benbecula in the Outer Hebrides, there to pick up Army personnel to fly out to the island of St Kilda, where they control a rocket range over the Atlantic. Having arrived, I shut down and have time to explore the line of cottages, previously the community, before the small island population of just 36 was evacuated to Mainland Scotland on 29th August 1930, at their own request. Returning to base, I fly over the jagged Cuillin Mountains of Skye, which are very impressive. Ann and I walked in the Cuillins in 1962, with both of us using the YHA property at Glenbrittle.

Mid-April 1980 and as a family we are off on a two-week holiday, a "Western Extravaganza" coach tour of the western USA. We fly in a BA Jumbo Jet from Heathrow to San Francisco, travelling in the top deck. I show the stewardess my pilot's licence and we are all invited to the Flight Deck while travelling over the North Atlantic. After 30 minutes, Ann and Christopher have had enough at looking at dials and they go back to their seats. The captain vacates his seat to go back in the cabin to talk to VIP passengers, so I am invited to sit there until he returns, an hour later. I compare this spacious and quiet cockpit with my current helicopter. It has an inertial navigator system, which can be used anywhere in the world. They are carrying diversion fuel to Los Angeles, plus 30 minutes' holding fuel. My helicopter fuel reserve in good weather is just 15 minutes, with no diversion fuel. Down below in the Atlantic, we can see what looks like sugar knobs, actually large icebergs. Every 30 minutes the co-pilot gives a position report on HF to a Flight Watch Radio Station at Gander in Newfoundland. After I finish a fresh orange juice served by the stewardess, the captain returns, and I go back to the cabin. Back in my seat and flying over Canada, I can see the transition from tundra vegetation to the start of trees, huge forests, and eventually fields and small communities.

We fill in arrival forms for immigration to the US, but are not warned about the first question by the grim-faced Immigration lady on arrival: "Are you or have you been a member of the Communist Party? What is the purpose of your visit?" My passport is checked against a list of criminals and handed back without a smile. "Welcome to the USA," is her parting remark. Now it is Ann's turn. No opportunity for conversation here, but our group of holiday makers are let through.

Exploring the San Francisco area, we are taken north by our Greyhound coach, out to a vineyard in the Napa Valley. Lovely views, lovely sunshine, lovely wine tasting. Back to the big city, we explore Fisherman's Wharf and ride on the cable car up the hills from the harbour. In the evening at the hotel, we hear a bang and experience a minor earthquake; just 3.9 on the Richter scale, we are told.

Next day we are driven down the coastal road, Route 101, to Los Angeles (LA). Christopher is looking at the coach driver's map book and making a mental note of where we are going. In the evening the Hotel fire alarm goes off; I call reception and it is confirmed as a false alarm. One of our group, an old gentleman, goes down the external fire escape, which he finds quite stressful. Next day we are visiting Disneyland, at Anaheim, southeast of LA. Having an eight-year-old child is a good excuse for mum and dad to tag along and enjoy the fun as well. The whole theme park is like a film set; castles, lakes, fountains, wild west train rides, decorated floats, and of course, meeting Mickey Mouse. One day is not enough to see everything, but next day we are at the Universal film studios in Hollywood. After a presentation, our group is taken around various film sets for live demonstrations. The first is "Jaws", the predatory shark – even made of plastic, it is frightening enough. Next, we experience a flash flood down a ravine, clearly a place to avoid. Moving on, we witness a shoot-out in Main Street of a western-style town. Making movies is big business, and no expense is spared in getting everything right. Their motto: "Lead, follow, or get off the set."

Next stop, Phoenix, Arizona. A very big city surrounded by desert country and mountains. Quiet night there, then on through Flagstaff to the Grand Canyon, where we have two nights in a hotel inside the Grand Canyon Park, prebooked entry only, because of the usual water shortage. Our 1st day starts with a guided walking tour of the South Rim. The scenery is breath-taking and we take many photographs. In the afternoon we are booked for a flight in a helicopter, a first for Ann and Christopher, and we are all weighed to work out where we should sit. I request to sit on the front seat next to pilot for the best view, and taking photographs, and produce my white pilot's licence. We all notice the coded warning over the radio to the incoming helicopter pilot − "There is a gentleman with an Air Transport Pilot's Licence who wants to fly up front with you." When he lands, we all climb aboard and are strapped in. We take off very gently as we head for the Canyon Rim. I introduce myself to the young pilot. Clearly, he is expecting some sort of authority figure and not a British tourist. Suitably reassured, he opens up. He is currently flying US Marine helicopters, and is doing this job during his leave. He offers to show us the caves just below the Rim, occupied by Native Americans in the past. We fly close and get good photographs. 6,000 feet below, at the bottom of the canyon, is the Colorado River, where there are a few sandbanks where you could land a helicopter if needed. I look for signs of groups rafting down the river, but none today. To keep separate from the fixed wing aircraft we fly below the Rim, and the fixed wing fly above. Whatever your viewpoint, the scenery is stunning. The many layers of exposed rock strata record the millions of years since the rock was initially laid down under the sea. Besides the main canyon, there are numerous side canyons, each with their own small river cutting down through the strata. Having come back to Earth, we all get out and a new group of passengers climbs in, rotors turning. This flight is so impressive, it must rate another visit in the future.

Next day, in the coach, we follow the canyon down to Lake Mead and the Hoover Dam. This was built to provide work during the Great Depression in the 1930s and was commissioned in 1936. Surprisingly, there was agreement amongst all the states affected to share out the electricity output and to share out the water flowing through. All very impressive. We press on to Las Vegas, gambling capital of the USA. There are lots of big cars, flash buildings, and casinos. Small boys are not allowed in, thankfully; Christopher would have witnessed many middle-aged ladies continuously feeding silver dollars into the fruit machines and pulling the big handle, in the forlorn hope of winning the jackpot.

We leave the bright lights of Las Vegas and press on to Death Valley, which, being below sea level, is very hot and very empty, with a surface of sand and salt. We make it to a small oasis and have lunch amongst the palm trees in a lovely cafe. The coach engine overheats as we climb a long hill out of the area, and we have to park up for 30 minutes to let things cool down a little. We soldier on, hoping to cross the Sierra Nevada Mountain Range, but we find all passes are blocked by snow. To get to Yosemite National Park we have to drive north to Lake Tahoe and have lunch in a hotel with a casino in the lobby. As a group, we pass through with Christopher hidden in the middle and make it to Reception. The next morning we have time for a swim in the outdoor pool and breakfast, then motor on to Yosemite. As we enter the National Park, we are all impressed with the U-shaped glacial valleys, the endless huge trees, and long vertical rock faces on the granite mountains. The notices inform us to be aware of bears and what precautions we should take if we were camping. Hopefully, we should be secure in our Lodge. Next day we are taken on a guided tour along the Mariposa Grove to see the Giant Sequoia trees in a Redwood Forest. They are the largest trees in the world, typically growing up to 280 feet, with a diameter at ground level of 26 feet. The biggest tree we see in the park is the Grizzly Giant. These trees can live for over 2,000 years and weigh up to 6,000 tons. Up close, the bark is thick, fibrous, and soft, a form of protection in the event of forest fires. We leave the park, heading for Sacramento (a centre for the California Gold Rush in 1849), then on to San Francisco to fly back to UK in the evening. It is the end of our tour around several states, and our courier asks us to guess the mileage we have done. Christopher, who has been monitoring the route all the time, comes forward with the nearest answer and wins a small prize, well deserved. At the airport we board a crowded jumbo jet and get thrown around by storms over Canada during the night. We are all firmly strapped in, the in-flight dinner is delayed, and we get a few hours' sleep before arriving at Heathrow. Nice to go away, nice to return home …

Back to work; on weekdays, usually two flights, sometimes three, a day. The hours build up through the summer. A technical problem on 19th Sep when I shut down offshore – the coupling gearbox, part of the transmission system, gives strange indications of serviceability, so I ask for technical assistance. The chief engineer is flown out with a bag of tools and winched down. Having inspected and checked out the system, I am cleared for a "Main Drive In" start – not the usual routine, but I get the engines and rotors going normally and we fly back to base with passengers no problem. That night a faulty actuator is changed. A few weeks later I am given an official report – pilot acted correctly – good to see endorsement for my actions. On 6th November a BAH S61N has gearbox problems on one of Shell's platforms and I am tasked with picking up four crewmembers by winching them up and taking them back to their base at Beccles. I learn that BAH have to do a Main Rotor Gearbox change offshore – a very complex and time-consuming job. Towards the end of December, I am tasked with transferring an underslung load from one platform to another, some years since I last did this, but no problems. At the end of the year, I have clocked up

500 hours on the Wessex, of which 30 are at night and 26 flying in cloud on instruments.

In spite of a new Conservative Government taking power, our local Grammar School is to become a Comprehensive Middle School, with a Sixth Form College to be set up somewhere in Great Yarmouth. Ann and I begin looking at Public Schools within 50 miles. While Christopher is at school, we drive out to various schools in the area for assessment. We see Greshams, near Holt, North Norfolk; the Perse School in Cambridge; and the Woodbridge School in Suffolk. All very impressive, with good personal development and academic results. We put Christopher's name down to join the Junior section of Greshams and pay a deposit. Christopher hates the idea of going away from home for his education. No need to take decisions yet, but Christopher's education is important. Meanwhile, Christopher starts going to Cubs, starts activities with other boys and begins to learn some useful life skills.

1981 starts with a three-week detachment in January to Skye and a refresher flight around the local area landing spots with the Chief Pilot, Captain John Waddington. Typically, I fly two trips a day, total flying two hours, all in daylight and clear of cloud. Scenery is breath-taking. Occasionally I shut down at the test centre and, surprisingly, am briefed as to what goes on and the results so far of the torpedo trials. Being in a remote area and having a long stretch of deep, sheltered water, Broadford Sound is ideal for the work being undertaken. I never see the submarines on the surface, but the range operators know where they are from the noise they generate being picked up by the hydrophones on the sea bed under the torpedo range.

Returning to North Denes, I have to fly an Instrument Base Check with Captain Ben Breach, which includes an ILS Approach at Norwich airport and a NDB let-down. A few days later I have a night flying check, circuits and emergencies. Luckily, the Wessex performs well on one engine, so operating at night and landing on oil rigs is not a worry.

In the spring there is a meeting at North Denes with Operations Director Mike Norris. My next posting, in August, after two and a half years at North Denes, will be either Nigeria, flying the Wessex, or Aberdeen, converting on to the Sikorsky S61N, to make use of my SAR experience. I choose the Aberdeen option and request a 10-year slot to settle into a community and make use of the famed Scottish education system. That evening I tell Ann and Christopher that we are on our way north in August. We need to make preparations – what academy, what community, what facilities, what sort of house should we buy? I am tasked to go to Skye in early May, so I drive up to the Bristow Aberdeen Operation, where I meet the Chief Pilot, Captain David Smith, who gives me a quick tour of the extensive complex. In passing through I collect some engineering spares destined for the Skye Operation, pick up the local Press and Journal newspaper for house sales, and drive west along the River Dee valley, looking at the numerous communities. Finally, I head off across the Highlands to the Isle of Skye for a 10-day detachment. At the end of this, my last detachment, I host a farewell meal with the Chief Pilot and learn a lot about Bristow's operations overseas. They are numerous, and cover SAR and aerial survey as well as supporting oil related activity, offshore and onshore. Task complete, I head home and then back up to Aberdeen, with the family, to look at academies, communities, and property for sale. Not surprisingly, the closer to Aberdeen, the more expensive the property. After talking to the Headmaster of Banchory Academy, where big improvements are scheduled in the next two years, we find a newly built four-bedroom Cala bungalow in a secluded cul-de-sac just five minutes' walk from the Academy. The owner is looking for offers over £55,000, and over the telephone we agree to buy it for £56,000. We inform our solicitor and arrange a mortgage through Lloyds bank, one of their first mortgages in Scotland. As the Bank Manager reads through the documents, we have to explain to him what the various terms in the text actually mean. He wants to offer us a mortgage of £45,000, way above the £25,000 we want. We also explain to the solicitor that we are happy to buy the bungalow without a survey, as it is only two years old and covered by a 10-year guarantee by Cala Homes. Job done, we head back south, happy with the bungalow we have purchased in the town of Banchory. With the oil boom affecting northeast Scotland, property prices are going up week by week. We feel pleased with the Academy, with its Junior School on the same site, being close to our bungalow. All we need to do now is to sell our house in Great Yarmouth and move to Scotland at the end of July ...

Ann has been taking Christopher to tennis coaching in Norwich and to swimming lessons in an indoor pool in Great Yarmouth. At weekends we explore Norfolk, the Broads, the beaches, and the towns. It will be many years before we would expect to be back in this area. My last flight is on 24th July. In two and a half years I have flown 1050 hours, an average of 420 hours per year, well within the maximum allowed of 800. I set my mind on operating out of Aberdeen and flying the bigger Sikorsky S61N, little knowing what would happen to the North Denes Operation or the fleet of Wessex Helicopters. As we make preparations for the move north, there seems to be a last-minute problem with our house sale in Great Yarmouth ...

Chapter 13: The Aberdeen Operation

(August 1981–October 1983)

2nd August 1981

"Welcome to our Aberdeen Operation," intones Captain Malcolm Soper, our Flight Commander for our S61N course of six trainees. "We are the biggest worldwide helicopter company. However, as such, we have lost two helicopters in the UK, with their crew and passengers, in as many weeks, including a Wessex from North Denes." This is news to me, which I will have to follow up in the next few days, time permitting. "Most pilots do around five years here at Aberdeen before moving on." I hope to do at least 10, if not more. "As aircrew we need to be ready to fly straight away when on duty in this building. We are here to serve the offshore oil industry, rain or shine, day or night, when things are going well and when things are going badly. We are the main helicopter operator here at Aberdeen, and we have an operation at Sumburgh in the Shetlands and at Unst at the top of Shetland. We have completed 10 years of operating with the Sikorsky S61N, and it has proved to be very reliable. We call it 'the Queen of the Skies'. In the coming years we plan to introduce the AS332L Super Puma," (Bristow Tiger), "and we will be the lead customer. I am your Flight Commander, come to me initially with any problems. Today, you are beginning two-weeks' ground school, including a procedure trainer and a flight simulator belonging to BAH, so slightly different instruments and central console to our aircraft. Once you are checked out after five Familiarisation flights," (or Famil flights), "you will start your line training as a co-pilot. Completing that, you will serve at least six months as a co-pilot, including a winter, before being considered for captaincy. There is lot to learn, and you will continue to learn every day, even after you have qualified. I will now show you round the Planning room, the Radio room, and the Operations room, and then downstairs, where our passengers are 'processed' before they fly. We will start at the coffee machine and get our free drinks before we move on."

We six trainee pilots start ground school looking at aircraft systems and their malfunctions, the most common ones being the undercarriage failing to retract and the No. 1 A/C generator failing, with or without a warning light on the Central Warning Panel (CWP). The S61N is amphibious, so can land on water, taxi around and take off. We will be shown this eventually on a local freshwater lake. The flight simulator is basic; the "visual" is just TV screens facing the cockpit windscreens with white lights against a black background, ideal for simulating night flying around an airport and flying procedures on instruments around any airport in Europe.

As we complete the ground school, we are introduced to the flight simulator and operating in the dark. It is good for practising all procedures and for experiencing emergencies that we can't practice in the air. With a colleague we are briefed for our first flight in the S61N (Famil 1) on 16th August. We are allowed to take passengers, as the flight is overland and just to show us all the local area. Ann and Christopher come along for the ride, plus several other family members and off-duty engineers. This part of Aberdeenshire is scenic on this lovely day, with an interesting coastline, castles, stately homes and gardens, and the valleys of the River Dee and River Don feeding into Aberdeen. The town itself has the University Campus to the north and the bustling harbour to the south. The big oil company premises are located around the edge, as well as newly built housing estates for all the "incomers." After we have toured round the local area, our instructor Captain Woodard disengages the auto-stabilisation and lets me fly the machine straight and level, then some turns, and finally climbs and descents. The people in the back are aware of the helicopter wobbling a little as I get used to the controls.

Compared to the Wessex, the S61N is bigger, and has less spare power and a slower control response. After 50 minutes we land back at Aberdeen airfield and taxi in past all the fixed wing aircraft and shut down on our allotted slot in dispersal. Suitably impressed, our passengers are taken back to our terminal and dispersal. Future Famil flights are over the sea, so no passengers allowed, but it is good for the family to see what my job is like and the noisy environment I will be working in.

The next Famil flight is about managing engine failures during take-off and in level flight. Initially, I am sat in a "jump seat" just behind the two pilots, so I get a good view of what is happening. As we climb up from the runway, Captain Woodard instructs my colleague to pull back on No. 1 "speed select lever" in the roof. As expected, the power on No. 1 engine reduces towards idle, but unexpectedly winds down to zero! Here we are over central Aberdeen, with No. 2 engine working hard to keep us airborne and No. 1 engine too warm to restart. He pulls out a cigarette, lights it, inhales a lungful of smoke, and we turn away from the urban area towards open countryside. A minute later he attempts to restart the engine in flight and is successful, so we carry on with the exercise. A lesson learnt for future reference. Now it is my turn to play with the levers, this time it all works normally, good.

In the next few days, I complete my training and become qualified to fly the S61N, by day and by night. My flying licence is annotated with this qualification, should anyone in authority in UK or abroad need to check. Training continues offshore with deck landings and take-offs, and I start my line training with Captain Hughes on 7th September by flying out to the BP Forties Field, 100 miles east of Aberdeen. There are four oil platforms there and we commence a "shuttle," conveying passengers to where they are required and refuelling on the last stop before departing to Aberdeen. The flight home is planned as an hour's flying, taking in an ILS Approach to runway 15, providing good training for bad weather.

The purpose of the line training is to experience landings and take-offs from the rigs and platforms in our local area. We also practice rig radar let-downs, using our weather radar to navigate and provide safe separation from the installation we intend to land on. Just before landing I need to note the name on the side and confirm this is our intended destination. After take-off for Aberdeen, I always need to check the compass is slaved with our detector unit in the tail, and aligned with the standby compass in the roof. Also, the radio compass needle should be pointing ahead to the powerful Non Directional radio Beacon (NDB) near the coast, at Scots-town Head, morse ident SHD. By day the position of the sun, and at night the coded flashing light from lighthouses, provides confirmation that the course you are taking is towards the coast and Aberdeen. In the early days, some crews did not align their compass properly and, after departing a platform in the middle of the North Sea, have ended up in Norway, a costly mistake.

Back at home in Banchory, we are settling into our lovely Cala bungalow. I bag the smallest bedroom for my office and my computer. We get a small TV and battery radio for Christopher's bedroom, sort out TVs around the house and a telephone next to our bed for when I am on night standby. The kitchen cupboards are very dark, and we resolve to change them eventually. Outside, we can get four cars on the drive and two in the double garage. We get to meet the neighbours, mostly oil-related incomers like us. In recent years, Banchory has doubled in size to 7,000 residents, needing improvements in schooling and recreational activities. Christopher is lining up to start junior school in September, just five minutes' walk away, so he can come home for lunch. We talk to neighbours about being prepared for winter. Apparently, the standard drill is to stock up in November with tinned and packaged food sufficient for two weeks, should the community get snowed in with deep drifts across the roads. Also, by not clearing any snow off the drive, you provide a degree of insulation, preventing sharp frosts freezing the water pipe to the bungalow, which is located under the drive. With any snow on the roof, we are to expect long icicles hanging down from the gutters. They can knocked off safely with a long handled brush.

First snow of winter 1981 but Ann can make it to the local shops.

We explore our little town of Banchory on the River Dee; it is very pretty and attracts holidaymakers from Aberdeen at weekends. We have all the shops we need, plus a bank, building society, and a garage that can service our Citroen GS. We set our sights on joining the town's tennis club, and the very popular golf club, set out alongside the River Dee. Five minutes' walk from the town centre, we can watch salmon leaping up a waterfall on the River Feugh. In the deep pool below the falls, so many salmon jostle for position that you could scoop them up with a net!

Aerial photograph of Banchory on the River Dee.

There are several walks from Banchory into the local country-side, and along a former railway line on the valley floor, heading towards Aberdeen, passing a sawmill, timber yard, and fields of lavender. We know that near the source of the River Dee is the ski resort of Glenshee, really busy in winter. In summer there are walks up the Glens, where the deer roam in great herds. Clearly, there is plenty to do when I have time off. The town of Aberdeen, called the Silver City because of all the granite-faced buildings glinting in the sunshine, is usually very busy on both the roads and the pavements. We only come in to talk to our Lloyds Bank, if needed, or to explore the busy docks or the deserted sandy beaches facing the North Sea. While the oil companies are expanding their operations in the North Sea, Aberdeen provides a good base, and profits from all the activity. A by-pass for Aberdeen is planned; the oil companies are pressing for dual carriageways for everywhere they need to take their bulky equipment. Much new housing is being built on the outskirts of Aberdeen and in surrounding communities to accommodate the incomers. All the local services – hospitals, schools, parks and golf clubs – are under pressure from the rising population. The local newspapers are clearly in favour of the oil boom, describing it as being, overall, a good thing. Hopefully, it will still be in place when we come to retire ...

After a decent interval, I decide to ring North Denes and find out about their accident.

On 13th August, a Wessex 60-G-ASWI crashed into the sea off the Norfolk coast. My logbook shows I flew it on 23rd July, a few weeks beforehand. The helicopter and the occupants, Captain Ben Breach, Crewman Adrian Amis, and 11 passengers, are never found. The company are looking at replacing the Wessex fleet with the Bell 212. The cause of the accident was not established. A memorial to all those who died is unveiled some years later in the grounds of Great Yarmouth Minster.

Eventually I am qualified to be released to the line, i.e. fly with other captains, but training continues with water landings on a local lake. Once you have seen it demonstrated it is quite easy to do, and once on the surface you can move around at walking pace. When stationary, the cabin floor is six inches above the water outside. This is without the extra buoyancy that can be provided by the built-in inflatable buoyancy bags on the sponsons. The take-off, moving forward, is different from a take-off from land, and you need the windscreen wipers on with all the spray thrown up.

Clearly, the S61N is well designed to operate over water and on water, with its boat-shaped hull and sponsons containing the landing gear. It performs well in rough weather, and with a protective shield in front of the air intakes, it copes well with snow and icing. Curiously, it flies best with a centre of gravity (C of G) towards the rear limit, and when back on the ground, with everything unloaded and in a low fuel state, the C of G is well forward, so taxiing in dispersal needs to be very delicate. I begin flying out to new and distant destinations, going to platforms which are nearer to Denmark than Scotland, a lot of fuel being needed for the return flight when battling into the usual head-wind from the west. Because of my experience with winching, I am shown "Public Transport" winching, which has a special application for the Beryl Field, about 150 miles from Aberdeen. The main requirement is being able to maintain a hover on the power of one engine, should the other fail for any reason. The ideal wind in which to hover over the Beryl Alpha mooring buoy, which makes random movements dependent on the wind and waves, is 15 knots. The stronger the wind, the more the movement, which makes winching people down onto its small helideck more difficult. Some pilots, in other companies, have been caught out when an engine has lost power, and the S61N has descended and the keel has touched a hard surface, causing extensive and very expensive damage.

Christopher joins his appropriate class and enjoys working with pupils from a wide range of family backgrounds. He finds out there is a Boy Scout Pack with a Scout Hut in the centre of town. At his age, it will be the Cub Pack first. We can see the work beginning on the Academy upgrade, which includes a swim-ming pool. Ann and I join the Parent Teacher Association (PTA), which is raising funds to help build a new sports pavilion adja-cent to the playing fields. Grampian Education Authority will build it if we raise £10,000 towards the cost. Various fundraising activities are proposed, and we start getting involved. We learn that, in line with many Scottish academies, we are a "commu-nity school," so outside school hours, various activities can take place in the classrooms, involving local people. Once the new swimming pool is in operation, it is planned to teach all pupils to swim. Also, the new computer room will teach people how to operate them, another invaluable life skill.

The town's tennis courts are in the centre of town, and on joining the tennis club we learn there are plans to build new all-weath-er courts on Burnett Park, at the western end of town. Again, most of the money needed will be supplied by the local authority, as long as the club raises £2,500 towards the cost. Being new-comers and very keen, Ann and I take up the responsibility for raising this money through a number of activities. At the same time, we learn that a new sports pavilion will be built in Burnett Park, adjacent to the cricket pitch. It's all happening thanks to the generosity of the local authorities and the push from the numerous incomers wanting better facilities in their expanding town.

Flying out to oil rigs and platforms and various checks continue at a steady pace. Eventually, on 3rd March 1982, I am deemed competent to act as a captain on the S61N, so now I am flying with a range of co-pilots with varying degrees of experience and skills. While things are improving for me at Aberdeen, the papers are full of the problems in the South Atlantic. Apparently, the Argentinian government is having internal problems and is looking at an action that will make them popular. Many Royal Navy captains are signalling to the Foreign and Commonwealth Office about the build-up of weapons and stores on the dockside of many Argentinian ports. On 19th March some scrap metal merchants are conveyed to an old whaling station in South Georgia and raise the Argentinian flag. This is followed on 2nd April by a full-scale invasion of the Falkland Islands, and of South Georgia the next day, catching the UK Government by surprise! It takes 74 days for the UK Task Force to achieve the surrender of the Argentinian Forces at Port Stanley. At the height of the debates in Parliament, when Margaret Thatcher outlines the sending of a Naval task force headed by two aircraft carriers, several of our ex-Navy Officers openly ring their old Operational Squadrons and offer their services for the duration. They spell out their contact details and state that they can report for duty within 24 hours when called upon. Amongst the many ex-military men, including me, there is speculation about possible calling up of the Reserves and what jobs we might be called upon to do. In the end, none of us are called up for duty, but all of us watch the news bulletins every night, to lament about information given out by the BBC which is of use to the Argentinian military.

Normal flying on the North Sea continues, but the S61Ns are being tasked to go up to the East Shetland Basin, a cluster of platforms and exploration oil rigs about 250 miles north of Aberdeen. We need to refuel at Sumburgh on the way out and the way back, giving a total flight time of six hours minimum. When the new AS332L (Bristow Tiger) and the Chinook are fully operational they will fly direct, bypassing Sumburgh, thus saving a lot of time and money for the oil company concerned. In the autumn, it is decided to check me and some colleagues out on SAR, as the company has a commitment in the Forties Field, and we fly several flights a day to that area. We take a S61N down to my former base at North Denes and spend five days training over the sea, involving both small and large lifeboats from nearby Gorleston.

All my former skills of hovering over water and small vessels on the move come back, and as always, smooth flying is the key. Back at base, I get prepared for a Captain's Night Line Check, using a handy oil rig just offshore for take-offs, landings, and circuits. At one stage my instructor takes out the auto stabilisation when on deck, and asks me to do a circuit. Fortunately, I have 1,000 hours of flying the Whirlwind, which has no stabilisation, so I was able to fly a perfect circuit, very pleasing. I resolve to keep my hand in, flying without auto-stabilisation, a skill I feel I need to maintain.

On the political front, Margaret Thatcher calls a general election for 9th June 1983. She is riding high following winning the war in the Falkland Islands the previous year. The opposition is split between the Labour Party and the newly formed Alliance (Social Democrat Party and The Liberal Party). The Conservative Party, with Mrs Thatcher as Prime Minister, wins a landslide majority of 144 seats and has the power to make big changes. The cutbacks planned for the Royal Navy are cancelled. All warships lost in the Falklands War are being replaced. The Falkland Islands will be defended long-term, with all the decisions that that will involve. The Armed Forces feel secure that they will not be disbanded. On the North Sea, the rush to explore for new oil reserves continues.

As they are found, plans are drawn up to exploit them, mainly involving establishing a production platform with associated sub sea oil and gas pipes to processing plants on shore. On schedule, Marathon's Brae Field is commissioned on 1st July. They have on standby many support ships and two S61Ns, on site for 48 hours, ready if needed. All of us involved are well rewarded and the task is completed on time with few problems. The UK is becoming self-sufficient in oil and gas, and some power stations are being converted from burning coal to either oil or gas. The UK economy begins to improve. What could go wrong?

Ann and I form a fundraising committee to raise the £2,500 needed for the tennis club. We approach the golf club, of which we are members, for support. Apparently, every year they have a sponsored golf match and donate the profits to a good cause. This year they will make the donation to the Banchory Tennis Club. They approach the local businesses to donate prizes for a sponsored golf match and are given numerous high value prizes – it's a new local facility that they will be supporting, and open to one and all. Our committee decide on a sponsored draw, and we approach the local shops for their support. One travel company offers a "Dinner for Two in Amsterdam," including flights from Aberdeen, a night in a five-star hotel and a dinner for two in of the best restaurants in the centre. This prize will be highlighted on the draw tickets and on our publicity posters. We set about selling tickets to the town's residents, sensibly dividing the town into sectors so that each of us have our own patch. Knocking on doors, we get various responses, from "No thanks," to "I would like several books of draw tickets, please." Most shops give us vouchers for their goods or services, and several are willing to sell the draw tickets for us and put a poster in their shop window. All of the committee buy draw tickets; Ann and I buy some each and some in Christopher's name. Eventually we have an open "Cheese and Wine" event, at which the draw will be done and the prizes presented. We ask our local District Councillor to draw the tickets out of a drum, and Ann and I match the ticket numbers to the list of subscribers. All is well initially, and the prizes are handed out to those who are present. Eventually, we get to the last and most important prize. Our Councillor reaches into the drum and pulls out a ticket and reads out the number.

Ouch! That number is our own son Christopher, and the Councillor announces "Christopher Lanigan. It could not go a more deserving person." Christopher comes forward from the audience and collects the travel shop voucher and looks very happy. As he returns to his seat, he is congratulated on his good luck by people who know him. Just as well Ann and I did not win it, and we are glad that some independent person drew the tickets for us.

Next week I have to go to the travel company and say that Christopher would like his dad to go with him to Amsterdam. All is agreed, and we have an interesting time exploring Amsterdam, around the colourful port area. In the evening, we have a table for two in the middle of the restaurant and we show the Head Waiter the voucher that Christopher had won to explain our presence in this expensive place. Promptly, he holds it up and in a loud voice explains it to all the other well-dressed diners. There is some applause and smiles all round.

Back at Banchory, the day for the sponsored golf match arrives, and the weather is bad. The stewards have a meeting and decide that it is important that the event takes place, and the golfers do their best, plodding round the sodden course. Prizes are awarded, and our tennis club collects a fat cheque. Enough money is raised for four En-Tout-Cas synthetic hard surface tennis courts to be built. As founding members of the new tennis club, Ann and I can go back and play there at any time in the future ...

It's October, and the training system is booking in all pilots for their pre-winter briefing; what to expect from the weather, the situation on offshore helidecks, and Air Traffic Control holdups. We are to expect rain, sleet, hail, and snow; our S61N can cope with this. Once airborne, we may encounter airframe and engine icing. We have a shield in front of the engine air intakes that protects the engines from slush or snow entering the engine and causing a flame-out. We have engine anti-icing to prevent build-up of ice in the front of the engine. At the pre-flight planning stage, it will be wise to check that the freezing level is above 500 feet over the sea, so if we encounter icing, we can descend into a warm layer and shed any accumulation. We will need the cabin heater on for ourselves and our passengers, it is effective and uses 100 pounds of fuel an hour. Operating onto helidecks, we need a wind less than 60 knots to prevent passengers being blown over, and on no account are ropes to be tied to the fuselage to help passengers find their way to the airstair door. No loose articles, clothing, hats, papers, or magazines; they will get loose and fly away. On landing offshore where a refuel is planned, keep the passengers on until the refuel is complete, so that their weight helps to keep the machine on the deck. Allow an extra five minutes for a turnaround on the deck, so an extra 100 pounds of fuel. Where the return flight to base is all over the sea with no alternates close by the route, and into a strong headwind, we need to bear in mind that in the event of an engine failure we may not be able to maintain the normal cruising speed of 110 knots. A table is issued giving the extra fuel required.

Returning to base, those movements requesting an ILS approach will be given priority to land over those requesting a "visual" approach. On the ground, it is likely that you will need extra fuel for waiting at a holding point prior to take-off, as those aircraft and helicopters wishing to land have priority, and in poor weather they are widely separated, so the wait is typically 15 minutes, sometimes more. It can happen that by the time you are allowed on the runway ready for take-off, you have used up so much fuel that you will need to return to dispersal to refuel! Plan all the extra fuel you think you might need, it will reduce the payload you may offer the oil company, but nobody will thank you if you run short. Enjoy your flight!

Chapter 14: Forties Delta Explosion and Fire

(1st August 1983)

"Forties Control, this is Four Zero Foxtrot with you at minute three zero, request weather, routing and return load." We are flying in Sikorsky S61N, G-BHOF and routing to the Forties Field, 100 miles east of Aberdeen, for the late afternoon shuttle flight and my co-pilot, First Officer Roberts is making the standard call.

The reply comes back: "Come straight to the Bravo platform, offload everything, go to the Delta, where there has been an explosion, and fire continues in the drilling derrick. Pick up the injured workers and bring them to Bravo for first aid."

I look across the cockpit at my young co-pilot – he seems unperturbed. I reply – "Willco, Bravo to offload. Will then go to the Delta and land on if the helideck is OK."

Closing with the Delta platform, we note the flames are confined to the drilling derrick, which has not crumpled so far, and the flames are not spreading out towards the helideck. The helideck is clear of debris and looks normal. As I commit to landing on, I am aware how momentous this decision is. Get it right, and the injured personnel will be in hospital within two hours. Get it wrong, and you will compound the problem. On deck, I feel no heat from the flame, and the power required to hover just prior to landing was normal. I keep the rotor revs up to pull down cold air onto the aircraft and be ready to take off if the situation deteriorates. I brief young Roberts to open the cabin airstair door, get the people on board, stay in the aircraft, close the door, and return to cockpit. I see a group of men being helped towards the aircraft. They have black patches on their overalls, faces and hands. I glance away and concentrate on the flying situation. When Roberts straps in, we take off using normal power and head for the Bravo.

I call, "Bravo, with you in five, with 11 injured personnel some in a bad way and they will need help to get off."

Control comes back with "Thank you for that, we would now like you to take some firemen across with equipment and bring back non-essential personnel, how many could you take?"

"Without baggage we can fill every seat, that's 19."

Firemen in bulky kit climb aboard with a range of hoses. We take off and return to the Delta. The fire looks the same, the drilling derrick is still looking solid. We land on, the fire crews offload and 18 chaps without bags are boarded. The take-off is normal and we return to the Bravo.

On landing, Control says "Keep rotors running in case we need to evacuate the Delta."

I come back with, "OK, can do, request fuel and some sandwiches and coffee."

A fuel hose is plugged in, and we load 2200 pounds, about two hours' worth, and wait for news, we can see the fire and smoke clearly about a mile away, no sign of getting smaller. After two hours rotors running, we request more fuel and my co-pilot heads out for the toilet; on his return, I do the same. Below deck, there are signs of frantic activity. We get given more coffee and sandwiches.

Eventually, Control comes up with, "An RAF Sea King SAR helicopter will be arriving in 20 minutes to assist. We want you take some slightly injured personnel to Aberdeen Royal Infirmary and some non-essential personnel back to Aberdeen Airport. You will be leaving in ten minutes for the Alpha platform for your final stop and refreshments for the flight home. Steak, chips, and all the trimmings plus white coffee suit?"

"Looking forward to that," I reply.

As we leave the Alpha platform, we hear the Sea King coming in and exchange information about the situation on the Delta. An hour later we land at night at the helipad at Aberdeen Royal Infirmary; luckily, I have been in there twice before in daylight. Our injured personnel are helped off into waiting ambulances. Ten minutes later we land at Aberdeen airport, drop off our remaining passengers and shut down – a long day, 7hrs 40 minutes flying.

Back in the flight planning room, we are halfway through completing the details when the Chief Pilot, Captain David Smith comes up. "I need to speak to you," pointing at me. "In the office now!" I follow him. "Don't sit down. I have had the Chief Executive of BP in London on the phone about your involvement with the Forties Delta today." He is looking a bit grim. "He is pleased to have the injured workers in hospital, he is pleased that the fire is dying down, and he thinks the platform will be saved from destruction and repaired. So, I am giving you and your co-pilot a bottle of Company Whiskey to remember your efforts today. I don't want a report." Very sensible, as we must have broken every rule in the book to do the job – everything has worked OK, so it's results that count. "Send your co-pilot in now." He opens the door, and I am ushered out into the planning room full of curious faces. My co-pilot returns a few moments later and, with the booty on display, we get offers for a tasting session on the spot – firmly turned down! I have to drive home, after all. Before young Roberts disappears, I make his day by publicly thanking him for his efforts. It will be a day I feel he will remember for sure.

Stripping off my rubber suit, I climb under a hot shower and feel the muscles relaxing in my back and legs. Getting dressed to return home, I pick up my flight bag with the special Company single malt whisky inside and make my way out to the car park. Now the real challenge begins – Aberdeen evening traffic, with the boy racers keen to get to hospital as soon as possible – watch out for them. As I turn into my neat and tidy housing estate in Banchory and park in the drive, I have a final thought. I am coming home very late, very tired, and carrying a bottle of whiskey. Have to think of something appropriate, otherwise my sensible Ann will give me chapter and verse and won't allow her breadwinner out of the house tomorrow for the 2 p.m. flight to the Beryl Field.

Post Script – Quote from Aberdeen Press and Journal – Wednesday 6 February 1985

Headline: Near Catastrophe – BP lapse led to blow out

18 months after the accident, BP admits 2 charges under the Health & Safety at Work Act at Aberdeen's Sheriff Court and are fined £15,000. While drilling on the Delta Platform they encountered a pocket of gas at 578 metres, causing a blow out and fire that raged for 9 hours. 11 men were injured in the initial explosion, flash fire, and were evacuated to hospital. At one stage the flames were 100 feet high, and beams in the drilling derrick buckled by 3 feet, but the derrick did not fall onto the helideck.

Chapter 15: The Falklands Experience

1984

Autumn 1983 – Getting the Contract

I am at a party in Banchory; the host is a friend of mine on another helicopter company, and he is in a good mood. After six months' work with the MOD he has got them to accept that "civilian" helicopter pilots can do a useful logistic job in the Falkland Islands, flying the well-tried Sikorsky S61N. He expects that a "contract" will be signed within weeks. He is in an expansive mood, and the more I express doubt, the more he insists on telling me every detail. Three helicopters would be required and would go out on a ship as deck cargo, in black plastic bags for protection from salt spray. The cargo ship would go from Southampton and the helicopters would be craned off at the quay in Port Stanley. Then they would be flown a few miles to their base at RAF Stanley airfield, shared with other fixed wing aircraft. Ground support would be provided in a number of ex-shipping containers. Accommodation and food would be provided free in an Army "Costel," an accommodation barge linked to the shore. At the end of half an hour I am swamped with detail, but I register the fact that the contract has not yet been signed.

Next day I go in early and ask for a talk with our Base Commander. I run through what I have learnt and answer most of the detailed questions he fires at me. Eventually, he says, "Leave it with me. I will inform HQ. If they like the idea, they will approach the MOD with a view to tender for the Falklands Contract."

A month later, the news is that we have won the contract and the company is looking for volunteers amongst ex-military people to go out for four months at a time. I mull it over, I meet all the requirements, but by the time I decide to apply the initial slots have gone. The soonest I can go is February 14th 1984. I am curious about the Islands, and I have experience of operating with the Army, in Borneo and Malaya. Flying mainly overland would make a nice change from flying over the North Sea. With my departure date agreed, I plan what I would need, and how I would get to RAF Brize Norton in Oxfordshire.

Ann's family are still in their old house, just 12 miles from the airfield, and I have a few days off before departure, so we all go down by car and prepare for the big day.

I get dropped off at the Passenger Terminal, say my goodbyes, and check in at Departures. My name is on the list, my passport is checked, my seat No allocated, my bulging suitcase, full of cold weather gear is taken away, and I join the throng in the departure lounge. Looking around, I do not spot any familiar faces, but clearly we are going to have a full aeroplane going to Ascension Island. On schedule, we climb aboard the RAF VC10, and I get an aisle seat. All seats face backwards, safer in a crash landing, but so far there has not been a crash landing to prove the theory. We take off on time with England spread out with a patchwork of fields, towns, and villages. Soon we are over the English Channel and lunch is being served; just five hours to go before our ETA. We land as scheduled, and are told we will stay the night before going to our various destinations next morning. With a few others I explore the Island, have a few beers with transit crews, and get an early night, ready for a wake-up call at 7 a.m. local time. Our passenger load for a Hercules – tactical transport aircraft – assembles, and we receive a briefing.

"When you leave this room, your passports will be checked, and you will be allocated a bus that will take you to the aircraft. There is a box of ear defenders which you can put in your ears to reduce the noise. You will enter up the rear ramp and take up your seat either side of the freight strapped down in the middle.

Once airborne, you can climb up onto the freight and stretch out if you wish. About three hours into the flight, we will start refuelling from another Hercules. You can watch that from the cockpit and take photographs."

Suitably prepared, we move out to the coaches, find ourselves an aircraft with lots of people around it, walk up the ramp and strap ourselves into the canvas para-troop seats. Then the noise and vibration starts; communication is now by sign language. We taxi out to the runway and take off with a roar, turning south and climbing up to cruising altitude. After a few minutes, our loadmaster comes round. She indicates we can leave our seats and stretch out on the freight, tied down with nets, in front of us. I find a suitable flat surface and make myself comfortable. I see that she carries on towards the back of the aircraft, using her torch to look for hydraulic leaks and anything untoward. A few hours later she wakes me up and indicates that refuelling is about to start. I clamber down off the freight and make my way up to the cockpit, joining a group of eager photographers, including some very senior RAF and Army officers.

Our aircraft is positioned to the right of the other Hercules. We can see a crewman at the window over there. As he waves, we see the refuelling drogue being fed out from underneath. There are no radio calls as our Captain brings our aircraft back and below the one ahead. I can see a yellow line on the belly of the one ahead, and our pilot is lining us up. I can see a green light on the Hose Drum Unit (HDU) of the one ahead. Our Captain holds the control column with his left hand and the throttles with his right. We begin to close on the drogue at walking pace; it is swaying in the slipstream, and our probe is out to the right, until at the last moment the drogue swings across to the right and our probe makes a solid contact. Our aircraft still advances, and the hose is wound in to keep it under tension. Eventually we stop advancing, the green light flashes, and we all understand that fuel is beginning to flow. Our Captain holds this position for the next 20 minutes, while we are looking up at a tailplane just 10 feet above our heads. As our aircraft takes on fuel, our Captain has to adjust the throttles, so we maintain position. Clearly, our Captain is concentrating hard, as beads of sweat break out on his forehead. No chance of using a handkerchief, though. Eventually the green light flashes again – no more fuel available – so we gently ease back, and as our probe is pulled out of the drogue, there is a little spurt of fuel. Well back, we slide across to the right as our co-pilot confirms that we have enough fuel to reach Port Stanley and our diversion airfield in South America. As we move ahead, the other aircraft turns left, away from us, and heads back to Ascension Island, job done. Again, no radio calls; our co-pilot takes over the flying controls as our Captain drinks a well-earned coffee. We photographers head back to our seats and a packed lunch is served. I check my camera, 20 shots taken of this unique event. Good, useful for a presentation at a later date, no doubt.

Four hours later, I am woken up from my comfortable place on top of the freight; the engines are making less noise, so we must be descending. Sure enough, land appears outside the window, and there is a settlement with a big church on a hill side above a quay, our first glance of Port Stanley. The harbour is full of ships, and as we swing round to land I see the airfield with its metal plate runway, more Hercules parked alongside, two Phantom Jets positioned near the eastern end of the runway, and some diminutive Harriers near a hangar. We thump down on the runway, the aircraft shudders as the brakes are applied, and within minutes all of us are trooping down the ramp and are guided into a building for a sit down while our bags are unloaded.

"Welcome to the Falkland Islands. I hope you have a pleasant stay." An Army sergeant is talking to us, while holding two small, round grey objects in his hands. "While the Argentinians were here they planted thousands of anti-personal land mines like these," he says, holding up the evidence. "Where we know many are planted, we have wired off the area and put up warning notices. Don't be tempted to cross the wire because sheep or wild-life are there – they are not heavy enough to set off the mines. Also, there are mines planted on most beaches, all battlefields, and near broken aircraft. To stay safe use only tracks, or travel in a vehicle. We are gathering up ordnance as we find it and destroying it using an old quarry near Port Stanley. You will hear a loud bang at noon every day. We are ready to repel any incursion by air or sea around the clock, and we deploy troops to key points at both dawn and dusk. Your bags are now ready for collection. Have a safe stay."

I find my bulging suitcase, meet Captain Beecher, the chief pilot of the operation, and in a Land Rover we drive 200 yards to where our three S61Ns are parked, next to an assortment of old shipping containers. Initially we file into the smallest, which is a combined operations room and crew room. I am halfway through a welcome mug of tea when in walks an Army Major. He is introduced as our Tasking and Liaison Officer.

"Welcome to the Falklands, David. I have come here to tell you what goes on and explain the part you will play." He has sat down opposite me, while Captain Beecher listens thoughtfully. "Your operation has got off to a good start, you are carrying 80% of our logistical requirement, your helicopters have proved to be very reliable and your crews very flexible; working through lunchtime, for instance. I look forward to your support for the four months of your deployment. Because you are often out of touch with base while you are flying in remote areas, if decisions have to made, please make them in the best interest of the Army's requirements. In the event of a major incursion, the Army will requisition this complete operation and offer all personnel the opportunity to carry on with an appropriate Army rank and doing the same logistics job."

Having served with the RAF, I remember I am on Reserve List Juliet, so no problems if my services are needed, I'm thinking.

He shakes my hand and hands over a piece of paper to Captain Beecher, apparently tomorrows tasking. I am allocated a locker and unpack my flying kit and cold weather clothing. I'm ready for the next surprise, a short journey to the Army Flotel (a block of accommodation sitting on a large barge, brought in by a special ship as deck cargo and then floated off).

Captain Beecher takes me across the access ramp into the foyer and then up wide stairs to a suite of rooms on the top floor. This is our company domain for the duration. My room is big enough for me, has a washbasin, a mirror, a wardrobe, and double-glazed windows, firmly secured as everywhere is air conditioned. Close by are the bathrooms and washing and ironing facilities. Captains have single rooms, co-pilots share a room. I feel I should cope, with a café-style Mess downstairs and a small snug bar for the officers, where alcohol is cheap and soft drinks expensive. Captain Beecher offers to escort me down to dinner and then to the "Snug" for a briefing on the next day's flying, which will be with him, taking me around the main locations that we use. I have a bath, a shave, and don clean clothes, ready now to meet the world.

Going downstairs, I find where food is being served, pick up a tray, and am soon sat down with Captain Beecher in quiet corner of the canteen. Clearly, food-wise, there is plenty of choice; fresh vegetables and fresh fruit, as well as tea, coffee, and soft drinks. With working through lunchtime being standard, I will need a good breakfast to keep me going all day. We make it up to the snug bar and I get an introduction on how things are run on this operation.

"Firstly, David, all flying is in daylight so that all military units can see you visually and know you are not a threat. For the same reason, we don't fly in cloud or above cloud, there are no letdown aids for us to use anyway. We navigate using maps, which have the Danger Areas marked on them. We fly with our landing lights on pointing forward, as well as using our flashing anti-collision lights. We also switch on our radar transponder with the appropriate 'squawk' for that airframe. As a civilian helicopter we use VHF radio frequencies; the military use UHF, so we don't hear them operating. The planned tasks and schedule you will be given assume a ground speed of 90 knots, 60 knots with underslung loads, and five minutes to turnround at each LP, if not shutting down.

"Try and keep to the schedule; arriving early or late at a destination can create problems. Your job is ferrying troops and freight to where they are needed, as well as delivering the post. Soldiers in remote locations look forward to receiving their blue aerograms from home, so that service makes us popular. Operating below cloud you may see Harriers operating at high speed and low level, often in pairs. Also, Chinooks operate from their base at Port San Carlos, named "Kelly's Garden", sometimes carrying shipping containers underslung going up to mountain tops. Keep well clear of them. You will also see the FIGAS aircraft flying from airstrip to airstrip. The Phantom jets and Hercules tend to operate well above you. You may occasionally see Navy Sea King helicopters and Army Gazelle helicopters carrying out their military missions. A good look out all the time, in all directions, is key.

"Our biggest problem is the weather. Generally, we have a westerly wind of at least 20 knots. That brings in rain, snow, and cloud covering high ground, requiring us to go round the coast rather than being able to fly in a straight line over the top. Some days, you will be notified, there will be live firing exercises involving Army and Navy guns. You will see the flashes as the shells explode, and sometimes the Peat catches fire and burns for several days. You will be helping with the construction of the Radar Stations on Mountain tops on East and West Falkland. All material comes in shipping containers flown in underslung by Chinooks. You will see towards East Cove, southwest of Stanley, a huge construction site that will become RAF Mount Pleasant when complete. Beyond that you will see the military port, with several ships there unloading containers. When routing round the coast in poor weather, it makes a good landmark. When we fly tomorrow it will all make sense. I will pick you up at the front door tomorrow at 8 o'clock and we will get airborne at 10.00. We fly with a cabin attendant who is also a technician and helps us with underslung loads. I will just check that your watch is set the same as mine, on Falklands time. I think that's all you need at this stage. See you in the morning."

I head upstairs, get myself sorted, set the alarm and put my head on the pillow. The quiet hum of the air conditioning lulls me to sleep in seconds

17th February, I prepare for my first flight in the Falkland Islands. Captain Beecher shows me our route, taking us round several LPs, and the schedule showing the pickups and drops as well as the timetable. We are refuelled to the standard overnight figure, with just bags of mail onboard, and our first stop is the grass area alongside the Governor's Residence in Port Stanley. Start-up is normal, we call for taxi and take-off, being close to the runway, and are cleared for immediate take-off. As soon as we reach 50 knots airspeed, Captain Beecher tells me to turn left 45 degrees to clear the centreline, so that if a Phantom- jet scrambles we are not in the way. A few minutes later, having stayed low over Stanley Harbour, we touch down on schedule and pick up five passengers in civilian clothes, bound for West Falkland. We head west towards the hills, staying low over the harbour until reaching the REME base at Moody Brook. As we climb up, following the slope towards high ground, I can see shell holes, trenches, and debris. This is the site of one of the battles of the recent war – Tumbledown Mountain. The heavy fighting took place on 13/14th June 1982; the position was taken by a combined attack by the Scots Guards and 42 Commando. General Mario Menendez surrendered to Major General Jeremy Moore at 9 p.m. the same day. When the opportunity arrives, I will try to get on one of the Battlefield Tours run by the Army, but today I need to concentrate on the task at hand. A few stops later we land at Goose Green, again the site of another battle, having been given 24 hours' notice by the BBC of the attack on 28th May by the 2nd Battalion, the Parachute Regiment. We need fuel at the next stop – Kelly's Garden – at Port San Carlos, where some Chinooks are based. While we are shut down, the Captain and I walk to the base canteen, collect some sandwiches and soft drinks for our crewman, and return to our machine, which is ready to go. Our task takes us up to Pebble Island, where there are several aircraft wrecks and a few houses dotted about. Today we have good communication with base on our HF radio, somewhat unusual apparently, and we report landing at an LP, all of which are only identified by a colour and a number, e.g. Yellow 3. As we head back east, we again cross over the Falkland Sound, and pass close to a Rapier Battery of Ground to Air Missiles guarding the San Carlos area. We carry on with our flight, which takes us to Teal Inlet and very open country (no trees, but plenty of sheep) towards Stanley. As we get closer, we can see intact and broken helicopters littering the ground, as well as vehicles. I learn that everything is being cleared up and what can be salvaged is being used by the Army. We land back at base on schedule, having flown 6 hours, 15 minutes, a normal day's workload. Over two cups of tea I get debriefed; nothing unusual happened, weather was good, the S61N was fully serviceable, is being refuelled and being checked over by the engineers, ready for tomorrow. After this Famil flight, I will fly tomorrow with Captain Bob Innes for a "Check Ride" to assess my competency. We flew together over primary jungle in the Far East in the 1960s on many sorties…it's a small world.

Next day we set off west, and Bob wants to show me how to navigate using the Fence Lines marked on our maps. The trick is to come down low and slow over the ground so that the fence lines can be followed and turns at junctions anticipated. One pilot does the navigation and instructs the handling pilot what to expect in terms of heading and which way to turn on approaching a junction. In poor visibility you need to come down to within 50 feet of the ground and airspeed back to 60 knots, half normal cruising speed. You need to know that the area you are operating in has no obstacles, and because you are following a Line Feature you need to keep to the right. After 10 minutes of practice in good weather, I ask if I can photograph some "Stone Runs", which are a unique feature of the Falklands landscape. From a distance they look like rivers of stones filling the bottom of some valleys coming down from mountainous areas. It is thought that continuous freeze thaw action moves the stones downhill inch by inch with every cycle. A friend of mine, a geologist at Aberdeen University, would appreciate all photographs from the air that I can manage. I manage about 20 in the end. From the air they look very interesting; on the ground, apparently, they are very difficult to traverse on foot, and impossible in a vehicle, but I never get the opportunity to try it out.

19th February, a long flying day, 7 hours 40 minutes, but we see yet more LPs, airstrips, and small communities. We also pick up 2,000 pounds' weight of fuel in jerry cans in a cargo net and fly it as an underslung load at 60 knots airspeed to a "Rebro Station" on top of a hill in the middle of nowhere. As we lower the load onto the ground, the weight comes off the cargo hook and it opens automatically, so we fly away without a stop. The weather is not good today, with cloud obscuring the high ground on East Falkland. This provides a good reason to demonstrate the low-level recovery route around the south coast. As we descend from 500 feet, I see a flashing light just to the left of the nose. Judging by the flashes, I report it as an anti-collision light, and sure enough a Harrier emerges from the gloom, passes down our left-hand side, with his No 2 a mile behind and out to one side. Seeing us, they turn away and stay low and fast. Glad we had all our bright lights on. We press on and follow the coast round past the military port; it looks busy with containers everywhere, cranes and bright lights, can't miss it. 10 minutes later we fly around Port Stanley to the South and are given clearance to land. We are the last ones back, and as we shut down the engineers swarm over the machine, doing their post flight checks and refuel. Inside, time for a big mug of sweet coffee and a short debrief. Apparently, I am judged "Good Enough" and competent to act as captain on subsequent flights. As a reward I have three days off to explore Port Stanley, the other Costels (RAF and REME), and to take a ferry across the harbour to the RAF SAR Operation. There is a lot to see, and I might as well explore and photograph everything while I have the chance.

Having walked a mile along a gravel road into Port Stanley, I find a coffee shop and offer my UK money to pay. This is not accepted, and I am directed to Government Offices 100 yards away, where I will be able to get Falklands currency. At last, I find the big door for the Financial Secretary, Mr H.T. Rowlands. A loud knock elicits a shouted "Come in!" I go in and introduce myself and my purpose on the Island.

"I would like to exchange £50 for Falkland Currency."

"You are in luck, David. Just today we have received a consignment of new notes from the UK. To celebrate, let me give you some examples." He reaches into some wooden crates and produces two one-pound notes and two five-pound notes. "I am the only person in the world who can over sign these, as that is my signature printed there." He signs the notes above his printed signature and gives them to me. "These are a present from the Falkland Island Government. Keep them as a memento of your visit. They will be worth something one day."

He then exchanges, one for one, my £50 UK currency. Just before I get up to go, I ask him about how the invasion affected him. "I was the only Government Minister kept back, as the Governor and all the others were flown out. General Menendez came to this office and asked me for Falklands Currency for his men. I showed him my empty safe, but he suggested that I run off some more! I showed him a note and pointed out that it was printed by De La Rue London. He said, 'Pity. When I am in my barracks in Argentina and I need money I get some soldiers to run off all I need!' How convenient." No wonder Argentina has runaway inflation. "David, you understand this oil business, one of the factors behind the war. Could you give a talk about oil to the Council this Thursday night? Say, 8 p.m. at my house, last one on the road out to the airport."

I reply, "Yes, I will bring along some 35mm slides supplied by Shell, if you can provide a projector and screen." I square my commitment with Captain Beecher and I will finish early that day and can use the Car, a Citroen 2 CV.

With the screen erected and my slides ready in the projector, I stand before an audience of around 20, all men, and introduce myself as a North Sea Helicopter pilot operating from Aberdeen and down in the Falklands for a four-month deployment. I start with some outline figures for the daily oil and gas produced from the North Sea. I can see on their faces outright disbelief, only slightly better when I run through the colour slides provided by Shell. They show the Demarcation Line between the UK and the countries surrounding the North Sea, the position of many of the major oilfields, and the pipelines taking the oil and gas to shore establishments for processing in Scotland, England, Norway, and the Netherlands. Only after 15 minutes' talking do I get the feeling that they believe something that I say about numbers of people involved, the complexity of the engineering, the cost, and the huge profits to the oil companies and taxes to respective governments. Currently, in 1984, it is still "Boom Time" for everyone involved. Fortunately, I have brought with me the latest UK Annual Oil & Gas Report, the famous Brown Book published by HMSO. It has a fold-out map about a yard square, which I open out and lay out on a table in front of them. As a visual aid it is very effective, not least because it is clearly produced by the UK Government to be presented to the public. I can see the concerns of the Councillors about any "Oil Boom" affecting the small population of the Falkland Islands. Port Stanley has very few electricians, mechanics, plumbers, welders, and medically qualified people. Most people have a day job and help out with other commitments at night. After a few questions, I wrap up the presentation, donating the "Brown Book" with its map and detailed figures to the Council for their future perusal. I learn that they are looking at issuing fishing licences for foreign trawlers to fish in their "economic zone." This will bring in long-term income to the Government, which is keen to build roads, a new school, a new hospital, and several improvements to communications. Following that experience, I maintain links with the Falklands for many years through Harold Rowlands and learn about the impressive improvements that materialise.

But it is not all work; on a day off I hitch a lift to Saunders Island, on the northern coast of West Falkland, to look at the large penguin colony there. There are hundreds of Adelie penguins roosting quite close to a wide sandy beach. With a colleague, F/O Holloway, we walk amongst them as they troop to and from the sea. We are cheerfully ignored as we photograph them; they have no fear of us, and we could reach down and pick them up. If we stand still, they come close and peck at our flying boots, then our flying suits. Only in the roosting area, where a few are sitting on eggs, do we experience any reaction and flapping of flippers.

Visiting a Penguin Colony on the Falkland Islands

On the way back home, we pass close to an albatross colony. They, too, are curious; some leave their nests, head out towards us, and fly alongside, looking at us for many minutes before turning away. It is slightly worrying, as they have a six-foot wingspan and we have a tail rotor at the back, which is not built to withstand a bird strike of this magnitude. Most birds we encounter head down towards the surface, away from our noise and whirling rotor blades. Sensible creatures.

A few weeks later, on a day off, I board a Hercules with 10 others, all clutching our cameras. Every two weeks an aircraft flies to South Georgia so that professional RAF photographers can get shots of all the beaches and hinterland. This is to check for evidence of incursions by sea (submarine) or by parachute drop. The flight crew will also drop, by parachute, some stores and post to the garrison there, most welcome in this remote location. As we arrive in the area, the rear ramp is lowered, and our stores are dispatched towards a boat waiting below. That done, the ramp is closed and a side door on the starboard side is opened, and a cargo net is secured across it. We are now invited to take our positions at the net, poking our camera lenses through. We fly round South Georgia twice, looking down on snow covered mountains and glaciers that flow all the way down to the sea. There is very little sign of life in this unforgiving landscape. One wonders how Ernest Shackleton and his five companions made it across the mountains in May 1916 to seek rescue for the crew of Endurance, which was crushed by sea ice in the Weddel Sea. Subsequently, the crew made it by small boat to Elephant Island, some 800 miles southwest of South Georgia, and waited there until Shackleton returned with a rescue ship. Overall, it has been judged one of the greatest ever feats of survival .

Rugged South Georgia still snowbound in the summer.

Back in the Falklands, I am made aware of the fact that REME has concocted a nine-hole golf course on the edge of town. There are holes in the ground where shells have landed; they serve as bunkers, and the greens are somewhat uneven. If a ball is within a club's length of the hole, it is classed as a "Gimme." Clubs, balls, and score cards can be collected from the Governor's Residence. So, with a young co-pilot in tow, we report to the front door of the residence, state our business, and a lady from the Foreign Office hands out four clubs each, some balls, and a score card. An hour later, we report back; a few balls missing in the undergrowth and a few problems with the sheep wandering about the place as if they owned it, but good fun and a unique challenge. As we hand in our clubs, we are invited in to meet the Governor, Sir Rex Hunt, in the lounge. He is behind the bar.

"What will you have? These drinks are on the Foreign Office, so put that wallet away."

"Gin and tonic, please," we splutter.

A bottle of Gordons gin is waved over two big glasses, followed by the same amount of tonic. "Good to meet you. What are you chaps doing in the Falklands? Army, Navy or RAF? I meet a lot of people from different walks of life coming out here, ships' captains, people heading for the Antarctic, and hosts of Civil Servants staying at the Upland Goose Hotel." He extends his hand and toasts, "Here's to you."

We go along with that, and conversation starts about the war and his part in it. "Don't look for bullet holes in the building, they have all been patched up," he says. As he speaks, another lady from the Foreign Office waves a piece of paper, a message from London apparently. "Please excuse me, I have to answer this now. Look after yourselves while you are here," and he is off to the Communications Room. We finish our drinks and head back to the Costel for lunch, wondering what we will tell our colleagues.

A week later we are at Fox Bay in West Falkland. Our schedule shows a one hour wait before carrying on along the route. As we shut down, I see a farmhouse close by, and speaking to our nine soldiers in the cabin, I propose that we pay the household a surprise visit. There is general agreement, and they are happy to check their rucksacks for chocolate, dried fruit, cans, newspapers, and magazines to use as an offering. At the head of the troop, I knock on the front door and introduce myself, my crew, and my nine soldiers. We would like to say hello and hear about their experiences during the war. Unfazed, we are invited into their parlour, told to sit down on the floor, backs against the walls. They are two adults and two teenage children. We proffer our presents and are offered tea and cake in return (there will be a slight delay while another kettle and some more mugs are found). While all this is happening, we are hearing about the dogfights between the Harriers and Skyhawks during attacks on the Naval Fleet in Falkland Sound supporting the landings near San Carlos. They have witnessed two Skyhawks on fire heading west and they know that they crashed about five miles away. I make a mental note to mark the sites on my map to look out for at some future occasion when I am passing through. We broach the subject about all the noise the military make around the Islands – low flying jets, helicopters whirling around, and live firing exercises in East Falkland. The reply comes back that the noise is welcome. It shows that the military are here, ready to deter another invasion, and they would like them to stay permanently. A big airbase, RAF Mount Pleasant, is currently under construction, and that shows long-term commitment. Time flies when you are having an interesting conversation, and during a pause I glance at my watch. Time to go and carry on with the task. I am not a popular man as I stand up, clap my hands and break up the party. When we depart, we just happen to fly past their farmhouse at 120 knots; they are all outside and waving. I feel we have done some good there as we head back east towards base.

Just north of San Carlos we see on a flat open area, a PSP strip oriented east/west, just one of several runways for the Harrier Jump jets to operate from if needed. As we reach Stanley Harbour, it is dusk; the streetlights are on, as well as the airfield lights and the lights on the anchored ships. Just before touchdown we fly past the two Phantom jets positioned at the eastern end of the runway, ready to launch at a moment's notice, day or night. We taxi into our dispersal at walking pace and are guided to our required shut down spot. On shut down the engineers take over the machine and are everywhere doing their checks. I sign in, machine fully serviceable, duty carried out, 6 hours 40 minutes flying, now where is that big mug of strong coffee?

A week before I am due to return home, a Liberation Memorial is unveiled on the 14th June at Port Stanley by the Governor, Sir Rex Hunt. This is the second Anniversary of the surrender of Argentine Forces, and this Memorial has been paid for by the Falklanders themselves. It commemorates the 255 military personnel who died and whose names are listed on the walls. A week later I complete my last flight, taking people out to nearby Volunteer Point to see the penguin colony there, a short flying day – just one and a half hours' flying. Time to pack my suitcase and a few mementos. I am warned about not taking back any firearms, ammunition, or brass shell cases.

Over the detachment, the tasks that we are asked to carry out have expanded in scope from just the ordinary internal and external loads to carrying the Army's 105mm gun. Being a heavy, dense load, it flies well as an underslung load, we easily achieve 80 knots speed in transit, and we can put it down exactly where required. Occasionally we are tasked with taking a rubber ball full of fuel and weighing 2,000 pounds out to Naval ships at anchor in Stanley Harbour. We carry this at the end of an 80-foot strop, and the best technique is to proceed very slowly, so the load does not swing and stays vertically below the helicopter. On approaching the ship, we identify the open space and a cross in the centre where the load is to be put down. Looking down, our crewman can see the shadow of the load on the deck, and that tells him the separation of the load from the deck. After the load touches down on the deck, it stays in position and a seaman is able to unhook the 80-foot strop and hold the end clear as we gently lift the helicopter vertically, ensuring that the hook does not snag on a part of the ship.

Picking up an underslung load,
RAF Stanley Airfield March 1984

One day we are asked to take two helicopters to Goose Green, load up with 15 soldiers each, and fly in formation to a Grid Reference, aiming to arrive at a specified time plus or minus 30 seconds. On arrival together, we are to offload the soldiers as quickly as possible, shut the cabin doors, take off separately and fly low level back to Goose Green. On arrival at the drop-off point we find we are just behind a line of guns, so we are part of a live firing exercise! The gunners wait until we are well out of earshot before they fire towards the danger area in the mountains of East Falkland. My fellow captain and I have not done this type of task since training up Australian soldiers in 1969 in Malaysia, before they went up to Vietnam to fight alongside the Americans.

I am conveyed to the departure lounge and have to open my suitcase and take out the contents. There are just a few questions about my headset and my flying suit. Luckily, our new chief pilot, Captain Mike Bill with four gold bars on his uniform, is there to explain my involvement in the Falklands. So, my suitcase is passed, marked with a blue chalk cross, and joins the others on the luggage trolley. As passengers we get a briefing; we will be refuelled mid-Atlantic and we will be fed and yes, we can make ourselves comfortable on the freight once we are airborne. It is good to be going home, after my detachment was extended by two weeks for administrative reasons.

This will be my only detachment to the Falklands, clocking up 344 hours flying, as the company is looking for people to commit to two years' involvement with a few short breaks at home. Not for me this time, I have too much involvement at home in Scotland. So, as we all walk out towards our Hercules, I glance around at the units I did not get to visit and remember my wish list of places to see. We strap in, the engines start, and within minutes we take off, turn over Port Stanley, and head out over the Atlantic Ocean. Only 6,000 miles to go before we make it to the UK.

Chapter 16: Aberdeen

(July 1984 – October 1985)

26th July 1984 – my first flight after coming back from the Falklands, and it is as co-pilot, owing to the fact that I am out of practice; it all seems very new and challenging. I have a whole month off, since coming back – readjusting to a new and nonmilitary, civilian situation – it is quite a culture shock. While I was away, the Miners' Strike, led by Arthur Scargill, got underway in March. Now back home, on television, one can see the clashes between the Flying Pickets and the police. Pickets are killed and injured as well as the police, and thousands are arrested. The strike is divisive across the country. Meanwhile the offshore oil industry continues to expand, with new discoveries being developed. The demand for helicopter services is at a high level. With the Miners' strike there is nothing we can do except watch – this is a battle between Margaret Thatcher, the Conservative Party, and the National Union of Mineworkers. It does not end well in March 1985. On returning to work, miners see their pits closed, and after a year-long strike most are seriously in debt. The strike is ending badly. The "Dash for Gas" power stations programme is started.

After a few days back I am called into the office and briefed on the fact that as I have served five years with the company, I am now fully established in the company pension scheme and could consider paying more into it by making Advanced Voluntary Contributions (AVCs), which can be taken as tax-free cash on retirement. After a short discussion with Ann, I sign up for this, as I am a 40% taxpayer. Also, I should consider taking on more responsibility and possibly converting onto the new helicopter, the Bristow Tiger (Super Puma). I don't fancy becoming a Line Trainer – they train up inexperienced co-pilots and introduce them to operating over the North Sea. Most of the young co-pilots have flown single engine helicopters, as single pilots, on short flights, in daylight, and overland. This is little experience on which to build for flying over the North Sea, where conditions could not be more different. I appreciate flying with experienced first officers; their knowledge and awareness is invaluable. I can see that the oil companies are switching to the Tiger because it is faster than the S61N, has a longer range and offers more payload. Similarly, they oil companies are looking at the progress of the BAH Chinook, which offers 44 passenger seats direct from Aberdeen to platforms in the East Shetland Basin at a good speed. BAH is placing adverts stating "We lead – others follow" with a Chinook in the background. There is clearly competition between these two helicopter types, and they are taking over from the S61Ns that have been in operation for over 10 years. Having spoken to several colleagues and instructors, the balance of advice is to volunteer to convert to the Tiger, as that represents the future. I put my name forward and join the list of volunteers. I will have to wait until January 1985 before I can begin the two-week ground school. Meanwhile, I can read all the reports I can get my hands on and gain some knowledge from other pilot's experiences. Clearly there is a lot to learn about the systems, which are computer controlled, and about the advantages of flying much higher than before. Also, the Tiger is not amphibious, but has inflatable stabiliser bags for use in an emergency water landing. Two weeks after starting flying again I am considered good enough to fly as Captain on the S61N, and on most of my flights subsequently I have that responsibility.

January 1985

With 3 others I begin the ground school for the Tiger; the usual electric and hydraulic systems, but the autopilot is new and so is the area navigation system, no more using a stopwatch to work out groundspeed from the DECCA chart. The area nav system combines information from Decca Chains as well as from VORs, with a Dead Reckoning (DR) back-up if inputs are lost. The area nav system gives good information as to position, ground speed, and ETAs, but no information about the terrain you may be flying over. Local knowledge is essential here. The power from the two roof-mounted engines feeds straight back into the main rotor gearbox and the noise from the engines feeds straight forward into the cockpit, so new Peltor headsets are the norm. The intercom is unusual in that it is off, no background noise, until someone speaks, when it switches on for the duration of the message. Takes a little getting used to. In terms of the tail rotor control system, one little fact gets stored in my mind: in the event that control of the tail rotor is lost for any reason, the default setting is equivalent to 8 degrees of main rotor pitch, which gives you 80 knots, a get-you-home speed.

Ground school complete, it's time for the flight simulator – luckily our own, so the cockpit is the same as the real machine and with sensible visual display outside. On this machine, for power settings, we fly on degrees of main rotor pitch, rather than torque feeding into the main rotor gear box, as per S61N. After take-off, the rate of climb is very good and initially a cruising altitude of 5,000 feet is quite efficient. As fuel is used and depending on local winds, 8,000 feet could be useful, and sometimes above the worst of the weather. The nav system works out the local wind velocity and you can use it to work out the time to return to base from an offshore location. The cruising speed is much higher than the S61N, and although the fuselage is smaller in size, it still has room for 19 passengers. My first Famil flight is on 19th January, flying circuits at Longside airfield near Peterhead, with my instructor Captain Mike Green. I continue with instruction until released to begin Line training on 20th February with Captain Woods. Most of these training flights with Captain Woods are direct flights to platforms in the East Shetland Basin, taking two and a half hours on both outbound and inbound legs. I appreciate the cruising speed being at least 30 knots faster than the S61N, and by going higher we can make use of stronger tailwinds and are often flying above the worst of the weather.

After a check ride with Captain Brian Backhouse on 15th March, flying out southeast from Aberdeen to the Trans World 58, with our planned diversion airfield in Denmark, I am released to the Line as a qualified co-pilot, able to fly with any captain to any destination. Although we all use standard procedures and specific aviation terms, each captain is individual in their likes and dislikes, depending on their background and experience on type. I am learning a lot from every flight, what works, what does not, and I write up every trip in a large notebook to help imprint the new information.

I feel I am learning to fly again from scratch, such is the jump from flying the S61N to flying the Tiger. The Tiger has a narrow track undercarriage with a nose wheel, so when light on fuel and with passengers unloaded, the centre of gravity is high off the ground, making it more prone to roll over when taxiing, especially when going round corners. To counter this, the requirement is to use the flight controls so that that the lift from the rotor is pointing into the corner. The S61N, by contrast, with a wide track undercarriage and tail wheel, is prone to nose over while taxiing when unloaded and with minimum fuel, with just the two pilots up front. As I gain experience I am checked out on winching, something I have previous experience of on SAR over the years. I demonstrate the skill of working with a winch operator and flying smoothly on a flight to the Brae Field with Captain John Whale on 27th June. Eventually, on 5th July, I am released to the Line as captain and begin flying with young co-pilots, mainly by day, to a wide range of drilling rigs and production platforms. They are at least 20 years younger than me, and this is their first commercial flying experience.

View from the helideck of a Production Platform

I need to make use of their strengths and guard against their weaknesses. Most of them see helicopter flying over the North Sea as a stepping-stone to a career in Fixed Wing based on Heathrow or Gatwick. Once there, they feel that their future will be more secure, and they will see the world and not just the North Sea. The cockpit environment will be a lot better, less noise, less vibration, and with no wearing of a rubber immersion suit, boots, or a life jacket.

Meanwhile, back at Banchory, Christopher finishes his initial two years at the junior section of the Academy, gaining the Junior Dux Prize as best pupil overall. Our local MP – Mr Alec Buchanan Smith – makes the presentations on Speech Day. We have to leave early to get Christopher and three others to the BBC TV studio in Aberdeen to take part in a interschool quiz. Christopher moves up to the senior section with his classmates and is streamed into the class that is working towards entry to university at the end of his school career. The town is keen on skiing, and every winter the ski club lays on a bus most weekends to take children and parents to the Glenshee Ski Resort near the top of the River Dee valley. Sometimes, if I am free, we go up together by car. On a fine weather day, the skiing is as good as an Alpine setting and is very popular. We need to watch the weather and road conditions carefully. One day I turn the car around with five miles to go to the Centre, as it is snowing very hard. Those that do make it to the Centre become snowed in, as snow ploughs cannot cope. It is the correct decision, but I am not thanked! Sometimes we have a skiing holiday in Austria, flying out from Glasgow. Ann doesn't ski, but walks along mountain tracks checking out the refreshment stops, while Christopher and I seek out the blue runs on the Piste and try and avoid the black ones, they have too many trees! He also joins the Cubs/Scouts/Venture Scouts; with their HQ in the centre of town, he can walk there easily. He mixes with boys from a wide variety of backgrounds and local dialects, and they all learn a variety of life skills, getting new arm badges every year. The town's golf club is very popular, and Christopher learns to play. Also, the tennis club provides tuition for him, so we are all kept active.

Flying continues at a busy pace, and as autumn approaches, I attend a winter briefing so that I will know how to handle rain, sleet, snow, and hail, coupled with gale force winds. On 1st October 1985 I set off with young F/O Jim Heanan, heading for the Thistle Platform in the East Shetland Basin, with 19 passengers, a planned two-hour flight. All is normal for the first hour, cruising at 3,000 feet and 130 knots. Then, just 18 miles from the "Beckett" reporting point abeam Sumburgh, a severe high frequency airframe vibration kicks in. Immediately I reduce power and start descending towards the sea, turning right to head into the southerly wind. I instruct young Heanan to transmit a "Pan" call to Highland Radar, who are providing us with a surveillance service. They acknowledge our emergency, and we request a rescue helicopter to be scrambled in case we end up with ditching in the sea. We notice that as power is reduced the level of vibration also reduces, so as we reach 500 feet, I slowly increase power to see if we can maintain height with a tolerable level of vibration.

Eventually, with 8 degrees of main rotor pitch, we can maintain level flight at 80 knots airspeed. We need to land as soon as possible while heading south into the prevailing wind. Our radar shows a coastline 45 miles ahead, just west of Fraserburgh, so we head for that, arm the emergency floatation equipment, and brief the passengers of our intentions. Out of the blue we are called by 95 Victor, a Bond Helicopter Super Puma. He offers to come alongside, report any damage and escort us to our destination. I welcome this offer and brief the passengers about this good news. I can see him ahead, turning towards us, and he comes in on our port side. Apparently, everything looks normal, and it is the same on the starboard side. From inside we can see the main rotor blades are following the same track, so our suspicions are that there is a problem with the tail rotor, something is out of balance and causing this vibration. *Let's hope the tail rotor assembly stays attached until we land.* We discuss the options facing us to work out which is the least-worst. We could, while we have control, deliberately ditch the helicopter, but the sea surface looks rough and in spite of buoyancy aids we would roll over, making it difficult for our passengers to get out. We could continue flying all the way back to Aberdeen airport, where crash/fire trucks are available. It would take at least an hour. Would our tail rotor assembly stay attached all that time?

Perhaps the middle way – landing in the first big open space after we coast in 20 minutes – is the least-worst option available. With luck, we will still have tail rotor control and stay upright during a minimum power running landing. That course of action decided, we inform our loyal escort and Highland Radar of our intentions. That done, 95 Victor proposes that he goes ahead and finds a suitably big and level field for our landing, and once found he will circle above it until we have it in our sights. He zooms off ahead towards the coast and as things are under control, I hand over the flying controls to my young co-pilot while I think through how to best carry out the approach and landing. Having settled on a plan, out of the blue is a call from the RAF

Rescue Helicopter on his way to meet us. I update him on our current position, coasting in about five miles West of Fraserburgh, and our ETA there. He says that he should arrive at the same time and will stay clear of our landing site. I confirm 21 souls on board. That settled, another call out of the blue. I recognise the anxious voice of our Chief Pilot on his way in a S61N with some engineers. He, too, is likely to arrive at the same time and will stay clear while we land. I can see our 95 Victor circling above a big green field with some cables at the far end. I confirm visual with the landing area and decide to carry out the pre-landing checks. That complete, I brief the passengers for the imminent landing and instruct them to adopt the "Brace" position so that they are best protected if we roll over. My young co-pilot is flying well to my instructions, leaving my hands free to pull on the Emergency Engine and Electrics cut off lever above our heads in the roof panel. I will pull this if we lose control or roll over on touch down. As we coast in, we reduce height and speed, aiming to touch down in the middle of the field. As we slow down, we need more power to maintain height, and the airframe vibration increases. At about 30 knots ground speed, we touch down, and as the weight comes on the wheels they sink into the soft ground and very quickly we come a stop, thankfully upright. I shut down the engines quickly and with seconds the rotors are stopped. Leaving my co-pilot to continue the shut-down checks, I get out and go round to open the passenger door. Most of the passengers are still adopting the "Brace" position, so I have to invite them to unstrap and come outside.

As they come outside and stand around the helicopter, the yellow RAF SAR Sea King helicopter lands close by and two crewmembers walk across, and I show them a broken control rod on one of the tail rotor blades. They shake their heads; they have never seen this sort of problem before. Before leaving us, I confirm that nobody is in need of first aid or needs to go to hospital. As they climb aboard their Sea King, belonging to my old squadron (No 202), our own S61N lands and shuts down. Out pour several engineers, with a stepladder and several toolboxes. They swarm around our machine as our Chief Pilot, Captain Smith comes across to ask us what happened. He too, sees the broken control rod, and three furrows in the ground where our wheels have sunk in during the landing. He asks us if we would like another crew to fly it back after it has been repaired. We have had enough excitement for the day, so happily accept that offer. As he takes away our 19 passengers and their bags, he promises that a small S 76 helicopter will be sent out with a crew for our machine and we would get a lift back to base. Within 30 minutes the two of us are back at base and I have to decide what to write in the technical log in terms of post flight snags. I write "See MOR" (Mandatory Occurrence Report). In the planning room I write a brief report, the MOR. We are told we will not be flying tomorrow, but there will be a debrief with a number of Directors, the meeting being chaired by the Company Flight Safety Officer. We are each given an audio tape, a copy of the Cockpit Voice Recorder, so we can write our separate reports, knowing the sequence of events, discussions, radio calls, briefings, and checks. It is invaluable, and our separate reports are closely matched. As I am about to go home, Captain Smith gives me two bottles of company whiskey to take across to Bond Helicopters for the crew of 95 Victor. They are airborne as I arrive there, but their Chief Pilot promises that they will receive the gift when they get back. Certainly, their voluntary involvement was very helpful in figuring out what might be wrong, and their presence alongside was reassuring to both passengers and crew.

The debriefing meeting goes well. We learn that the passengers reached their destination later that afternoon. The helicopter was repaired and flown back to base and the nosewheel assembly was changed, as it may have received a shock loading during the landing. The helicopter is back in service and already flying. The tape is played to the meeting, stopping only so I could explain a decision, or describe what was happening outside at the time. The outcome of the emergency was that the passengers were safe and reached their destination, the helicopter was repaired and back in service, and the crew had given a full explanation of their actions and had acted sensibly on the information that was available to them at that time. Job done, we have the rest of the day off, but are back flying the next day early in the morning.

Two weeks later, I am informed that tomorrow will be a special day. No flying, but instead young F/O Heanen and I are to go to a posh restaurant in Aberdeen in our best uniforms for mid-day, when there will be a special lunch and presentation. As we turn up, we are ushered into a small dining room, where there is a long table with many of our colleagues waiting for our arrival. We are to be seated either side of our Base Manager. As we sit down, he stands up and says a few words about our little episode.

"Good crew co-operation, good decisions and a good landing. We are here to celebrate the actions of one of our crews two weeks ago." He holds up the first of two solid silver tankards and reads the inscription. I am pleased that my co-pilot is also receiving recognition; he performed well while under stress, and completed a running landing on a grass field, during which the helicopter stayed upright. The tankards are filled with lager and lunch begins. With a mix of captains and co-pilots, the atmosphere is relaxed and informal. Clearly, we are all pleased to be here. The Tiger, being new, is having teething problems, and crews are learning from each other's experiences. When I get home I examine my tankard; clearly not many of these are presented, and it is inscribed "Bristow Helicopter Group – Safety Award." This is followed by a few words about the incident. I like it, and it gets cleaned and polished every month thereafter. A few days later I am given a copy of a letter from the farmer in whose field lots of helicopters landed and one put three long furrows in it. He is pleased with the flowers, the substantial cheque, and we are welcome to drop in as needed, any time we like in the future!

CITATION

BRISTOW HELICOPTER GROUP

SAFETY AWARD

CAPTAIN D.S. LANIGAN

Whilst Captain of Bristow Tiger G-TIGM

On 1ˢᵗ October 1985

Displayed a high standard of professionalism

following a tail rotor control failure

when 45 miles offshore subsequently

achieving a safe landing of the helicopter

and its 19 passengers.

Chapter 17: Aberdeen Operation

(October 1985 – September 1988)

Life continues normally – that is, excitement every day at work, flying out to oil rigs in the North Sea, and at the end of the day the quiet, ordered environment at home. Some days, 70 flights are scheduled, with the flight planning room full to bursting. As we taxi out towards the runway we expect at least 15 minutes waiting in the queue before we can take off. Only when we use the ILS approach to land do we have any sort of priority over other traffic. Plump for that every time. Speaking to our neighbours, many of whom are directly involved in the oil industry, I get an understanding of the scale of investment that is being made by American banks. British banks don't like pouring money into a hole in the ground, especially if it is underwater and a hundred plus miles offshore – there is no collateral to call on if the loan defaults, don't you see? I thought that helicopters were expensive, but for oil companies, all their transport requirements are less than 2% of their annual expenditure. One neighbour, an accountant, signs big cheques every day for goods and services against invoices. He can authorise up to a million pounds on his own signature. Above that figure, he needs the signature of a colleague on the cheque, who independently checks the invoice. He looks relaxed enough as he is charged one million pounds a year to have the use of a helicopter and two thousand pounds for every hour it flies.

Another neighbour tells me about a presentation he has recently given to Senior Management about what is needed on a new production platform to be sited at the northern end of the East Shetland Basin, over 100 miles from the nearest land. Top reliability is needed for every process, every item of equipment, and even the pipelines to the shore. To achieve this, at least three separation process lines are needed to separate the oil from the gas, water, and sand that are all part of the crude oil that comes up from the well. Everything needed to support the operation is at least duplicated, if not triplicated. By the time he has finished, the total bill is close to one billion pounds, but Senior Management see the sense of his case and authorise the expenditure. With the average cost of extraction of North Sea oil at 13 US dollars a barrel and the World Spot price in excess of 35 dollars a barrel, all planned projects are going ahead. As more and more exploration rigs come in, we are sent all over the place, including the Norwegian Sector. Most days when we plan our emergency diversions, we find that the Norwegian airfields of Floro, Bergen, and Stavanger are often the airfields we can reach the quickest if we have a problem. When we are in the flight simulator doing our instrument rating tests, I practice using the ILS approaches into these three airfields. Suitably experienced, I never have to call upon this knowledge, but it is comforting to know that there is nothing tricky I need to remember. All I do need on the day is contained in the book of airfield approach charts that all our helicopters carry.

6th November 1986 – I am at home watching the six o'clock news. I sit up when it is announced there has been a helicopter crash into the sea just two miles from the Sumburgh airfield in Shetland. Only two survivors are picked up by the rescue helicopter and they are taken to Lerwick Hospital. Many bodies are picked from the water by small boats; many are missing. The helicopter is a tandem rotor Chinook belonging to BAH, on its way back from the Brent Field. Tomorrow, I have a check ride early in morning flying out to the Beryl Field. After I have finished that I will find out more details.

The flight goes well, no surprises, finishing with an ILS approach to the runway at Aberdeen airfield. Everyone is quietly professional in the air and on the ground; even the planning room is subdued, and the crew room is deserted. Nothing to keep me there, so I go home. Once I have changed my clothes, Ann and I complete our usual half-hour walk around the edge of Banchory, noting the planned developments and some interesting gardens. It is a reassuring feeling, being part of the community; we are involved in numerous activities that keep my mind busy during my time off. I will need to go to bed early tonight, as I have an early take off tomorrow, going to the Auk Field with a young co-pilot. It's our job to provide a service to the oil companies, whenever and wherever they need us. We both concentrate on the task, and it goes well.

The local evening TV news is all about the Chinook crash, the worst helicopter crash so far on the North Sea. Of the 47 on board there are only 2 survivors. The captain is one of these and is helping the inquiry. Offshore, the pilots who fly the small shuttle helicopters within the Brent field and their engineers indicate that they would prefer to fly home in a different helicopter, such as the S61N or Super Puma. That view is taken up by passengers, and even the intervention of Robert Maxwell of the Mirror Group has no effect. Everyone effectively boycotts this helicopter type – the BAH Chinook pilots are rapidly retrained onto the S61N, and continue to provide a service from Sumburgh to the Brent Field. After many months it is confirmed that the Chinook broke up in mid-air and crashed, out of control, into the sea. The remaining Chinooks are effectively grounded and are never used afterwards to carry passengers in the UK. The captain, meanwhile, recovers from the accident and expresses a wish to carry on flying. He is put through a series of tests, both physical and mental, and then retrained on the Sikorsky S61N. He ends up flying as a captain again, based at Sumburgh and flying out to the Brent Field. Some dedication and perseverance there.

Back at Banchory, in Burnett Park, the all-weather tennis courts are built, as well as a new cricket pavilion overlooking the pitch. In the same park is a curling pond, which sees much use in the winter. The large car park is often crowded with all the activities, and children are frequently involved. Christopher joins the town's under-18 cricket club and plays in matches all over Aberdeenshire. Ann plays tennis for the Banchory team and is involved in many matches. They must be memorable events, because I am lulled to sleep at night by ball-by-ball accounts. I can play rounds of golf with the retirees and eventually get a high handicap. One day, playing on my own, I tee off on a par-3 short hole, laying off a little to compensate for a crosswind. Luckily, there was another player on an adjacent hole who saw my ball bounce on the green and roll sideways into the hole. First and last time that happened! My witness signed my card and eventually I get my Hole-in-One tie. Was that luck, or good judgement? Suffice to say, it inspires me to play golf for many years afterwards.

Our local MP, Mr Alec Buchanan Smith, Conservative, becomes the Energy Minister under Margaret Thatcher's government. The offshore oil industry is providing jobs for tens of thousands of people in the UK, helping to make UK less dependent on oil from the Middle East and providing government with a "windfall" of many billions of pounds a year. Unfortunately, being a "petrocurrency," the pound sterling increases in value, making imports cheaper and exports more expensive. Our manufacturing industry is badly hit, and unemployment reaches three million. Around the Oil Capital of Europe (Aberdeen), everything continues to boom. More houses, more schools, more leisure pursuits, more congestion on the roads, at Aberdeen Harbour and of course at Aberdeen Airport. When I speak to a CAA Flight Inspector about helicopter flight safety following the Chinook crash, he informs me the acceptable level of fatal accidents, for the risks being run, is one per year. Often, a year goes by with no accidents, so the "Light Touch" regulatory regime is set to continue. There are no plans for a SAR helicopter to be based at Aberdeen to support the offshore oil industry, but improvements for ATC would continue. A second ILS system is installed at Aberdeen and Sumburgh will get its first ILS system for its westerly runway shortly. I can't fault the logic of what has been said. Clearly, my safety is very much in my own hands, so I need to concentrate when planning to fly, during the flight, and in writing up reports afterwards. I am pleased to be flying a helicopter that requires two pilots, one of which is the "handling" pilot, responsible for flying correctly (height, heading, and speed), and the other pilot (the non-handling pilot) monitors the handling pilot and looks after the navigation and radio calls. Some of the smaller helicopters have only one pilot, and problems are still occurring when operating over the sea in misty conditions. Looking outside to judge height and airspeed is confusing – it all looks the same at 50 feet or 500, especially if inadvertently descending. Fortunately, my helicopter is fitted with a radio altimeter, which gives height above the surface directly underneath. Also, it is fitted with a "bug" which can be set on the dial, typically at 200 feet, so that there is a voice warning of "Check height" if you descend below it. Before every descent over the sea, or before an instrument let-down over the land, the settings of the "bugs" are part of the required checks. Only once do I get the voice warning: when in a level turn over the sea, I let my height drift below the 1,500 feet setting. I apply power immediately and bob up. Pleased to know that it works, but I must not rely on it.

As I approach my 46th birthday at the end of June 1987, life seems under control, and I am happy with what I do (learning new stuff every day) and living in the small town of Banchory (which continues to expand) situated on the River Dee. On the morning of the 26th I team up with F/O Bill Burborough, a very experienced RAF Puma pilot, and we set off to the North West Hutton Platform situated in the East Shetland Basin. Everything is normal until we are flying back past Sumburgh. We have just checked that we have sufficient fuel to reach Aberdeen with 30 minutes reserve fuel. Bill is the handling pilot and the autopilot is holding our height and heading. Suddenly the nose pitches down, two hands grab the stick. We look at our attitude indicators, they both show 5 degrees nose-down, but we are maintaining our altitude, albeit with a gentle nodding from the autopilot. Bill checks in his small rear-view mirror; there is no sign of the horizontal stabiliser. Clearly, with that gone, the helicopter would adopt a nose-down attitude, and the autopilot would produce a gentle nodding. There is no alternative; right turn towards Sumburgh and a "Pan" call to declare an emergency and to request a rescue helicopter. We are cleared descent to 500 feet, to be clear of any cloud. I look back into the cabin and see that some of our passengers have pulled the hoods on their survival suits up over their heads so they can't hear our messages to them through their headsets. With things under control in the cockpit, I check with Bill that he is happy that I go back into the cabin to sort things out. Should take no more than five minutes. The nine passengers seemed pleased to see me as I check their seat belts are securely fastened, pull back their hoods, replace their headphones, show them the Emergencies card, and check that only small passengers are next to the small windows at the back. As I climb back into my seat, I can hear the rescue helicopter saying he can see our lights. Bill tells him that we think we have lost our horizontal stabilizer on the port side, and we are flying at 120 knots with everything under control.

The rescue helicopter comes alongside and announces, "You haven't lost it, it's tucked in close to your fin. You slipstream is holding it steady in that position. I will escort you in and tell you if anything changes."

Ouch! Not the news I want to hear. We can't land at 120 knots, and as we slow down for the landing, will the stabiliser start wobbling and fall off, possibly interfering with the tail rotor? If that is damaged, it becomes unbalanced, and within seconds the whole assembly will wrench itself off. We could lose directional control on final approach. We have 10 minutes to sort out a plan of action, keeping in mind that we might lose directional control at any time before touch down. Bill is very experienced at flying the Puma, of which we are flying a development, the Super Puma (Bristow Tiger). We run over our options and agree on a plan of action, meeting two requirements: we need to land as soon as possible (our situation can only deteriorate) and we need to be able to cope if we lose directional control at a moment's notice. We plan an approach to runway 06, the short runway, but into wind. On the final approach, speed will be reduced from our current 120 knots to 80 knots (minimum power speed, therefore minimum torque) as we cross the threshold of the runway. Maintaining a few feet above the runway, airspeed will be gradually brought back to 60 knots (50 knots ground speed) and the helicopter slowly lowered so that our tricycle undercarriage makes gentle contact with the runway. If everything is stable, brakes will be applied, we come to a stop and shut down. If we lose directional control, we need to reduce power to zero in a bid to keep straight, and the cockpit roof-mounted emergency engine and electrics handle will need to be pulled. As we approach the airfield, the approach checks are carried out and our undercarriage is confirmed down. I brief the passengers about our running landing and to stay inside the cabin until the rotors have stopped turning. Bill instructs our escort SAR helicopter to move away to a safe distance and tells Air Traffic to keep all vehicles well clear until our rotors are stopped. Should we roll over on touchdown, or crash, our rotor blades will fly off in all directions away from the helicopter. As I line up on finals I brief the passengers to take up the brace position for the running landing and I concentrate on making a fixed-wing-style landing.

Suitably ready for all contingencies, everything goes to plan and we shut down about halfway up the runway. As the engine noise dies away, I am aware of a drumming noise from the cabin. Looking back, I can see our passengers stamping their boots on the floor and punching the air like footballers. I'm glad they enjoyed it! Something to tell their families about when they make it home later today. With the rotor stopped, I get out and open the cabin passenger door and beckon them to come out into the fresh air. We all can see the stabiliser, still attached but out at an angle to the fin, now there is no slipstream to hold it in place. A big tractor type vehicle draws up towing a large Rigged Inflatable Boat (RIB). Sumburgh airfield is surrounded by water, so I guess it might be needed one day. Eventually a large passenger coach turns up for our nine passengers, their bags are loaded, and they head off to the air terminal. No doubt, after a loo stop and a coffee, they will be boarding a fixed wing airliner and completing their journey to Aberdeen Airport. With them gone, a company vehicle turns up with a towing bracket for our undercarriage. Bill goes in the vehicle, and I sit in the cockpit as the helicopter is towed across the airfield to our hangar. In the small operations room, I take a call from base. Bill and I are booked on a fixed wing back to Aberdeen, check-in time 1 hour hence. The helicopter is not to be touched; the investigation team will fly in tomorrow morning. Bill and I down a coffee and present ourselves at the departure desk, our flying licences, which we always carry, serving as ID. The fact that we are wearing our rubber survival suits and aircrew lifejackets is not commented upon. Joining the other passengers, we troop aboard and find our seats, our lifejackets going into the overhead locker. I sit back and enjoy the short flight, letting other pilots take the strain as my cup of Buck's Fizz brings a smile to my face, the first one of the day.

Arriving at Aberdeen airport, we walk across to our operation and present ourselves to the Chief Pilot. Apparently, the CAA will be part of the investigation and may want to talk to us at some point (The passengers are safe, and all the evidence is there for any investigation, so not a problem). We will not be flying tomorrow, but filling in a MOR and talking through what happened. This is the first occurrence of this problem, so it will be important to find out the reason for this structural failure and to prevent its recurrence. When we both get back home, we find that our respective wives have had a quiet lunch together while we were having an exciting time at Sumburgh. It's a small world …

Next day, Bill and I run through the flight and our actions during the emergency. We learn that a new stabiliser will be fitted, and the helicopter will return to service. We learn later that the AIB at Farnborough had found a corrosion pit, and a fatigue crack had started from there, resulting in the eventual failure of the main spar. The CAA issue an emergency airworthiness directive to all operators, to be complied with within 10 flying hours. Within a few days I am heading out to Croatia for a well-earned break, but Ann tells me to get out and enjoy the sunshine, not hide away reading a book. Bill, eventually, heads out to the Middle East to take up a post as a VIP helicopter pilot for a royal family. No rubber suit, boots, or lifejacket when flying over the dessert. Not much wine at the end of the day though. He and his family tough it out for several years, then return home.

When I return to duty, I am not allowed to fly until I am checked out by a doctor, A.V.M. O'Connor, based in Harley Street. The company book flights from Aberdeen to Heathrow and off I go, not knowing what to expect. I find his practice and check in at reception. He is an expert in neuropsychiatry and a consultant to the CAA, with citations all round the room. I am welcomed into his surgery. He says that I have had serious problems with flying the Tiger and that I had expressed a wish to fly the SAR S61N with the updated flight control and navigation system. This is true, I have always liked SAR and I found the S61N very reliable in all weathers, day and night. Not only that, the S61N cockpit is a lot quieter to operate in, and I am finding that I am developing tinnitus, a constant background high pitched noise caused by exposure to excessive noise and/or severe stress. I am a little surprised when he asks if he can speak to my wife Ann, on the phone. I see no reason why not, so he calls her straight away and I can hear her voice on a loudspeaker. He asks how she feels about her breadwinner being a pilot and flying over the North Sea, day and night. She says that she was quite happy to marry me when I was a jet pilot and quite proud of me when I saved many lives during my seven years on SAR. She had every faith in my ability and my commitment to flying several helicopters on a range of tasks, in the UK and abroad. As support goes, this exchange could not be more helpful. Job done on that front. We chat on about my flying history from my first flight at the age of 12 to my two recent incidents with flying the Tiger over the last few years. He mentions that his main job is with airline pilots, some of whom find the responsibility of their job just too overwhelming. Quite a few of these pilots come from the Middle East. When asked if I could offer a reason, I cannot think of one. He accepts my honesty. After half an hour of general conversation and trying to fix his photocopier, he says that it was nice meeting me and he would be in touch. As I walk out through reception, there is a young man, smartly dressed, clearly from the Middle East, waiting to see him. He does not look very happy. On the other hand, for some reason, I am feeling quite buoyant as I make my way through crowded streets to the Underground and then to Heathrow for the flight back to Aberdeen. Within a few days I am shown a letter from him, recommending that I convert onto the S61N and receive training for SAR to make use of many years of experience in that area. I could not have been more pleased. There is a difficulty for the company; it will take some months to train my replacement, so in the meantime I will fly as co-pilot on the Tiger. Now I know my future is settled, I can concentrate on my new role and fly with experienced captains, learning from every flight, even diverting to Bergen in Norway for the very first time.

On 7th July 1988, I am listening to the early morning news while eating my early breakfast before flying. There has been a catastrophic explosion overnight at the Piper Alpha Platform, about 100 miles northeast of Aberdeen. The fire is still raging, and there are reports of survivors being picked up from the sea, having jumped from the helideck (at 175 feet above the sea). There is assistance almost alongside, coming from a specialist semi-submersible rig, the Tharos, which is using its high pressure fire hoses to control the flames. Its helideck is not affected, so survivors are being flown out to hospital by RAF rescue helicopters from Lossiemouth and our own S61Ns from Aberdeen. Controlling the rescue effort from overhead is a Nimrod, a large maritime reconnaissance aircraft from RAF Kinloss. Our planning room is awash with rumours, and I have to wait five minutes before the duty operations officer becomes aware that I am waiting patiently to be given my task for the day. He breaks away from the group of oil executives who are shouting the odds about routing helicopters around the North Sea (controlled by Aberdeen ATC), over which, as a helicopter company, we have no control. I am teamed up with Captain Seide and our task is fly to the Beryl Field, our route out taking us within three miles of the burning platform. We are requested to fly as high as possible or in cloud, so our passengers don't see the 350 feet high flames and the mile high column of smoke. We are not to mention it in our passenger briefings or draw attention to it during the flight. We are due a second flight in the afternoon, by which time there may be temporary routes in operation, outbound and inbound. Check the operations board before starting planning.

Suitably briefed, we take off on time, and climbing to 5,000 feet as we coast out near Peterhead, we can already see the dark column of smoke 80 miles ahead. There is no cloud around, so we just press on. We can hear our radar controllers talking to the rescue helicopters and the Nimrod, and as a precaution we put on our forward-facing landing lamps so we can be seen from 10 miles away. As pilots, we can see everything clearly, and our course takes us clear of the smoke plume. We complete our task on the Beryl Field. We are not asked to give any information by their radio operator, and we don't offer any. Everyone is calmly professional and as we fly back, we can see a jumble of debris and the platform is not recognisable. By afternoon, a new route out and back from the Beryl Field has been authorised, adding 15 miles to the distance to be flown – no problem with that – and the flight is completed as planned.

The local BBC Television News that night shows footage from the door of the RAF rescue helicopter as it winched up survivors from the sea, bathed in the light from the massive fire. The Piper Alpha is one of the biggest platforms on the North Sea and controls 10% of the output of UK offshore oil and gas. Over the coming months we will learn how many died and how many survived. Clearly, this is worst offshore disaster for the UK up to now, and there will need to be a public enquiry to find out what went wrong and what steps will be required to prevent a recurrence.

A few days later I have a meeting with our local MP at his regular monthly surgery for residents. I speak to him about my feeling that helicopters were flying overloaded as the "notional" weight used for passengers, the airline figure, was far too low at 165 pounds. Could government, in the shape of the CAA, conduct weightings of passengers and aircrew as they walk out to the helicopters, complete with survival suits, lifejackets and flight bags? If the CAA came up with a standard weight for helicopter passengers and flight crew for offshore destinations, it would be accepted by all companies. He tells me to put my suggestion on paper and send it to him at his Department in London. The letter is sitting on my desk ready to go, and I ponder whether to send it, as his hands will be full at the Department for Energy. I decide to send it, half expecting no reply, or a possible rebuff, given the circumstances. A week later, I receive a short letter from him, written by his department. He has spoken to his opposite number in the CAA. They are aware of the problem, and they have been thinking about taking action for several months. They have decided to conduct a survey starting within a week, and they will consult with all parties concerned so that their conclusions are immediately accepted.

Sure enough, we are all weighed as we walk out to the helicopters, in my case 200 pounds, a good 30 pounds over my body weight. All my survival clothing, boots, lifejacket, headset, and flight bag clearly add up. After a month, the new "notional" weight – 187 pounds – is published and brought into use. The day we first use the new figure, I notice that at the normal cruise power setting we have gained five knots airspeed and the vibration level is significantly less. This improvement is the first of several flight safety related changes that come in, like anonymous reporting of incidents, and the correct distances on the planning forms to oil installations north of Aberdeen. Now the passengers get a video safety brief in the hour before they board the helicopter they are going to fly in. Every month there are improvements in safety related issues, for passengers as well as aircrew. All welcome and most well overdue.

Eventually I get a date for my S61N conversion: mid-September 1988. Something to work towards, and now, with things going well, I must not relax and spoil my copy book. Still learning, I complete my last flight on the Tiger on 15th September and dig out my S61N Pilot's notes. One door closes and another opportunity beckons..

Chapter 18: Converting to the S61N and SAR

(October 1988 – November 1992)

Suitably briefed, I slip back into flying the S61N again. All the old handling skills come back, and the standard operating procedures have changed little since I have been elsewhere. I look at the list of S61N pilots that I will be flying with in the coming months. At least five of them, like me, have come from the Tiger, having experienced problems with it, such as the high cockpit noise level. All the captains are aged 40-plus, and most of the co-pilots are in their 20s. After three weeks of check flights, I am released to the Line on 7th October as a qualified co-pilot able to fly in all weathers, day and night. My SAR training is promised in six months' time, I just need to prove over the coming winter that I am up to speed in all areas of operations. Sensible, really, so no complaints.

Most of the flights are to rigs and installations within 150 miles from Aberdeen, and as winter comes on, we pick up light airframe icing if we fly in cloud. There is an increase in airframe vibration, and we need extra power to maintain our usual 110 knots cruising speed. In our fuel planning we allow for light icing and needing the cabin heater on for ourselves and the passengers. I am pleased that the S61N has a big deflector in front of the engine air intakes, keeping out rain, sleet, hail, snow, and slush coming off the cockpit roof. At low temperatures we turn on the engine de-icing, which heats up the first stage of the compressor, preventing ice from forming and affecting the engine. The engines are proving very reliable after 10 years of operating over the North Sea, and I feel quite safe and secure when flying in all weathers, day and night.

At last, the Public Inquiry into the Piper Alpha Disaster gets under way in mid-November. Lord Justice Cullen sets out the basic facts; of the 226 people who were on the platform, 165 died and 61 survived. My next-door neighbour, a solicitor, attends the inquiry, and over the weeks that follow I am given an update on all the failings that are coming to light. It will be a long, in-depth inquiry, hopefully leading to improving offshore safety. The local newspapers are full if it, as the work continues to extinguish the flames and recover all the bodies.

On 10th December I fly with Captain Whitehouse across snowy Scotland to RAF Stornoway, in the Western Isles, where the company has a SAR S61N unit with the latest automatic pilot and navigation system. As we are staying overnight, I have time in the afternoon to go on a training flight, sitting just behind the two pilots on a "jump" seat. It is instructive to watch the helicopter carry out a let-down and coming to the low hover over the sea just using the automatic pilot. The flying controls move, the engines change power as both pilots have their arms folded across their chests, carefully watching the winking lights on the autopilot control panel. As one of them says, it is sobering watching the autopilot flying more smoothly and accurately than him, even after years of training

The next day there is forecast heavy snow across the high Scottish mountains, so we plan to go back to Aberdeen, following the coast at 500 feet above the sea. My captain is buying flats near Aberdeen University for students to rent. His bank is happy to loan him whatever he wants as long as they hold all the mortgage documents as collateral. Clearly, a second career beckons …

Every six months we carry out "base checks" in the S61N flight simulator. We use the one belonging to BAH and the instrument layout and position of switches is different to our own machines, so I have to memorise the differences. Also, we carry out emergencies that we can't practice in flight, such as engine fires or switching off flying control hydraulic systems, which either makes the controls very heavy or very light, and at the same time losing the autopilot assistance. No one expects great accuracy or smooth flying, just being competent is enough. The usual routine is that we depart from an airfield (any in Europe), and about five minutes into the flight we experience an emergency that requires us to return using either the ILS or an a NDB approach. If a NDB approach, we can expect the autopilot to fail, or the Auxiliary Hydraulic System. On overshooting from the approach, the emergency is cancelled and at some stage during the ILS approach the engine will fail or catch fire, or both, depending on the whim of the instructor! All approaches seem to require an overshoot (go around) as the non-handling pilot cannot see the airfield approach lights, something that rarely happens in reality. Good practice, though, for that day when it might happen!

With winter over, I fly a series of check rides to assess my capability. Finally, on 24th April 1989, I fly a check ride with our Chief Pilot, Captain David Smith out to the Ocean Nomad drilling rig near the location of Piper Alpha. Although the weather is good, he instructs me to carry out an ILS approach to a runway at Aberdeen Airport.

At the debrief at the end of the flight I am assessed as competent as a captain on the S61N and will shortly receive SAR training. Next day I am with a young co-pilot heading out to the Tharos, still close to the remains of the Piper Alpha. The weather is poor on our return, so we need an ILS approach, which my co-pilot flies very competently, and as I see the airfield approach lights, I take over control for the landing. Next week I am to begin my SAR training in northwest Scotland. The three SAR units that the company are operating – Stornoway, Sumburgh and Lee on Solent – are providing a service for HM Coastguard. As most helicopter SAR call outs are for maritime incidents, HM Coastguard are looking to become responsible for providing a comprehensive service for the whole of the UK. Our company hopes to provide the helicopters, the bases, and the air and ground crews to man such a task. At present the SAR S61N is providing a very reliable service in all weathers, day and night, though it will not continue for ever as the manufacturer, Sikorsky, have dropped hints that support for this machine will come to an end in the next few years.

In early May, I drive across Scotland and catch the ferry across to Stornoway in the Western Isles to find our SAR unit on the huge airfield of RAF Stornoway. I check in at the unit, meet the chief pilot, stow my flying kit, and get a briefing on the new autopilot and its capabilities, very impressive if you are flying in fog or at night over the sea. I am booked into a good hotel for the duration of my training and spend the evening looking at maps – lots of coastlines, beaches, open moorland, and high ground; Ben Nevis and the mountains of Skye are within our operating area. I have been there on foot, so it will be good to see the summits from the air. I should have brought my camera, but perhaps I need to give full attention to the training. There is clearly a lot to learn about the area they operate in and the capabilities of the new autopilot.

5th May 1989: my first flight in the new SAR S61N with Captain Lee. Out in the open sea we spy the paddle steamer "Waverley" and ask if we can do some Decks training while it is proceeding at 10 knots into the prevailing southwesterly wind.

Paddle Steamer SS Waverley under way near Stornaway.

To make it realistic, we will lower our winchman down to the open space at the stern of the vessel, he will come off the hook, and we will leave him there for a few minutes before we come back and collect him. Once on deck, our winchman calls us on his small radio; he is getting the ship's captain to change course slightly to make it ideal for winching, which is wind direction plus 30 degrees. We see the ship alter course and get the call to return. While we in the helicopter are pointing into wind and getting the benefit, with less power being needed, our captain in the right-hand seat has a clear view of the vessel, all of the obstructions and can manoeuvre well clear of them all. With our winchman back on board, we say farewell to the Waverley, and it resumes its original course. My captain tells me that most vessels that they come across are only too willing to indulge in Decks training; it is good for the ships' crews to be acquainted with helicopter procedures. Also, it is good for the helicopter crews to see as many vessels as possible, making a judgement on each one as to where the best place is for the winchman to be put down (as big an open uncluttered space as possible).

Something completely different for the next flight. After take-off we head east to the Scottish mainland and inland towards a prominent mountain that rears up from the landscape of lochs and heather, Suilven. It is a very prominent mountain and its long ridgeline (two kilometres) is over 2,400 feet (723 metres) above sea level. Lots of walkers and climbers scale its peaks, especially in summer; a few come to grief and need to be rescued and flown to hospital. This area is part of the unit's patch, so whenever the weather is good enough, they fly in and practice rescues along the long ridgeline.

Today, there is a gentle 20 mph wind blowing from the west, so only moderate turbulence and down drafting; even so, our captain has to work hard to maintain the required position when in the hover. Our two engines rev up and down together as their computers work out how much power is required at any given moment. I hear the continuous instructions from the winch operator to our captain, who responds smoothly so that the helicopter is at the height and position required to give our winchman an easy arrival on the mountain top. Good crew co-operation is key to effective rescues, the pilot not being able to see underneath and being totally reliant on the winch operator. My job as co-pilot in all this is to look after any radio calls, monitor the temperatures and pressures, and deal with any minor emergencies, enabling the captain to concentrate entirely on flying smoothly and accurately.

Next day something different – the mountains on the Isle of Skye. It's 26 years since Ann and I walked up to the peaks from the youth hostel at Glenbrittle. We were engaged then, and due to get married in August 1963, so as we reached the ridgeline we paused and took a break, leaning up against some big rocks and looking at the impressive scenery. As we moved off, we heard a loud noise; the slab of rock than Ann had chosen to lean against decided to topple forwards down the steep slope. Suitably impressed, we carried on our exploration, making the ridgeline with a view down the other side into Loch Coruisk, a valley clearly carved out by ice. Time to return, so we picked a route down to Glenbrittle, taking our time over the rough terrain. Halfway down we realised that Ann's waterproof trousers, which she had tied around her waist earlier, were missing. There was no way we could find them in this rough country, so they were abandoned for some walker to discover at a later date …

From the air, the ridges are as sharp-edged as I remember them, and the up and down drafts coupled with turbulence are the same as I had experienced in Snowdonia many years previously, flying the RAF Wessex. Now I am in a much heavier helicopter with less excess power to play with, so I need to plan escape routes if I get caught in a strong downdraft, making an approach to a mountain top. Most days the peaks are in cloud and the mountain rescue teams (MRTs) on a call out will be dropped off some way up the mountain for them to continue on foot to the casualty, carrying their stretcher. I am shown the LPs alongside the Mountain Rescue huts dotted around the mountains. The civil MRTs are busy summer and winter, and the rescue helicopters are used to convey the casualty to the nearest suitable hospital, often the new Raigmore hospital at Inverness.

9th May, my first callout on this unit and this time to the Skye mountains, an easy pick-up of a mountaineer who had twisted his ankle and was immobile. The winchman uses the stretcher to bring him up to the cabin and within 15 minutes we are landing at the hospital near Broadford to transfer him to the waiting ambulance. 11th May, next call out, to a Spanish trawler 30 miles out in the Atlantic. The casualty, a seaman, was found unconscious, either from drugs or illness, and needs hospital treatment. The sea is rough and there is a gale blowing and our winch operator uses a 100-foot "high line" to get initial contact with the trawler's crew on the stern of the vessel. Our winchman goes down with 45 minutes of deck time before fuel considerations mean we will have to leave for a refuel. Just 20 minutes later our winchman comes up with the casualty in the stretcher, still unconscious, and we head off east towards the Raigmore Hospital near Inverness. As we proceed, our winchman gives the casualty oxygen to help his breathing. After threading our way through the Scottish Mountains and along the Great Glen, we find the hospital helicopter landing pad and transfer our patient to a waiting ambulance. We will have to wait until he is discharged before we will be told what was wrong with him.

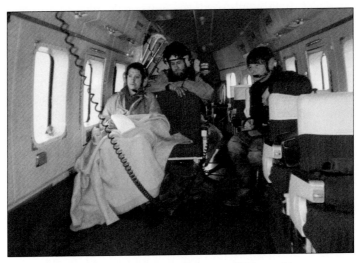

Casualty being kept warm after rescue, off Western Isles

Next day, time to return home for a two-week walking holiday in Austria, flying out of Glasgow. My job is to drive carefully, in my Citroen GS, through the Glens, concentrating on the driving and not the fabulous views. With this detachment over, I am programmed to get checked out at Sumburgh in the Shetlands and at Lee on Solent in Hampshire. So far, the SAR flying is much more interesting than the boring grey North Sea, with the boring grey clouds and the sea mist that go with flying offshore.

24th June: I am heading up to Sumburgh by fixed wing for a week's training on the SAR Unit based there. I am met by Captain Miller, the chief pilot, taken to the operation and introduced to some of the crew members and engineers. At 5 p.m. I am taken to a nearby hotel, where I am lodged for the duration – transport will be provided whenever I am needed. At dinnertime I meet up with the other guests, mainly BAH helicopter crews who fly the daily shuttle flights out to the large Brent Field. At the moment they are using S61Ns, but they plan to introduce the Super Puma, similar to our own Bristow Tiger. They anticipate using our Tiger flight simulator for training (we use their S61N flight simulator). Their Chinook simulator is gathering dust at Aberdeen and looking for a good home; the Chinooks themselves are back in America, carrying logs in remote areas. Compared to the S61N, the Chinook was very noisy and had a high level of airframe vibration. They even had vibration absorbing devices fitted to the cockpit seats to reduce one's eyeballs bouncing up and down, so that the instruments could be read. By comparison, the S61N is quiet and smooth, especially if flown within the normal cruise power setting. A variant is judged reliable enough for American presidents to be flown in, so good enough for me.

Next day I am checked out by Captain Leask, the Training Captain. We do drums and decks where, as pilots, we depend on the instructions of our winch operator. Not using any of the automatic functions, I carry out low level circuits and come to the hover over the drum in the sea and hold my position and height as instructed. As I receive the instruction "Up gently," I apply power and slowly gain height vertically, waiting for the instruction "Clear forward," before moving slowly forward and gaining height. That exercise completed, we move on to working with the local lifeboat, which we ask to take up a course of the surface wind direction plus 30 degrees at 10 knots forward speed. My captain, sitting in the right-hand seat, can see the lifeboat clearly and using the fore and aft axis of the vessel (boat's axis) can respond to the instructions of the winch operator. Seated on the left-hand side of the cockpit I can see nothing, but I can look after the radios, check the temperatures and pressures, and anticipate any requirements of the captain. Later we ask the lifeboat to stop going forward and drift with the wind and current. As pilots, we lose sight of the vessel as we come to hover over it, so must use "aircraft axis" for directions from the winch operator, using the sea surface for guidance for height and position. Looking well ahead gives a good feel for attitude, and one's peripheral vision gives good height guidance. The more one practices the more skilled you become, and you can train from either side of the cockpit. Another five years and I will have cracked it …

By contrast, we have a gentle afternoon flight looking at our local area, stretching up to Sullum Voe and the island of Unst in the north, to Sumburgh Head in the south, with the capital, Lerwick, in the middle. There is a lot of oil tanker traffic going in and out of the oil and gas terminal at Sullum Voe, and a lot of commercial, fishing ferry, and cruise ship traffic using Lerwick Harbour. To support offshore oil operations, there are numerous small airfields operating both fixed wing and helicopters; we need to be in touch as we pass by. Our second company base is on Unst, which provides a helicopter service to oil platforms in the north of the East Shetland Basin. Passengers are brought in by fixed wing from Aberdeen and flown out to the oil installations by company S61Ns. The NDB, which is located close to the westerly runway threshold, is very useful for homing to the airfield in mist or low cloud. With so much maritime traffic plus yachts in our patch, there are many call-outs for our rescue helicopter. The unit has two water pumps, which can be easily loaded onto the helicopter and winched down to any vessel which is taking on water. The pump comes with instructions, appropriate flexible pipes, and a full fuel tank. They are in frequent use for yachts and small vessels. We also have several multi-seat dinghies in the hangar ready for immediate use as well.

Moving forward to 5th January 1993, the massive oil tanker "Braer", on her way from Norway to the USA, suffers engine failure and, carrying 85,000 tonnes of light crude oil, drifts ashore onto rocks in west Shetland. The ship is abandoned, and the 44 members of the crew are winched off by our rescue helicopter. A week later, the ship breaks up and the light crude oil spills out and is blown across open fields and evaporates. The subsequent inquiry blames the ship's captain for fundamental failures of seamanship. Later, HM Coastguard acquire large vessels that can tow stricken ships out of danger should they lose engine power …

With two call-outs for yachts with problems, during which we work with lifeboats, my stay at Sumburgh is completed, and I fly in a Vickers Viscount back to Aberdeen and a few days off, then back to the "day job" at Aberdeen, flying out to the usual rigs and platforms. My stint at our SAR unit at Lee on Solent is slated for the end of July; my home area, as I grew up in Southampton, and with my elder brother sailed in the area amongst the big ships heading for the docks. On 25th July I board a train in Aberdeen, heading for Fareham in Hampshire to be picked up by Captain John Whale and whisked off to the SAR unit on a Royal Navy airfield. After checking in at the operation, I am taken to the Officer's Mess and with 4 gold bars on my shirt epaulettes I am mistaken for a Royal Navy Captain. Even when I explain that I am a helicopter pilot working for HM Coastguard there is still lingering disbelief. Also, at mealtimes when I chose to sit alone, within a few minutes I am joined by junior Naval officers, keen to make their mark. My room is big, well furnished, and I am well looked after. Next day I am flying with Captain Thomson out in the Solent, working with the local lifeboat doing drums and decks. We listen out on the Coastguard radio frequency and inform their rescue centre that we are training in the Solent and available immediately for any rescue situation. With yacht races around Cowes and normal commercial traffic going into Southampton, the Solent is a busy place. From time to time, we receive a call saying that our presence in this hazardous area is appreciated. Eventually, we get a call to look for a yacht which is four hours overdue at its berth at Hamble. I copy down all the details, and we head down towards the Needles to begin our search. There are numerous yachts that have a superficial resemblance, and we have to descend to low level to read the yachts name, usually on the stern, making sure we don't blow them over with our powerful rotor downwash.

Eventually the search is called off, as the yacht is found in Cowes Harbour, so we return to base. As we coast in, we pass over a wide slipway which is being used for hovercraft trials by the Navy. The hovercraft are being built in a big hangar in Cowes and are being exported all over the world. Eventually, the RNLI get several small ones to operate on the Thames in London, on Morecombe Bay, at Hoylake and at Southend-on-Sea. Because they can operate in shallow water and on mud and sand, they can reach areas which are inaccessible to conventional lifeboats. Having bought the T-shirt and a few mementos from the unit's goody store, I am good to go after one week at Lee on Solent. Everyone enjoys their job here and their location on the south coast. Another tick, then, in the box for SAR locations visited. Next location I am told will be our operation at Unst, a two-week stay this time, starting on 2nd November. Time to get together my cold weather kit, anorak, scarf, thick gloves, and woolly hat.

Back to the normal job at Aberdeen. As S61N pilots we get the "Winter Operations" briefing. We can look forward to rain, sleet, hail, and snow, coupled with strong winds. On the ground, slippery conditions underfoot; in the air, airframe and engine icing are to watch out for. We will need a lot of extra fuel to meet all contingencies, as well as keeping the passengers on board when on a helideck offshore, during strong winds, until we have re-fuelled, gaining at least 2,000 pounds in weight, and thus sitting on deck more securely, rotors running. All flying proceeds normally without incident until 18th September. While operating in rain in the Forties Field, the cockpit begins to fill with smoke. I declare an emergency and inform Forties control I am making an immediate landing on the nearest platform, Forties Charlie. My co-pilot switches off the windscreen wipers and the heater blower motor (known problem areas). Having made it to a deck, I shut down, and keeping the passengers on board with my co-pilot, I go below to get to a telephone and call base. I get clearance to do a 15-minute ground run with the two suspect items switched off, and there is no smoke. I follow this with a five-minute flight, again, no problems. So, we load up with passengers and make the one-hour flight to Aberdeen without windscreen wipers or any cabin heating, not comfortable at all. On the ground the engineers find that the windscreen wiper motor has burnt out and it is replaced. However, for the next two weeks the windscreen wiper system plays up and many parts are replaced, adjusted, and checked before it finally performs in the correct manor.

Meanwhile at home, Christopher decides which university he wants to attend to study Politics. He has done well at Banchory Academy, being awarded the Senior Dux Prize for best all-round performance. Again, the end of term prizes are presented by our local MP, the Rt. Hon. Alec Buchanan Smith. After visiting several universities, Christopher picks Newcastle; he likes the planned course and the gig culture of the town. Ann and I take him down to his Hall of Residence and change the plugs on his electrical devices back to the 3 pin round plugs. Everything works; kit unpacked, it is time for him to meet his fellow students, so Mum and Dad can go home, job done.

It's 3rd November, time to board the Dash 7 fixed wing aircraft to fly from Aberdeen to Unst, at the top end of the Shetland Islands. I am told it will be cold and windy for my two-week stay, so I have packed everything I could need for winter conditions. On arrival I am met by the chief pilot, have a brief tour of the operation, then off to the local hotel to settle down for the night. Next morning, I meet the other pilots and am slotted in for two flights acting as co-pilot. Our main job is supporting the Ninian Field, about 110 miles out to the northeast, carrying passengers, baggage, and freight. The Decca charts have our routes plotted on them and the NDB, near the threshold of the westerly runway, which we mostly use, gives us good guidance in misty conditions. This is my first flight to the Ninian Field, with its three platforms; the central one is huge and sits on a support column of concrete. The other platforms have the usual fabricated steel structures. All of them have their names displayed on the helidecks as well as on the sides of the structures, so no excuse for landing on the wrong one, as can happen in misty conditions. We shuttle from one platform to another, landing in the centre of the yellow circle with the nose into the wind and the yellow line passing underneath the cockpit. Job done, we are refuelled and given refreshments; we give our departure message, which is recorded, and take off into the prevailing westerly wind.

The calculated flight time to base is 1 hour 20 minutes. On approaching the shoreline we are cleared by ATC to come in low level, simulating misty conditions. The needle of the NDB points straight ahead and I can see the start of the runway about a mile beyond it. As we continue, we pass over the aerial of the beacon; the pointed end of the needle swings round to point behind us, the other end pointing towards the runway. By tracking it, we end up at the threshold of the runway, where we do a gentle run-on landing and turn off to the right into dispersal and shut down. During a sandwich lunch with the engineers, I find that most of them are ex-Navy, are paid very well to work in this isolated spot, and have plans to run B&Bs in Devon or Cornwall as soon as they have accumulated enough money. Later on, I meet the pilots in their hotel. Like me, they come up for a spell of duty then return to their homes in the rest of UK for their time off. Given the choice, they prefer to fly from Unst rather than Aberdeen. There is far less traffic, so no delays on departure or returning, and with the airfield close to the flat coast, they can operate safely in bad weather. Most of them have served overseas with the company in some very remote areas, where the main problems tend to be concerning the heat!

After a week flying as co-pilot, getting to know the local procedures, I am assessed fit to be a captain and start flying with the young co-pilots. They are quite with it, and are experienced in operating in the area, so good value. Most days, two flights, always to the Ninian Field, from where we can see the platforms in the Norwegian Sector. Many oilfields straddle the dividing line, and much Norwegian oil and gas is pumped ashore to the UK, that being the most convenient thing to do. One notices that there is very little flaring off of excess gas in the Norwegian Sector, as it is pumped back underground. On the UK side you can see numerous platforms in the East Shetland Basin flaring gas, especially at night. When landing and flying past a big flare, you need to keep looking forward to the faint edge lights of the helideck and ignore the powerful flickering light over one's right shoulder! Similarly, on take-off, after the initial vertical climb, you need to select 5 degrees nose down, retaining full power, and the airspeed and height slowly increase as you climb initially to 500 feet before turning. Returning to base at night you are often the only movement, so no delays. On shutdown you often see the Northern Lights flickering, very impressive.

After two weeks away I am given a week off; time to complete the Christmas shopping, a few walks locally in the snow, and even a few rounds of golf on a frost-bound course with a bright orange ball. The River Dee, which skirts the town, has ice along the river bank and sometimes freezes over, but never tempts me to walk out onto it.

In November, the long-awaited Cullen Inquiry into the Piper Alpha disaster finally reports. The local papers are full of the 106 recommendations, all of which were accepted by the offshore industry. The responsibility for implementing safety regulations is transferred from the Department of Energy to the Health and Safety Executive (HSE). The offshore industry is acting urgently to carry out the 48 recommendations for which they are responsible. Meanwhile, on the aviation side, things continue to improve: an ILS system is installed for Aberdeen airport's north-facing runway; at Sumburgh airport, an ILS system is installed on their west-facing runway; and the Robert Gordon's Institute of Technology (RGIT) brings in video briefings for helicopter passengers. All passengers are to be briefed in the one hour before take-off for the helicopter type in which they will fly, the briefings to be given both onshore and offshore. The passenger survival suits are improved and now have the inflatable lifejacket incorporated.

As the year ends, my services are required at Sumburgh for SAR duties, a long deployment. The weather generally is bad, low visibility, strong winds, rain, sleet, and snow. I am pleased to be flying in the S61N, which was designed to operate in this sort of weather, so no problems. The new navigation equipment, the new colour radar, coupled up with a new autopilot all work well and enable the pilots to concentrate on the task in hand. Very early on the morning of 5th March, our crew are called into the unit by HM Coastguard to standby to assist in a big rescue situation off John o' Groats. The P&O freight ferry "St Rognvald", sailing between Aberdeen and Lerwick, has been hit by a freak large wave that had smashed into the bridge. With windows broken the sea had poured in, disabling internal communications and steering. The ship is three miles offshore and drifting towards the coast. The captain has sustained an injury. We are briefed by the Coastguard that the RAF had scrambled a Sea King SAR helicopter, RH 137, which was on location and had put their winchman on board. Our captain, Paul Bentley, confers with the Coastguard and they agree that the best place for us to be on standby is within 10 miles of the incident, ready to assist at a few minutes notice. That agreed, we launch at 5 a.m. in the dark and the rain. 30 minutes later we arrive on scene, our infra-red camera and nose mounted radar guiding us in the darkness. We speak to the captain of RH137; they have had a hard time with the ship bucking in the waves, as the ship was moving in a circle. All three of their 100-foot long lines had broken under strain and they were returning to RAF Lossiemouth to collect some replacements; their winchman was still on deck and working the Coastguard frequency. The Coastguard task us with going to John o' Groats, landing in an open area, and picking up several hand-held radios to replace the lost ship's internal communications. On returning, we call the winchman, and he confirms that he is on the stern of the vessel, so we suggest that we lower three long lines joined together, making 300 feet, with a weight at the end. Having done that, we lower our winchman, attached to the top of the long line, and he is hauled into the rear of the ship. He hands over the radios and begins sending up two survivors at a time in double strops. A total of 10 are transferred, leaving just four crewmembers to man the ship. As the survivors are flown to John o' Groats for transfer to the Coastguard, the RAF Sea King arrives and is able to winch down a replacement captain. The ship is brought under control and is able to set course for Aberdeen, where it is able to dock successfully. Having dropped off our survivors, we need to refuel, so we head up to Kirkwall's airfield and refuel there. Some 30 minutes later Sumburgh airfield comes into view in the pouring rain; we land, shut down, and the helicopter is towed into the hangar to dry out. We have flown five hours, five minutes and relied on the new navigation system and autopilot to help us. Very impressive to experience. Next day the unit receives a message from HQ: we have all performed very well, in bad weather at night, coping with a complex rescue mission. Next day the ship is unloaded, trucks are on their sides, contents spilt and contaminated, but at least the ship did not end up on the rocks.

That detachment over, it is back to the daily grind at Aberdeen, but back up to Sumburgh again in April for a short deployment. With the hours of daylight longer, that is a plus, but the weather, low visibility, rain, and strong winds are the same as usual. On 5th April we are scrambled to the west to a two-masted sailing vessel, the Enterprise, which reports that it is taking on water. There are eight souls on board, including 3 children. The

P&O ferry "St Rognvald" is standing by in the area. On arrival at the scene, it is clear that the best thing to do is to lower our pump on the end of the winch cable, with a 100-foot long line attached underneath. The crew are able to catch the line and pull in the pump to the cockpit at the back. Within minutes we hear that the pump is working and that that they will motor to the nearby harbour of Scalloway, the ferry following, as it is getting dark. Captain Brewster, our pilot, decides that we will return to Sumburgh, refuel, and remain at immediate readiness to scramble until we hear from the Coastguard that the vessel has berthed. Our report states the benefits of our radar, and our forward looking infrared (FLIR) camera, which can guide us in poor visibility. Our flying is logged as two hours 15 minutes, of which one hour is night. Detachment over, it is back to Aberdeen and flying out to the Forties Field, which I am getting to know very well after more than 100 trips.

However, on 2nd September I am back up to Unst to help out for two weeks. The job is the same as before, just to and from the Ninian Field and nothing else. I am flying with new captains, including Gordon Mitchell, who commanded the SAR unit at Sumburgh and is originally from Shetland. There is clearly a lot of work going on offshore, and to save time we keep a helicopter there overnight. We get to see what it is like to work, relax, sleep, and be fed on a working platform. It is continuously noisy, with the public address going all the time, directing workers to their required stations. The food is good and there is plenty of it available round the clock. Sleeping is more difficult because of the noise and vibration, of being onboard a working platform.

Most workers come offshore for two weeks and then have two weeks on shore, being ferried about by helicopter. Most put up with hot bunking – having their bunk for 12 hours a day, with fresh sheets available when they take it over from their partner. These chaps are well paid, work hard, and come from all over the world. When they have time off there is the cinema, with a programme running round the clock; likewise the games room. In all, I am offshore for a week, with not much flying to occupy myself, and you are not encouraged to explore.

Back to Aberdeen with a new challenge: find a drilling rig which is on the move to its planned destination, 120 miles northeast of Aberdeen. It has no NDB which would help us to locate it, and no fuel available either. In planning our fuel required, we have to assume it might be at the furthest point from Aberdeen, in which case we need fuel for the outbound and inbound flights plus deck fuel plus reserves. It comes to a lot of fuel, some of which we will need to jettison if it turns out that it is still close to Aberdeen. We plan to fly out along its planned route at 1,000 feet, to be clear of cloud until we find it. Then we will need to work out how much fuel we need for the return journey and jettison the rest if they want maximum payload on the return flight. We find it about halfway along the route, and we calculate how much fuel needs to be jettisoned; on this occasion, 1,000 pounds, all from our central tank. We land on the drilling rig, still under tow but well within the maximum pitch, roll and heave limits. With our passengers on board plus refreshments, we lift off and land at Aberdeen 40 minutes later. Glad the visibility is good, and the flight is by day.

Christopher, meanwhile, has been working away on his studies at Newcastle University and has taken his final exams. The results are pinned up on the notice board. He has got a First in Politics, the only one on his course. Graduation day is in July, and Ann and I make arrangements to go down for the day, remembering the camera. The ceremony is in the Hall and the Chancellor, Mathew White Ridley (4th Viscount Ridley) presents the certificates. Photographs are taken of all undergraduates shaking hands, so we will get some of these. Afterwards, some light refreshments, and we meet some of his tutors. Then outside into the sunshine to take some more photographs of Christopher and fellow undergraduates. Christopher is going on to Durham University to do an MA. Everyone is happy, a day to remember.

Christopher is happy after three years hard work.

At the end of October, Ann and I are walking our usual route around Banchory. The town is still expanding, with a new primary school being planned. There is a nine-hole golf course being considered west of the village. Our own golf, on the established town course, is progressing, and with handicaps we can enter competitions. The news from Christopher at Durham University, doing his MA, is that he is enjoying his course, sharing a rented house with some other students, and participating in gigs at local pubs with his band. The prospects are good. What could go wrong? Then the phone call at the weekend ...

Chapter 19: British Airways Helicopters Aberdeen

(June 1993 – December 1993)

A phone call from my contact in HQ: "You need to think of another career. Update your CV, you may need it." Click.

When I check the flying programme on Sunday, I am not flying Monday but am to report at noon, in best uniform. I arrive, and the crew room is in turmoil as senior pilots, made redundant, settle down before going home. I have seen this situation before, so I start talking to those affected. Apparently around 30 pilots are being made redundant at Aberdeen, all over age 50, including Line Trainers but not QFIs. Cutbacks are necessary because demand for our services from the Oil Companies has slackened off and exploration rigs are being laid up. The cutbacks are across all helicopter types.

Long-service old pilots cost twice as much as short-service young pilots. Most senior pilots joined as captains, on two annual pay increments (for myself, three), and then received an annual increment thereafter. Some are now on the maximum of 18. Every year their pay and salary related pension entitlement goes up. Old pilots (over 50) can be given immediate pension and might be willing to be daily contract pilots in summer, when the demand is highest. This is the third redundancy programme I have seen during my company service to date, and many pilots have been rehired sometime later, when the situation has improved. But I can look for a job with BAH, Bond Helicopters, or elsewhere, as I am qualified and experienced on both main helicopter types, the S61N and the Super Puma. Possibly, overseas helicopter companies need my SAR experience. Too young to retire; there must be a flying job out there somewhere.

At 2 p.m. it is my turn for the interview with Chief Pilot David Smith and Ops Director Brian Norris. It is clear that they have had a stressful morning, and the atmosphere is brisk and business like. Firstly, I am asked for my security tag, then a letter is read out that I will receive in a week's time. I will be entitled to six months' pay, tax-free, an immediate pension which I can commute and get a tax-free lump sum, and all my AVCs back tax-free.

Mike Norris says, "Once you receive this letter you can sign up for employment with a rival helicopter company, but you can't fly or use their simulator until then. There may be opportunity to fly with the company at a later date. We would be in touch. This is a sad day, for all of us. Thank you for your dedication and professional service. Would you send in Captain…"

I have kept my cool throughout, though my unhappiness must have shown. No point in burning my boats by having a row. Nothing they can do to change things. They are the unfortunate messengers bearing bad news, and I might need them at another time. I come out of the room, have a coffee, compare my situation with other pilots. We are all in the same boat. We are all experienced, with good safety records, and keen to fly. Then, having calmed down, I drive home carefully, concentrating on the traffic.

I arrive home mid-afternoon. Ann comes home, having played tennis. I blurt out, "Sit down, I have something to tell you – it's early retirement with a redundancy payment." All our plans are up in the air, there is still a mortgage to pay, and at 51 it is too early to retire. Perhaps companies overseas need pilots; I can produce a CV. If we stay put, I will be available for any helicopter job at Aberdeen or in the Shetlands and can operate overseas if required. Christopher is continuing with his studies at university, so he is self-supporting. With him away, perhaps we can make use of the spare bedrooms and do some gentle B&B for long-term clients. We have space for two extra cars on the drive, so they can come and go as they please. We need to look at the local papers to see what the going rate is for accommodation.

Next day I order Flight magazine, with flying job adverts at the back, as well as the local paper for B&B adverts, to get a feel for the market. I speak to the bank re: advice for investing lump sums; they can do little until we get the letter and the payments into our bank account. I prepare 20 CVs and letters to go out to helicopter companies worldwide as well as at Aberdeen. I start looking at office jobs in the paper, but they are mainly looking for computer experience. I ring up the Job Centre in Aberdeen. To register for Job Seekers Allowance I need to turn up with my letter, so I book an appointment for two days after I assume I will receive it.

I send off 20 CVs with cover letters to helicopter companies around the world, including those based at Aberdeen. The letter from the company arrives – no surprises, but I need to decide what I want to do about claiming my AVCs back and how much of my indexed linked pension I wish to commute for a tax-free lump sum. That decided, a letter goes back with details of my bank account; it should all happen within a week. Meeting a Job Centre youth of 20 years, I show him my letter of redundancy. He asks me to make my first application for Unemployment Benefit by filling in Form UB 40. I explain how this is the first time I have been unemployed, having been continuously employed since 18. We go through the form together, and I can claim for self plus wife, £70 per week, sent every two weeks. Besides the benefit, my NICs will be paid, so my State Pension will not be affected. There will be a review after six months. He is pleased to have helped a well-mannered applicant, and we shake hands. At least some money is coming in on a regular basis.

A week after the redundancy interview, I get a call. There will be a lunch at a hotel in Aberdeen at which all pilots made redundant will receive a silver item for their long service, plus a bottle of wine and an 80 shopping voucher. Also, please ring to fix a date to hand in flight kit and get flying logbook checked. I go in best uniform, hand in my immersion suit but keep my black flight suits, thermal underwear, and all items of uniform. The planning room is quiet as newly promoted young captains grapple with flight planning problems. I resist the temptation to offer advice; I am not in the company any longer. My logbook is checked and the figures noted. I am asked if I am likely to stay local, as I might be offered short-term employment in the future. Then I am escorted out of the building. It has been a formal experience, so no emotion after serving 11 years on that operation. From the car park I can see many helicopters parked in dispersal, not in the air earning money. However, at the end of the month I will receive my first pension payment and the tax-free lump sums. As one door closes, another one is bound to open.

The atmosphere at the lunch is good; the fresh-faced young captains have had a week in the hot seat and are still excited with the trust placed on their shoulders. At the end of the lunch the leaving captains are presented with a piece of silver marking the occasion, a bottle of wine and the shopping voucher. We are invited to say a few words. Not an occasion to offer advice, but a few jokes about the fact that after 11 years in the saddle, my wife, my son, our engineers and fellow pilots are still talking to me, so I must have made some sensible decisions! Now I am free to work for the opposition (BAH and Bond Helicopters) or even the CAA!

"I wish you all the best of luck, look after yourselves in the air and on the road. I will probably hear you over the airways sometime in the future. It's a small world after all..." Then I sit down, and another captain is called up. I go home by bus, clutching my booty, and glad the driver is taking the strain. Home at last, where's that pot of coffee?

On the B&B front, a journalist from an Aberdeen Paper checks us over, likes what he sees, and signs up for continuous occupation.

He is followed by a chartered accountant working on projects for the Grampian Regional Office. They get on very well together and come and go at different times. More money coming in, so raising our morale. The future looks better, but keep trying for the next flying job.

Calls from overseas: Court Helicopters, operating out of South Africa, say they like my qualifications, but are worried that, being a Brit, I might head back to UK if violence breaks out with Nelson Mandela coming into power. Also, I would be paid in Rand, which I can't take out of the country. However, we will stay in touch. Next call from Irish Helicopters. They provide SAR cover for the Republic and like my experience. However, I would lose 50% of my salary to income tax – but if a position comes up, they will be in touch. The helicopter companies at Aberdeen will put me on their list and will call me if pilots are needed. The rest of my letters and CVs are ignored.

1993, June: Ann takes a call from BAH at Aberdeen. They are looking for short-term (three months) contract pilots to fly the Super Puma or the S61N. Call back if interested.

I call back and speak to their Chief Pilot. He confirms their requirements and suggests a date when I can make an interview, with my flying licence, logbook, and passport.

I arrive in my best formal suit and meet up with five other ex-Bristow captains. We are all offered slots, mine on the S61N, which suits very well. Then we are introduced to the crew-room so see if anyone has an objection to any one of us. We all pass muster, so we get issued with uniforms, badges of rank as First Officers, ID, and immersion suits. Training in the flight simulator will begin straight away, followed by the real helicopter. I will spend some time up at their base at Sumburgh in Shetland, for which I will get a daily allowance. Time for a coffee and to meet some of the pilots, mostly S61N but some on the Super Puma. We are welcome because they are busy and could do with a few more hands to help out. My training on the flight simulator will begin on 22nd June, and it will involve flying circuits around the airfield with emergencies, such as engine problems and auxiliary hydraulic failure in the flying control system. This failure makes the flying controls very heavy, and it is easy to overcontrol. Sometimes you might need the assistance of the other pilot to help you move the controls. I get through without crashing the flight simulator, so that is deemed as pass.

My next experience will be instrument flying, ILS and NDB procedures, plus some rig radar let-downs (where the non-handling pilot gives a talkdown to guide the handling pilot to a position where he can see the offshore installation when half a mile away and at 200 feet above the sea). The two-hour training session goes well, with the instructor sitting where he can reach all the levers and switches. Simulator session over, we debrief the flight; the basics are there but there is room for improvement, which will come with practice.

Finally, I am signed off as competent and released to the Line to begin earning money for the company. It is comforting to see training in depth and assessment of my handling of the helicopter. My handling meets the standard, but there is room for improvement. I am happy to work on that, to volunteer for trips to widen my experience of working the company procedures and operating in new areas, like the Brent Field. With the appropriate signatures in my flying licence, I am packed off to Sumburgh for four weeks, to make my contribution. I meet my Line Trainer, Captain Martin, and begin new preparation for flight procedures. I am impressed that fuel requirements are worked out carefully so that the client (Shell) is offered the maximum payload for the prevailing weather conditions. When the client does not use up all the payload, extra fuel can be carried, giving more options when operating offshore. The in-flight shuttle form has all the required reporting points, radio calls, and weights for passengers, baggage, freight, and fuel. As the flight progresses, the form gets filled in. Just before each offshore take-off we transmit a departure message (which is recorded), so everyone in the area knows our intentions.

July is a busy month, and I am flying two flights a day. While I am away from home, I am happy to fly all day rather than sit on the ground reading a book. At breakfast I have a big meal; if I am busy, lunch will be missed, though I will get some coffee from somewhere. Most days a senior pilot will come up from Aberdeen and will be seen in the crew-room and talking to the pilots between flights. I can't help overhearing the conversations, which are mainly about administrative matters, rosters, leave, allowances and flight kit. Each pilot is addressed by his first name, and it is clear that the senior pilot is fully aware of where the pilot has his family, and what his career intentions are. Quite a few intend to go to fixed wing, if possible British Airways itself; we are operating in their helicopter division, after all. Clearly, senior management cares about its pilots, and works at keeping them happy and feeling supported. There is no mention about the BAH Chinook accident or its aftermath. A lot of the pilots at Sumburgh who obviously flew the Chinook are now back flying the S61N. In crew-room conversation the subject is not mentioned, so I keep quiet about my applying to fly the Chinook for the RAF in 1968 and volunteering to go to Philadelphia for six weeks training. In the event, the RAF cancelled its first order for Chinooks and my career progressed down the SAR route. One day I fly with the captain of the Chinook that crashed; he was one of the two survivors and is now flying the S61N again. The flight goes well and my logbook shows a second flight a month later. When the senior pilot speaks to me, I confirm that I am happy flying again after six months off and that I am happy flying two trips a day to gain experience. He asks me if I would be willing to continue beyond the initial three months contract into the winter months, and I confirm that I want to fly on for as long as possible. He nods his understanding and moves on.

On that first detachment in July, I complete 16 flights and 50 hours of flying, of which 10 hours were flying on instruments and included four ILS approaches. So it's back to the Aberdeen Operation and living at home for a couple of weeks. It seems so civilised after operating in the Shetlands, and home life is very comfortable. Checking on advertisements for flying jobs, there seems nothing suitable so far, so I keep on checking and updating my CV. I am grateful to be back in flying practice; it makes getting another flying job that much easier.

Back to operating out of Sumburgh, I find that the room I am allocated has a computer, covered over with warning notices: "Please don't touch." I don't, but there are magazines about portraying small electronic companies. Perhaps this pilot is, like others, working on a small business venture, which he will take up full time when he gives up flying. One night after dinner, conversation drifts on to the Government Privatisation programme, with the first one being British Telecom with its "Tell Sid" adverts. Some people have sold their shares as soon as they received them. Some, like myself, have hung and watch the share value grow and have received dividends. Also running at the same time was the "demutualisation" of many Building Societies. For £100, you could become a member and participate in the share out of the Reserves, typically giving a return of £1000, sometimes more. Very safe and very rewarding.

The Daily Telegraph published a comprehensive list of Building Societies and their stated intension to demutualise and the proposed date for starting the procedure. My experiences of these schemes are listened to thoughtfully. Meanwhile, as we progress into autumn the weather becomes worse and we spend more time flying on instruments, using our weather radar to identify the offshore installations and the radio to keep track of other aircraft movements nearby. I am flying two flights a day, usually flying with the same captain all day. I am teamed up with all the captains, so that they can assess my competence going into winter. To me, everything is new and exciting, and each captain has a different view where discretion is allowed. One captain chooses not to carry more fuel than is strictly necessary. His view is that the lighter the helicopter, the faster it will go and with less vibration. I fly with him several times and we always land with our reserve fuel intact, proving his point. I am happy to fly with any captain in terms of fuel requirements as long as we start with at least the minimum. Given the choice, however, I would take an extra 15 minutes' fuel, say 300 pounds. It is not my choice, and as on other matters I keep my opinions to myself until I am asked. The more captains fly with me, the more I am asked about my North Sea experience of flying to different platforms and into different airfields.

Back at Aberdeen, the company rolls out a Cockpit Resources Management (CRM) course. After many decades of aircraft operating around the world, authorities have realised that the way crews work and make decisions could be improved. The two-day course is largely common sense, so I have little trouble with the course questionnaire at the end and duly get the certificate for my flying logbook. We also get a pre-winter briefing, nothing new there, but we will be using more fuel, for the cabin heater and engine anti-icing. Also, we need to ensure that at 500 feet above the North Sea the ambient temperature is above zero, so we can, if required, descend to 500 feet and melt any airframe ice we might have accumulated. Flying continues at Aberdeen up to 2nd December. When I come back from my second trip the chief pilot tells me our short-term contracts have come to an end. Time to hand in my immersion suit, make up my logbook and clear my locker. The short-term contract, for all of us, has lasted many months more than expected. Total flying has been 372 hours with 20 ILS approaches, a valuable experience in a very reliable helicopter. Time off over Christmas and time to talk to an Australian ex-Bristow colleague who, rumour has it, is flying in the Netherlands. Could be another opportunity, now where is his phone number …

Chapter 20: Joining
KLM Helicopters

I call my Australian colleague, Martin Donohue, and fix to go to his house for a long chat. We discuss the ad in Flight magazine: "Wanted: S61N pilots for European Operation, apply Box No..." He describes his involvement with KLM Helicopters, based at Schiphol Airport near Amsterdam. They need pilots to man a UN operation in Croatia, as their own pilots are reluctant to go. Objections are around mountain flying, no radar inland, and no let-down aids. Also, the helicopters will be flying across the ceasefire line; not something they have signed up for. Management feel that British pilots with an ATPL, IR, and military experience might be suitable. He has flown there for over a month following extensive training. I write down the place names, the type of flying involved, accommodation, pay, and allowances. He is flying as a captain but is not well-briefed or looked after on the ground. The flying is good, but the ground organisation could be a lot better. Suitably briefed, I apply for the job in the magazine and within a few days get a phone call to go for an interview at Norwich Airport.

As there is extensive flooding in Norfolk, I decide to fly down rather than drive. I arrive, am given a coffee, and meet up with ex-Navy Geoff Newman. At the interview with two directors, I explain what I like about the operation and where my SAR and military experience could be useful. It is clear they have not been to the operation, so were pleased to be told what goes on. After meeting several other candidates, I return home to sit by the telephone for the next few days. Sure enough, the call comes through: an offer of employment as a First Officer (co-pilot) for the duration of the contract, a nominal two years. Although I was aged over 45, in fact 52, they liked my experience, my qualifications and my enthusiasm. Initially, after training, I would serve three weeks in Croatia, followed by two weeks back in UK. If acceptable to me, I could start by flying out of Aberdeen to Schiphol and start training.

Within a few days I am flying in an Air UK Fokker Friendship with my suitcase. I meet up with my company contact and am driven to HQ to be met by Geoff Newman. Younger than me, he is going to be a captain, and we are the only two that are being hired for the moment. We have a lot of training before we can fly in Croatia. Firstly, Geoff and I have to attend a medical at the Central Aviation Unit, where they do all medicals for civil and military pilots. We are given a hire car for the day; Geoff drives, I navigate, and we get there for our 10 a.m. appointment. We check in, each given a folder, and go from room to room being checked out by a range of doctors. The new items for us are blood tests and assessment of the tendency to be affected by flashing lights. For this test, a crown of equipment is placed on the head, lights are flashed at irregular intervals, and the brain waves are measured. Ideally, the brain activity should die down within three seconds of a flash. For some people, irregular flashing lights can upset their balance and leave them feeling disoriented. Luckily, as helicopter pilots Geoff and I are used to flashing lights caused by the main rotor blades, so we pass. The blood tests are apparently to check for dread diseases. We pass on that one as well. 4 pm, and I am in front of the chief doctor. I am assessed as very fit for my age. He likes my walking for exercise, he likes my moderate drinking, and he likes my not smoking. His message: carry on the good work. When he asks me what my job is going to be, he shows concern that I am going to Croatia to fly for the UN. To reassure him I have explain that this is not Bosnia, and a ceasefire has been agreed between the combatants. Our job is to help keep the combatants apart by serving the armed battalions from various countries that are stationed there as Peacekeepers. Duly processed, Geoff and I head back to base.

Tomorrow we are headed for the National Aviation Training School near Maastricht to learn Dutch Air Law.

In the classroom we are mingling with young men and women set for a career in aviation. In most cases they have got "Career Learning Loans" from banks or Mum and Dad to pay for the expensive course. They accept that they will be co-pilots for at least 10 years before getting a command, but the pay and allowances are good, as well as the working atmosphere. They are enthusiastic and keen to learn, inspiring to us older guys. After two days, Geoff and I take the exam, a question of ticking the right answers. I pass with 81% and paste the certificate in my flying logbook. Back to base, then the morning flight on 14th February, with instructors, up to Stavanger. On arrival we climb aboard a taxi and head for a five-star hotel in the centre of town, a very pleasant location. Quick lunch, then off to Helicopter Services to view their S61N flight simulator for a long gentle briefing, and then an hour sitting in the cockpit getting used to the cockpit layout and the wrap around visual in front. We will be practicing using airfield approach aids at Rotterdam and Schiphol Airports, as we might operate there in the future. Geoff, as he is wanted as a captain, is to be given priority; I will act as co-pilot, providing support and learning all the time. The simulator flies well and can be landed on the sea, rocking gently on the ocean swell as we shut down. Besides us, flying the S61N simulator, there is a group from the RAF using the Super Puma flight simulator. At lunchtimes there is a chance to meet up. The RAF have had the Super Puma and the Chinook for many years, and I find one or two of my RAF SAR colleagues are now flying these Army support helicopters, mainly around Salisbury Plain. It is a small world.

Croatia – One typical day in 1994

"Zagreb Tower, this is UN Oscar One Nine Zero requesting start up for flight to Knin."

There is a dull pause while the Croatian Air Traffic Controller considers our flight plan into the Serb-held area and its centre at Knin. Finally, "The One Nine Zero is clear start up and taxi to holding point Charlie, call reaching."

We begin the start up checks challenge and response, setting the levers and switches, ready to push the button on the first engine. Now we going at last, the worries melt away. With both engines and rotor running smoothly on our KLM Helicopter Sikorsky S61N we signal chocks away and move gently forward, checking the brakes immediately. We note the watching bystanders, the engineers, the boss, and a few flight crew and exchange brief waves. We taxi past the American Operation with their Bell 212s. At the end of the day we will compare our day's experiences, with the weather, our various air traffic regimes and our spy in the sky – the AWACs aircraft. As we taxi, we pass a big Mill 26 (Mi 26 Halo) helicopter from Ukraine – a mechanic rushes out to signal that we are taxiing well clear of the rotor blades. We know that, but it is comforting to get confirmation.

As we approach holding point Charlie, we receive our departure clearance – normal route to cross the Ceasefire Line, initial height 2,500 feet. We confirm and wait to enter the runway for a take-off to the east. While waiting, we note the cargo jumbo on the far side of the airfield, still unloading it's military cargo 24 hours after arrival. We are cleared to line up and take off. We check the runway both ways for other aircraft – all is quiet – we line up and lift into the hover. With temperature and pressures all checked we move forward, gaining height and speed.

At 200 feet, the instruction, "Turn left now onto north, climb to and maintain 1,000 feet." We acknowledge and turn away from the runway – perhaps one of the fighters on quick reaction alert has been scrambled and we are in the way? We don't ask – just obey. Eventually we are cleared for normal routing, the two GPS systems both agreeing and both aligned with the map as we pass over the same river bridge as we have done many times. Time to get established with the AWACs circling over the Adriatic Sea at 30,000 feet. We give a position report, aircraft squawk code (radar identity), souls on board, and ETA.

"You are identified," booms a South African voice; that's a new one to us in the cockpit but we don't comment. On track, approaching the Ceasefire Line crossing point, we change frequencies and call the Serb-controlled airfield we will pass in 20 minutes. Today no reply, so we maintain our authorised course over the ground. Sometimes they reply, sometimes they don't, but we know they always listen out. Rumour has it that they are not being paid, that could account for it.

A welcoming smell of coffee penetrates the cockpit. Hans, a new crewman from Schiphol, pushes forward the plastic cups and they are drunk straightaway. The passengers were looked after first, and being a large helicopter, we can supply this service. I look back into the cabin and the passengers are reading papers, books, or briefing notes. None are looking out at the lovely vineyards, and hilltop villages we are passing, but below there is also destruction – houses, hotels and factories in ruins, no road traffic, no farmers' tractors, all is quiet, quite strange. We are flying towards the mountains and can see low cloud hiding the tops and the passes we hoped to use. We exercise the option of climbing and transiting above it all. At 8,000 feet we are clear VMC on top, but we can hear our American cousins battling through the bad weather below.

Now we are high, we can call our destination, 100 miles away at Knin. It is the Canadian Battalion base that we are talking to.

Their weather is good and the surface wind light and variable. We are happy with our navigation, with both independent GPS systems agreeing our position and our ETA. With 30 miles to go, the cloud below thins, and we can see the old town of Knin ahead. There is some road traffic, but no trains, and the rails are rusty. With smoke drifting up from a fire on the ground, we note the surface wind direction and opt for an approach down a long valley ending up at the landing area. This, a huge slab of concrete sitting on top of a reservoir that supplies the military base, is now part Serb-controlled and part UN. As we finish our approach and come to the hover, we are aware of armed guards looking at us as we touch down on one of the helicopter pads. All is well and we shut down completely before the passengers disembark into waiting coaches. We refuel and our crewman, also a mechanic, supervises this. All postflight checks complete, the crew stroll down to the UN base below, sticking to the paved surface in case of land mines being planted in the grass. We pass some Canadian soldiers, who guard the base, cleaning their vehicles, which are brimming with both cannons and machine guns.

UN armoured Patrol Vehicles at UN Base at KNIN

We say good morning, and because we are displaying our UN ID badges, we are not challenged. Arriving at the Canadians' Orderly Room, we are told that our return flight departs at 4 p.m., but to remain on-base on standby in case there is a medevac requirement. Time to kill, so first to the outdoor café, run by a Serb and his Croatian wife. Two years previously they had been running a small hotel on the coast, then, as the civil war broke out, the family were given 24 hours' notice to quit or have their hotel burnt down around them. They boarded a bus with other Serb families with all they could carry and were dumped near the front line. Eventually they got to Knin, established a café on the UN base, and began to put their lives back together. They produce good coffee, and we sit in the shade of a thatched open wooden building discussing the latest company news – we are up for sale apparently – but there is nothing we can do except carry on with the task and enjoy it while we can.

Relaxing in the sunshine at the UN Base at KNIN

An hour later we can check in for lunch at the UN canteen. One US dollar for a hot lunch for UN-badged people. They have come from all over the world, with a range of clothes and languages. Some UN observers are in, dressed top to toe in white, with their binoculars, radios, and notebooks, but no weapons.

UN Observers, dressed overall in white and unarmed

We find some Canadians and sit down. They are discussing an incident the previous night, when one of their patrols laid an ambush and surprised an armed group who they challenged. The response was a burst of automatic fire, and a serious firefight erupted. A minute later, six gunmen are dead; they are checked for ID, they have none. The weapons are gathered up and the bodies are buried on site with no marker. These encounters are not unusual, and the Canadians have gained a reputation for being serious about their responsibilities concerning armed bands roaming the countryside in their sector. We don't wear any body protection in the cockpit, but the floor of the cabin and cockpit has a layer of Kevlar to protect everyone from small arms fire. So far, the two machines have only collected one .22 bullet in the tail, probably from a shepherd in the hills who we may have annoyed by overflying his flock one day.

An hour before take-off we are given our route, initially to Split airfield, which is joint civil/ military, shut down for half an hour, then return to Zagreb up the coast, not above 1,500 feet, via Šibenik, Zadar, and Crikvenica, where we will coast in. The weather is good at Zagreb. We load up the helicopter with the pax and freight, no medevacs today, and start up. As we lift off, we pass over the Serb store of artillery and tanks, all looking ready to go.

Before we have time to lift the undercarriage, AWACS booms, "We see the One Nine Zero lifting from Knin for Split call level."

"Roger wilco," is our reply as we run through the post-take-off checks. After 10 minutes crossing semi-desert countryside, we approach the ceasefire line with a chain of white UN observation posts strung along it. The observers will have seen our lights for at least 10 miles before the beat of the main rotor becomes apparent. As we pass overhead, we check we have our squawk responding, and call Split on their approach frequency with our position report and ETA. Again, there is a long pause as the Croatian controller considers our flight plan. Eventually we are cleared for VFR entry for the easterly runway to call three miles. The weather is fine, and we can see the airfield and the mountains behind and the azure blue sea; I make a mental note to return some day on holiday when this is all over. As we are cleared to finals, I look to the right and note the helicopter base, full of military machines which operate into Bosnia on a daily basis. We carry out a running landing on the runway and taxi off right towards a crowded aircraft parking area, and are marshalled to a shut-down spot close to the control tower.

The one runway airfield at Split, base for flights into Bosnia

Pax and crew stream into the terminal and are met by a Norwegian logistics team, headed by a very young lady with her clipboard. She gives out her instructions in perfect English, so we all know what we are doing. I go to the tower to confirm the UN flight plan already submitted. As I walk across the dispersal, I am stopped twice by armed soldiers checking my UN ID badge. They let me through to the tower. There I speak to the airfield controllers, confirming our route, weather, and souls on board. The dispersal is full of Lockheed Hercules transports, both RAF and RCAF, with cargo being unloaded everywhere.

All back together in the helicopter, we are cleared to start up and taxi to the holding point just before the runway. Checks complete, we take off towards the mountains and turn right, and are cleared en route, not above 1,500 feet; no problem, as we have a beautiful coastline to look at, with some lovely old fortified towns carefully preserved. Then we fly over a modern shipyard with a half-completed vessel rusting on the slipway, the cranes stationary, and nobody about. We turn right to track up the coast, passing over many islands. The sea is deserted, the modern marinas are empty, the roads quiet, but the limestone-based scenery is lovely to gaze upon. Many small towns pass by, along with major towns with extensive harbours such as Šibenik and Zadar; the latter has an airstrip, and most nights a small fixed wing delivers mail from Zagreb. The airstrip is close to the ceasefire line, so landings are made without using lights, so far without problems.

As we progress up the coast, cloud appears, and we choose to climb above it, initially to 6,000 feet. Air traffic clears us to route northeast towards Karlovac and on to Zagreb, climbing as necessary to stay above cloud, as the outside air temperature is dropping towards zero and we want to avoid icing. Along the coastal mountains is a long sheet of cloud, and we climb to 10,000 feet, our maximum, to stay well above the gleaming white expanse. Even though our airspeed is reduced, our speed over the ground is 200 knots, with our navigation systems showing a tailwind of nearly 100 knots, although we experience no turbulence. As the air beneath us passes over the coastal mountains, it descends, heats up, and the cloud evaporates, leaving just a thick haze. We request and are granted descent to 5,000 feet and request an ILS approach to Zagreb's easterly runway. For some reason, this is not available at this time, but we are offered a step-down radar approach instead. All is well until, approaching a mile from touchdown in thick haze, we are informed the runway threshold is 20 degrees off to the left. We turn and continue descent, being in contact with the ground, but cannot see any approach lights. We check with the tower and are informed they are changing runways for a fixed wing, probably Croatia Airlines, coming in at the other end, so the lights for our approach have been switched off. We find the runway threshold in the murk, touch down, and taxi off the runway, stop, complete our landing checks and begin a gentle taxi towards the UN dispersal. Across to the right are parked large white Ilyushin passenger jets that may have made the trip into Sarajevo today. They are not always welcome there and occasionally return to Zagreb with multiple bullet holes. The crews are issued with flack vests, which they position under their seats!

The crews from Ukraine are paid well and after two years can retire comfortably … all being well.

We taxi slowly into our crowded dispersal, stop, shut down and then unload our passengers. They stream off and are looked after by the UN logistics team. As the crew leave the helicopter, I see our Dutch captain reach forward for a small teddy, which he puts in his flight bag. "It has always brought me good luck and brought me home safely." I can't argue with that as we all stroll into the hangar, check in with the engineers, and sign up the flight authorisation sheets.

The boss looks up as we go into the crew room. "Drinks are in the fridge – top shelf. If you want coffee it's on the Cona machine."

I opt for a beer, which just disappears, change out of flight gear, and check when I will be required to check in tomorrow – 10 a.m. – gentleman's hours. Things are improving already as I prepare to walk home to the British pilots' house, a mile through fields into the nearby town of Velika Gorica, putting my UN pass out of sight. As I pass a pizza place I decide to pop in; I am surrounded by burly men and shuffled to a round table. As I sit down, glasses of beer arrive and I glance at the faces around me; some look familiar, possibly some of our engineers. They speak English to me; they have been changing a rotor head today, the chunky bit at the heart of the rotor. It is heavy and delicate and needs careful handling, but it all went well so they are celebrating. We discuss what the company is up to – nobody seems to want to buy it yet. The EU and its machinations come up for comment, as well as the activities of the UN. Nearby is large field full of white motorbikes and vehicles that have not moved for months, but it retains an armed guard around it day and night. They have been told that the fields around the airfield boundary were sewn with anti-personnel land mines during the civil war, so no exploration off tarmac surfaces in future.

Suitably fortified, I head for home and find it immaculate. Our housekeeper, a Croatian teacher, looks after us and the house, and with excellent English tells us about the shooting that went on during the civil war. When her house came under attack one night, she bundled her children under the bed as bullets took out the windows. As well as looking after us pilots, she acts as interpreter for the UN mission, where she is well regarded and rewarded. Her husband helps service the Russian-built transports that fly into Bosnia from Zagreb, repairing them when necessary.

As ten o'clock approaches, I prepare for bed, set two alarm clocks for 8 a.m., and place them out of reach from the bed. I phone home in Scotland; calls are free but probably monitored, being an UN house, so I keep my conversation discreet. All is well at home – lots of small problems but all can be fixed – due home in a few weeks, so some treats being bought. I feel the adrenaline running out, and in bed I settle down with some light reading – UN Standard Operating Instructions. Then, for no good reason – alarm clock! *You cannot be serious!*

We have a ground taxiing accident on a very hot day, using a temporary parking area. The co-pilot is the handling pilot and there are no white lines for guidance. Main rotor tips strike an extension to a former Air Traffic Control tower, knocking out bricks and pieces of concrete, some smashing through the windows of our operations room. The helicopter is towed into hangar for damage assessment, rotor blades all bent back, clearly needing replacement, but what else has been damaged internally? An engineer from Sikorsky comes out with a jig to see if the alignment of the main rotor gearbox to the fuselage was undamaged. It is not distorted, but the main rotor gear box has suffered a shock loading and will be replaced as part of the repairs. These will be done in Holland, and the helicopter will be transported by air in a Russian Heavy Lift aircraft, an Antonov AN 124, with nose opening cargo door. It is parked on main dispersal and the S61N is winched in backwards, rotor blades secured alongside. The nose door is closed and the huge aircraft taxis out and lumbers up into the sky. Two weeks later, our helicopter is replaced.

The AN 124 heavy lift cargo plane with our helicopter inside.

Chapter 21: Operating in Croatia

(1994)

9 a.m. 2nd April 1994: Martin comes back from the ops room with today's task. We are taking the Force Commander to Klisa, about 100 miles east. Because of security considerations, travelling by helicopter is the best and quickest way to travel. The scheduled take-off is 10 a.m., time enough to have a good look at the weather forecast. It is bad, rain and low cloud, especially over high ground. Wind from the west at 30 knots, no improvement until nightfall. Because we have been tasked, we feel we need to give it a try. Our passengers are the French UNPROFOR Commander, General Bertrand de Sauville de la Presle, and six staff. They arrive in a convoy of vehicles, board the helicopter, and are seated so that they can communicate to some degree. Start-up and taxi are no problem, and we request a VFR departure to the east at 1,000 feet, staying in sight of the ground. Initially we find no difficulty, with the Sat Navs working in agreement and easy-to-spot pinpoints on the ground. We pass over the VOR aerial, now switched off deliberately but still serving as a reporting point. The weather deteriorates as we progress east, and we are forced to descend to 500 feet above ground to remain clear of cloud. It does not look good, as we know there is high ground covered in trees further east with no low-level passes. It is the classical situation: ground rising, cloud base coming down, and a strong tailwind. We are discussing turning back when suddenly we are enveloped in cloud. We know we can't proceed in cloud because we have no let-down aids at the destination, so we both shout "Full power!" and Martin starts gaining height rapidly, turning right onto reciprocal heading. Safety height off the map is 3,000 feet and Martin levels at that, still in thick cloud. I talk to Zagreb control; they can see us on their radar and clear us for an ILS approach straight in on their westerly runway. We pick

up the localiser beam and then the glide path, noting the weather has deteriorated since we left. Still, the ILS should get us down to 200 feet above the runway, even though it is raining hard. At 250 feet on final approach, I report approach lights seen and at 200 feet Martin looks up and continues descent to the runway in pouring rain. Because we can't see the control tower, we report our touchdown and request the normal taxying to our UN dispersal. So cleared, we taxi in and close down. As the rotor stops, a convoy of cars draws up and the General and his entourage disembark, not glancing back but driving off to sort out different travel arrangements. We walk into the shelter of our hangar and into our crew-room, half expecting criticism of our actions; 1 hour 30 minutes' flying and nothing achieved. But over coffee we hear that the General is pleased that we tried; we took the right decision to turn back, and he is going by road.

Another VIP trip occurs on 14th June. I am flying with Captain Jacques Van-de-Bliek and I have no inkling of the importance of the return flight from the joint UN/Serb barracks alongside the town of Knin, 100 miles south of Zagreb. He is less conversational than usual on the outbound journey, but we arrive on time, shut down and refuel. Only when our crew of three are sitting together over a coffee does he reveal that we are carrying the US Ambassador to Croatia back to Zagreb with his support group of six. There are no other passengers, so it is likely they will be working together during the flight. Sure enough, when they board at 3 p.m. they choose the two double seats that face each other, with three single seats just across the aisle. They board with their attaché cases, strap in, and start exchanging paperwork as we start up. Ten minutes into the flight our crewman serves them coffee and biscuits and gives them our ETA at Zagreb. They carry on working away for the whole journey; fortunately, the weather is good, the helicopter remains fully serviceable, and our Serb Air Traffic Controller cheerfully ignores our radio calls as usual as we fly through his sector. On arrival at dispersal we see the VIP cars and military escort vehicles lined up. As we shut down the engines, with the rotor still turning the guard waves the vehicles forward under our rotor blades, which bend up and down as we slow the rotor with the brake. Not the thing to do, and in the cockpit, we can only hope that a vehicle is not struck. Our group climb into the vehicles and head off behind the escort vehicles with their blue lights flashing and sirens blaring. We must remember in future to control the outside environment until the engines are shut down and the rotor stopped.

One day I am in the house, not required for flying, and our housekeeper arrives. As she speaks good English, I start a conversation about the general situation. She is guarded with what she says, so I offer to make us both a coffee and even find some biscuits. I explain what I am doing, here in Croatia for three weeks then back to Scotland for two. My logbook has a photograph of a white S61N with big black "UN" letters painted in prominent positions. She says that she has seen them flying about. I mention about flying down to Knin, the centre of the Serb-controlled area, and she clearly does not believe me. So, I get out my maps, lay them on the dining room table and show her the routes we typically use and the towns we overfly. More than that, I produce a batch of photographs of the places we stop at, like Split, and the coastal towns we often overfly. For the past two years these places have been off limits to the general population. Some of the photographs show towns intact. Others show factories destroyed, bridges down, and residential properties burnt to the ground. She finds it difficult to believe that UN helicopters can cross the Ceasefire Line without delay, knowing that on the ground UN convoys can only cross at agreed crossing points, sometimes with long delays as the local politics are sorted out. Some aid convoys carrying food and medicine to cut-off communities on the wrong side encounter pop-up check points on the road. After the appropriate "gift" has been handed over to the local militia, the convoy can proceed. In order to get some aid through, a high loss rate en-route is accepted. She mentions her family and the frightening time they experienced while the

Civil War was raging around them. Since the Ceasefire was negotiated and the UN moved in things have stabilised, although there is still tension in the air. Families are split up; many are refugees in their own country, and unable to go back to their previous communities.

I offer to meet the family one evening at the local pizza place. She says the food there is trash, far better that I meet the family at her apartment and have some proper homecooked food. He husband will pick me up and return me by car. It is an offer I can't refuse, and we agree on a Saturday night as we don't usually fly on Sunday, as essential maintenance and cleaning of our helicopters is carried out. At the agreed date and time, a big Citroen car arrives with the correct number plate and I climb in with my flight bag. My driver does not speak English, so I just concentrate on where we are going in town. We draw up at a block of apartments and I follow him to the lift. As we enter the apartment, I am grabbed by "Grandma" and kissed on both cheeks. I was not expecting that as a form of welcome! In the room are my housekeeper, her husband, Grandma, and two boys around mid-teens. Everyone is curious about what this British helicopter pilot from Scotland is doing in Croatia. I gently explain, and every sentence I utter is translated; her husband clearly understands English but chooses not to speak it. After a few minutes I get out the maps and lay them on the floor so all can see. There is rapid excited conversation around me. When that dies down, I get out the photographs, mainly taken from the air. They are passed around and the places recognised. For two years they have not been able to travel in their own country, and here is a stranger flying around over land and sea on a daily basis. It is an odd situation, but maybe the UN will sort out the situation eventually. With a flourish we are summoned to the dining room. There are bottles of wine on the table and cans of soft drinks for the boys. The pizzas arrive, and my glass of potent red wine is topped up. The atmosphere is good, and I can see from the glances that I am accepted, indeed, being made very welcome. As we finish the meal and are served coffee, I am told there is going to be an important announcement on State Television by their First President, Franjo Tudman. I can tell by his gestures and powerful voice that matters are serious, and volunteers are needed for the Army to defend the country. The teenage boys hold their hands up and shout in support; clearly, they want to volunteer, in spite of the risks. Mum and Dad nod their agreement. The boys have a few years before they are old enough. Perhaps things will settle down, the tourists will come back, and they will be able to travel both inside and outside the country. I don't remember the rest of the evening, but I must have got home somehow, finding my bed and sleeping soundly to mid-morning.

The evening of 20th November, I am waiting for a call from Geoff Newman as to what my task is the next day. After an hour's wait, I call Ops, and am told there will be no UN helicopter flying anywhere in Croatia the next day. Not had this before, but I don't argue or question. I will probably walk into the base mid-morning for exercise and get an update; I have got the task of doing the amendments for our books of airfield approach charts, so I will be kept occupied. At 6 p.m. I check into Ops for next day's programme; again, there will be no UN helicopter flying in Croatia.

So, I ask, "What is happening?"

The Ops officer is guarded, but says, "There has been a NATO airstrike today on the Serb airbase of Udbina. In the past few weeks this base has been used to carry out air strikes in Bosnia and Herzegovina. This NATO raid hopefully will deter further attacks."

Not surprisingly, helicopters are not allowed to fly into Serb-held areas for three weeks while repairs are being made to Udbina airfield. However, we are tasked to fly to Split, and by following the coastal route we can stay above areas controlled by the Croatian Government. News leaks out that the raid on Udbina was the biggest air combat operation in Europe since World War II, and the largest combat operation in NATO's history. Grounded for three weeks, I use the time to replace the maps on the crew-room wall showing our main routes, and I go through and check the boxes of emergency maps held in each helicopter. Sitting in our crew-room I see engineers from the American units alongside us in the hangar pop into our engineering stores for the odd roll of paper, some nuts and bolts, and barrier cream for their hands. Out of curiosity I ask one of our engineers to show me the room, with its benches and shelving. There are a lot of spare parts, tools, and equipment essential to service two helicopters, in all costing the equivalent of a million pounds; sobering for a pilot whose job is to fly the helicopter during the day and hand it back to the engineers at dusk to be refuelled, cleaned, serviced, and re-paired as necessary to be ready next morning for the next day's tasking. With the helicopters being grounded I am able to spend some time conversing in English with our engineers. They are on permanent career contracts and would, if necessary, serve in the fixed wing side of the KLM airline. Many have been abroad, and they like this overseas operation, going back to their fami-lies in Holland from time to time.

Towards the end of the year, Geoff Newman takes over as chief pilot. It makes sense, as all the pilots are now British, and some have brought their wives out to stay with them in Croatia, rent-ing their own accommodation. Plans are being discussed about Christmas and New Year. The families of the engineers based in Holland are invited down for both festivities to see what their menfolk get up to. The families squeeze into their accommoda-tion and come up to the unit every day. The UN allows us up to two passengers on our flights down to Knin or Split, giving the chance of a return flight over the coast on our return. The wives are most impressed with the scenery and plan to come back on holiday when things are back to normal. I feel I have to hand out large maps of Croatia to the boys to go on bedroom walls when they get back. I have a quiet Christmas on my own, relieved by a long telephone call to Scotland. Over New Year I am invited to a colleague's house for the celebrations. As we approach midnight, about 30 of us stream out onto the lawn to watch the fireworks. The rockets go whizzing up, the bangers are loud, and we see the glow of bonfires. After a few minutes we begin to hear what is clearly machine-gun fire, with tracer bullets flying skywards. One of our ex-Army pilots identifies the guns involved, and our housekeeper explains that during the Civil War most men kept machine guns in their house basement, the bigger the better, from a status point of view. With bullets dropping out of the sky, we are ushered back into the house to watch events through the windows; the children are excited but hang on to mother's hand for security!

One of the company directors is with us for a few days. He tells me that I will be promoted to Senior First Officer in the New Year on the anniversary of joining the company. My pay and life insurance will both increase significantly. Because I still carry life insurance from Bristow up to age 58, I am now worth a lot more dead than alive! Comforting in a way, but not worth worrying about. 1995 has started well; I have been a permanent resident in the British pilots' house for some time, enabling me to build up my stock of clothing, shoes, books, and food. The contract with the UN is due to last to the end of August, a long way away. For exercise, I walk the mile into the UN base in the morning, and most evenings I walk home, feeling totally secure. The future looks good, but I know there will be surprises, just have to take them in my stride …

Our Sikorsky S61N on the landing pad at KNIN.

Chapter 22: Leaving Croatia

We are all gathering in the passenger lounge at Split airport. Around the room are air crews from various Air Forces, flying the Hercules tactical transport aircraft, and ourselves, distinguished by our various flight suits. Conversation is muted; crews keep to themselves, seated around tables nursing soft drinks or coffees, all of us waiting for news. Eventually a spokesman from the Logistics team claps his hands; the place is silent.

He starts off, "There has been a rocket attack on Zagreb and the airport. In the Central Square, seven people have been killed and hundreds injured. The airport has been damaged. When I have further news I will bring it to you. You should all stay here until you receive details of your next task. That is all."

There is a murmur of conversation across the room. We all knew that something was happening. Perhaps after another coffee we can get a call through to Geoff Newman back at base to find out more details. Our captain, John Allan, heads off to the Logistics Office and comes back 15 minutes later looking a bit grim. He has spoken to Geoff Newman, who is at his desk wearing a tin hat and thick clothing. Our helicopters and crews are all safe and secure, though one pilot's car has a window shattered by flying debris. There is damage on and around the airport. The company has decided to pull the operation out of Croatia; details of how this will be done will follow later. We are to stay where we are until the details are agreed. Another coffee then, and a quick look at the lunch menu; we could be stuck here for some time. After lunch, our captain tries again. The news is we are to take off late afternoon and head across the Adriatic Sea to Italy and land at Ancona Airport. After overnighting there, we are to fly direct to Graz in Austria, bypassing Zagreb Airport. The unit will assemble at a hotel and details of our ongoing journey to Holland will be worked out. Meanwhile our kit in our accommodation will be collected and brought to us at Graz. The Dutch Army is helping us with moving aircraft spare parts and personal items. We will be paid for any food and drink that we have left in our accommodation. Once we are in Italy, we will be updated.

Now we know what's required, John and I head out to our helicopter and open the emergency map box. We take out what we need and plot a course for Ancona, and in Air Traffic Control we file a flight plan. We are cleared to take off at dusk, and with the forecast wind the flight should take one hour and thirty minutes. We have four hours' fuel endurance and the details of the airport and approach facilities in our handy airport guide. The weather forecast for the sea crossing is good, so at 2,000 feet we should be clear of cloud and in sight of the surface. As departure time draws near, we check out with the Norwegian Logistics Team and walk out to our helicopter as the sun is setting. As we start up, I put our flight details into the Sat Navs and read off our first course, northwest across the Adriatic Sea. We are saying goodbye to Split Airport, which we know well, heading to Ancona Airport, and landing there in the dark. At least all the lights should be on.

The take-off and departure are normal as we head out over the dark sea, eventually being handed over to Italian Air Traffic Control. As we approach the coast, we can see the bright lights of Ancona; we need to go 10 miles past it before we turn left, see the runway approach lights and call the tower for landing clearance. We are cleared to land and follow a small vehicle with a flashing light to our shut-down spot, well clear of the main parking area. As we shut down, a fuel bowser turns up. I check that it is jet fuel and show the man the pressure refuelling point on the port side of the fuselage, and within minutes all our tanks are full. Quick, safe and no spillage. I am ready to sign for the fuel we have picked up, but the bowser driver has noted that we are UN white all over, with 191 in black figures for identity. That's all he needs. He calls the tower and asks for a car from the airport service company to come over and pick up our crew. Within minutes we check in at Air Traffic Control and agree we will submit a flight plan tomorrow for our trip to Graz. Our car takes us into town, to a big hotel and at reception we ask if we can go into the restaurant for a late dinner. Yes, we can, but it will be a fixed menu: lasagne, ice cream, coffee and biscuits, and house wine. We can cope with that. It feels strange sitting in our grubby flying suits, all on our own in a well-appointed restaurant. All of us have big glasses of wine, which wash away our anxieties. Tomorrow is another day, and it will look after itself.

I don't remember the room or the bed, but the knock on the door at 8 a.m. tells me it's time to get up and get some breakfast. Two hours later we report to Air Traffic Control, check the weather forecast and calculate the flight time to Graz of 2 hours, 30 minutes. We note the reporting points en route and submit our flight plan. Thirty minutes later we are ready for take-off, which we can do from where we are because we are in a helicopter with nobody else near. Climbing to 5,000 feet, and heading northeast, we are heading towards Zagreb; there are no problems with the radio calls, all in perfect English. As we pass the city we can make out the airport in the distance, the runway, the hangars, the passenger terminal; it all seems peaceful, but we see no aircraft flying.

Passing across Slovenia, we are handed over to Austrian Air Traffic Control and cleared descent to 2,000 feet and to contact Graz. So doing, we are identified on radar and guided in for a straight-in approach to their north-facing runway. As we descend below 500 feet on final approach, we can see another white helicopter in an area well away from the main parking area. Sure enough, after landing we are directed over to that area, and under the guidance of a marshaller we taxi to a spot alongside it and shut down. It is good to see familiar smiling faces. We hand the helicopter over to the engineers, climb aboard a vehicle, and head to a lovely hotel in the centre of Graz. We meet up with Geoff Newman and are treated to sandwiches, coffee, and cake. That should keep us going till the briefing before dinner!

Our crew are allocated a lovely room each with a bath and a shower, no expense spared for the few days we are going to be here. Time for a shave and a hot bath, but no change of clothes yet. We will find out everything that is happening at the mass briefing at 6 p.m. in the conference room. As we assemble, I spy a collection of suitcases at the back of the room. Mine is there, so I open it and find fresh clothes, wash kit, towel, and in a discreet pocket, an envelope containing my allowances. Lucky boy, to hang on to that. After the briefing there might be time to spruce up before dinner, but in the meantime I get out my notebook and pencil; I have a feeling there will be a lot to remember.

The room is crowded with pilots, cabin attendants, engineers, and wives as Geoff Newman stands up to talk. "Tomorrow we will load up our two helicopters with the spare parts; those not required to help have a day off in Graz. The hotel reception has maps of the town. We will meet up again tomorrow at 6 p.m. The plan is that that the helicopters will depart for Holland, via Germany, during the morning of 5th May. Those with cars will be able to depart on 5th or 6th May as you think fit, meeting up at our HQ at Den Helder Airport in due course. We have some suitcases at the back of the room, with most of your kit, so claim your own. The Dutch Army are going back through the accommodation we have used and will bag up any personal possessions that are left, leaving behind any food or drink, for which you can invoice me at a later date. The personal possessions will get to us eventually. Any questions? No? OK, let's go into dinner; the tables are ready, and the wine bottles are uncorked. Enjoy!"

I get my early call for 8 a.m. and have a big breakfast and two large coffees. Next, I check in with reception, collect a tourist street map, mark the hotel's position and phone number, and circle the two best things to see: the Castle Hill and Graz Old Town. I am told that my Deutschemarks will be accepted. Back in my room I get prepared for a tourist day out in Austria's second city. I have my camera, money, and map, and the weather is good, so with no more excuses, off I go. Using the sun to orientate myself, I head north to Castle Hill and its viewpoint, with an impressive clock tower. It is long way up to the top, but worth the climb. The view over the Old Town is very impressive. I know I will not be able to capture the panorama on my camera. However, I take a good dozen overlapping shots, which should give others a feel for the view. The authorities have done well in preserving this mix of Gothic, Baroque and Renaissance architecture, not one concrete and glass structure in sight, and everything intact. I feel it is unlikely I will be here again, so indulge myself at the smart viewpoint café. Sitting in the sunshine, soaking up the view is very relaxing. I could spend all day there, but there are other sights to see, so reluctantly I pay my bill and set off downhill towards the Old Town.

It is almost like a film set, walking amongst this collection of very old buildings. Only the pavement cafes, occasional cars, and tourists with their cameras make you realise you are living in the 20th century. I make my way to the bank of the River Mur, alongside which is a busy road. I need to look both ways before crossing and keep on the pavement. You can see why the town and castle were built here many years ago. It is a lovely spot. I wander on, soaking up the views; I may not have the opportunity to come back here again. Vienna is on my wish list though. I am spoilt for choice for a place to have a light lunch and a cold beer, followed by coffee and cake, spending an hour watching the world go by. Suitably impressed, I check my map and work out how I will make it back to the hotel through the maze of streets. I have plenty of time and being on foot can afford to explore side streets and gaze into shop windows. They cater for everyone, from the rich tourist to the penniless student. It is reassuring not seeing broken buildings or people in uniform. Civilisation has a lot going for it.

At 6 p.m. our briefing kicks off. Tomorrow I am flying with Peter Whalley, taking a helicopter loaded with aircraft spares to Holland. The first leg will be to the airport at Egelsbach, near Frankfurt, where we will stay overnight. Next day we will fly across Germany to our base at Den Helder, in North Holland. The other helicopter will follow at a later date. For Peter and me, our check-out time will be 10 a.m.; initially our transport will take us to Air Traffic Control, where will work out the best route and submit a flight plan, using the aircraft registration PH–NZR as our callsign. Then we plan to get airborne an hour later. Some people plan to start driving off across Europe in the morning. We will meet up again eventually. At dinner the mood is subdued; our operation in Croatia is finally breaking up and our futures are uncertain. Only when we get to company HQ will we learn what lies ahead.

Peter Whalley and I meet the Air Traffic Movements supervisor and spell out our requirement to get to Egelsbach as soon as practicable. The supervisor suggests flying beneath an air corridor with its known reporting points. We mark out that route on our maps, highlighting the reporting points by name and position (latitude and longitude). He suggests a cruising altitude of 8,000 feet initially, well above the Austrian mountains we will cross over. We agree the squawk code for our radar transponder. All approved, we submit a flight plan and head off to the helicopter, where we meet the engineers. It has been prepared for flight, and the fuel tanks are full. The cabin is full of boxes placed under nets secured to the floor. We are not taking a cabin attendant. A quick walk round for an external check, all looks normal; Peter and I climb in, close the cabin door and begin the start-up checks. Soon we are calling the tower for taxi clearance and moving towards the active runway. We get our "departure clearance" – our initial route and cruising altitude. As we approach the start of the runway we are cleared to line up and take off. Passing 500 feet, we turn right and head north to our first reporting point. It feels good to be flying again; the scenery below is wonderful, but I need to concentrate on the navigation using the two sat navs, backed up by map reading. It all agrees, and we are making good our planned groundspeed of 100 knots. Soon we are passing Salzburg and transferred to another controller, who asks us to squawk "Ident." We press the appropriate button and a few seconds later he confirms we are identified on his radar screen, gives us the pressure setting for our altimeters, and clears us to our next reporting point. Crossing into Germany, we change controllers and are cleared to continue at 5,000 feet, well clear of the ground but giving a better ground speed.

As we near our destination we descend to 2,000 feet and see many red and white electricity pylons; we must be close to the airport. Once we see the runway we are cleared to land, no other traffic, and we touch down close to a vehicle, which guides us to our shut-down spot in the General Aviation area. It has been a long flight, four hours, but the weather has been good and we have been able to see the ground all the way. A few plane spotters come out to inspect our white helicopter as we accept jet fuel plugged in to the port side. We fill right up to full, and the fuel bowser man requires a signature from Peter, as well as noting our registration and company. At least we have not been asked to pay – my bank manager would not be pleased! The airport ground service company takes us to Air Traffic Control, where we meet the supervisor and discuss tomorrow's flight. We agree that it is best we do the flight planning in the morning, when we have seen the latest weather forecast. The next leg will be shorter, probably three hours' flying. Our ground service vehicle takes us to a lovely hotel close to the airfield and we agree a 10 a.m. morning pick-up time. We check in and have time for a shower, shave, and change of clothing before signing in for dinner. The hotel is very orientated towards flying, with numerous photographs, pictures, and models. Time after dinner to take it all in.

In Air Traffic Control, Peter and I study the weather forecast; it is good, broken cloud and a slight head wind. We should be able to see the ground to confirm our position as we fly our planned route. We are soon airborne and heading North across Germany, staying clear of cloud and in sight of the ground. As we approach Holland, we change Air Traffic Controllers and again are identified on radar. When we state our destination – Den Helder – in Northern Holland, our controller says that he will route us around the busy Schiphol Airport, taking us well east and descending us to 1,000 feet. This will keep us well below the airliners making their approach to the westerly runway in use. This diversion adds 10 minutes to our planned flight time, but we have plenty of fuel, so we can relax and enjoy the stupendous view of Amsterdam.

Soon we are handed over to Den Helder. We recall the layout of the joint use airfield, and with no other traffic we land on the main runway and taxi slowly in to stop alongside one of our company helicopters. We walk into our operation and are welcomed loudly! We have not seen some of the staff for over a year. They are pleased to see the helicopter back, still painted white all over. It is filled with very expensive spares, which everyone is most pleased to see. A director pops in and tells us we can go in company transport to a local hotel for the night. We are to get a good night's sleep and report at 10 a.m. to get updated on future commitments.

Next morning Peter and I are asked if we would like to serve short-term at Norwich, Norfolk as pilots on the S61N; we would be flying the machines that are coming back from Croatia. The task is to fly workers out to offshore gas fields, six days a week. As I have landed on these platforms 15 years earlier with Bristow, flying the Wessex, I am happy to serve and because of my experience request a captaincy. The company will consider this, and the decision will depend on how well I perform in the flight simulator in Stavanger, and during line training at Den Helder afterwards. Meanwhile we are being sent back to UK for three weeks' stand down. After that we will be contacted, and training will begin. Until then, we can go back to the hotel whenever we wish and will be picked up at 10 a.m. tomorrow for our flights home. I have a brainwave: I locate the box of maps in the helicopter we brought back, select what I might need, and offer the others to the long-term pilots and engineers. It was just like Christmas, with lots of maps being laid out and discussed. Quite a few are going to end up on their children's bedroom walls.

In the morning the company transport takes us to Schiphol Airport for our flight to Heathrow and then, in my case, a linking flight to Aberdeen. This may be my last look at Duty Free for some time, so good brandy is the favourite this time around. As we taxi out and the hostess come round and checks our safety belts, I give her my flying licence and ask if I can go up to the cockpit after take-off. She takes it and 10 minutes into the flight she comes back and takes me up to the cockpit. I am offered a dropdown seat and sit just behind the 2 pilots. I introduce myself and give a brief rundown of my activities in Croatia. We are flying in a Boeing 737. The cockpit is spacious, quiet and with little vibration compared to the helicopter I have recently flown. I am asked if I would like to stay in the cockpit for the landing at Heathrow. I would be delighted! I note the air traffic instructions coming from Heathrow Radar Control are very professional. No more words than needed. All the various aircraft being controlled comply immediately with instructions to climb or descend and with changes of course and speed. I see aircraft in the sky around me, but the crew say that we will have at least 1,000 feet vertical clearance. The big jumbo jets look very close and almost hanging in the sky as they turn onto required headings. As we approach London from the east, we change to tower frequency and confirm we will carry out an ILS approach to their westerly runway. We are given clearance to land in turn and to turn off at the end of the runway for our terminal. I count the aircraft ahead of us, five that I can see. As we touch down, the runway ahead is unobstructed, so we could do a rolling landing and get airborne again if we had an emergency that required that course of action. Not required this time, and we exit the runway quickly, then slow down for the taxi to the passenger terminal. Safely on the ground, I have a two-hour wait for my flight to Aberdeen; time for a coffee and a sandwich in a crowded departure lounge. I buy a national newspaper and look for news from Croatia following the rocket attack on the capital, Zagreb, and the airport. Absolutely nothing! Either it didn't happen, or the news was supressed. No worry, I have my future mapped out around flying from Norwich Airport. Quite a big change from what I have been doing, so it will be a challenge to get everything right.

After a few weeks off it is back to Stavanger and the flight simulator, all familiar stuff. We have the simulator all to ourselves for two days, so normal briefing, flight simulator, then debrief, then a break. After that, same again. What I appreciate is landing on water without engine power and rocking gently in the swell. We carry out many Standard Instrument Departures (SIDs) from Schiphol and Rotterdam followed by ILS approaches and go-arounds with an engine failing at some stage. We also practice rig radar let-downs, where we use the helicopter's weather radar to home in on an offshore rig and then carry out a missed approach if we fail to see it when we get down to half a mile from it. Over two days we log eight hours' simulation, at the end of which my instrument rating is renewed and written into my flying licence. The next step is flying down to Schiphol and continuing my training at Den Helder. There is a small problem: there is an industrial dispute limiting passenger numbers on the aircraft, a BAE 146. Being aircrew, I am offered a seat in the cockpit as supernumerary crew. As I strap in and put my headphones on, I get a briefing on how to exit the cockpit through the roof in the event of a crash landing, including use of a thick rope to get down to the ground. The flight proceeds normally, and I experience Dutch Air Traffic Control as we fly into Schiphol on a busy day. You do need to be experienced and patient while being controlled on the ground. Getting to your gate to offload your passengers takes a lot of time. Eventually, on 17th June, I am heading out from Den Helder with my instructor to the nearest gas rig for five landings, including engine failures after committing to the landing. We carry out rig radar let-downs and an ILS approach on returning to the airfield. My flying is assessed as satisfactory, and I become qualified as a captain. Very good. After all that training I am ready for the real thing.

I meet up with Peter Whalley and sign up for a room in his planned pilots' house in Norwich; there will be four of us altogether, all old pilots and a little deaf! With so many cars needed I chose to park on the street, rather than the drive; it is a quiet neighbourhood, apparently. Eventually, after a week on the ground at Den Helder, we are cleared to ferry a helicopter across the North Sea to Norwich. On 1st July I fly with Ian Morrison, and we pass over the gas platforms that we will be flying out to within a few days. Once at Norwich, I have time to fly Air UK to Aberdeen; one day at home, then I drive the car down with the food and kit I will need looking after myself.

On 5th July, I am back in the harness; it is a good feeling to be flying with Geoff Newman. We complete three flights out to the Leman Field, and having a cabin attendant to sort out baggage, freight, and manifests means neither pilot needs to leave his seat. These short flights complete my Line Training. Not a lot has changed since I was operating out here 15 years ago. I am given a black book of clear plastic folders to make up my own aide memoire of SIDs and arrival procedures, maps, radio frequencies, distances to diversions, including Holland, SOPs and performance graphs. You need to take it with you in your flight bag, along with your flying licence, passport, some cash, and a credit card. Be prepared for every eventuality. Also given to me is a big notebook for recording new briefings, other people's experiences, and anything I need to recall. As I am checked out to be a captain, I can fly with any co-pilot or as a co-pilot to any captain. Besides a feather in my cap, there is a substantial increase in pay. On 9th July I fly with Jill Pemberton as my co-pilot and Terry Trip as my cabin attendant. She is experienced in operating the new cassette recording system, which saves a lot of paperwork after landing on a helideck.

The locals are complaining that helicopters taking off early morning (7 a.m.) are waking them up as we head east out to the oil rigs. We may have to alter our departure routes and heights. Eventually, Norwich Air Traffic Control require us to climb to 3,000 in the vicinity of the airport before heading east for the rigs. Sometimes, when we are recovering to Norwich, the Jaguar jets taking off from nearby RAF Coltishall might be in conflict with us, as their runway points towards the airport. Occasionally, when we approach the airport from the east, we are held at 3,000 feet until radar sees the jets departing the area, then we are cleared to spiral down for our landing.

With some of our captains being sent to the USA for training on the Sikorsky S76, we become short of pilots and some Dutch pilots are drafted across to the "British" operation, staying at the hotel at the airport. Sometimes we are tasked with flying out to oil rigs in the centre of the North Sea. The surveillance radar has no height information on the military jets operating in the Combat Training Area above, so we are often warned of potential conflicts, when the jets are 10,000 feet or more above us. We press on, staying at 1,000 feet, clear of cloud, and maintaining our planned course and speed both out and back.

Flying continues through the summer, normally two trips a day, sometimes three, picking up an ILS approach most days to stay in practice. Our pilots being sent off to the USA to do a conversion to the Sikorsky S76 will be flying a smaller and faster helicopter, with a single pilot being the crew. If this is going to be the future of the operation, I will not be staying. I am wedded to the two-pilot model of operating helicopters over the sea, with the handling pilot concentrating on flying on instruments while the non-handling pilot looks after the radio and navigation. Also, having a cabin attendant means the two pilots can concentrate all the time on aspects of flying. I have grown to like flying the S61N; very reliable in my experience, with a spacious cabin, relatively quiet cockpit, and a low level of vibration. Checking my logbook, my total flying hours now exceed 10,000, of which 5,000 are on the Sikorsky S61N, the Queen of the Skies.

On long flights, when talking to young co-pilots about their future intentions, most see themselves graduating to fixed wing airline flying, if possible, with KLM itself. Some of them are very gadget-minded. One of them operates his hand computer all the time on the ground. When things go wrong and he ends up with a blank screen, he soon replaces the lost information. A wrong selection is not a problem. However, one day when we are together in the cockpit and starting up, with me controlling the engines and rotor, he says, "I know what's wrong," and makes a switch in the roof panel. There is a flash of light in the cockpit, the intercom and radios go dead, and the warning panel lights up with many captions. Fortunately, I can close the engines down and stop the rotor. We inform our passengers we have a technical problem and report to our ground engineers. Operations gives us another helicopter and we are soon airborne on our task. On returning three hours later, we both go to the hangar to find out from the engineers what went wrong. Apparently, there was a voltage surge in the DC electrical system. That damaged many items beyond repair, some light bulbs and wiring. The cost of the repair is at least £250,000 and seven days will be needed for the work schedule. Very sobering for both of us, as we realise there will be an inquiry; two days later we are interviewed by the chief pilot.

He intones, "It appears that the non-handling pilot decided to take emergency action which was not stipulated by the handling pilot. There was a surge in electrical voltage, which caused many failures, and damage to cabling. The estimated repair bill is £250,000 and the helicopter will be out of service for at least a week."

This is not the first time for this type of accident (un-commanded emergency action), and it won't be the last. Only a few months ago a Sikorsky S76 lost an engine on take-off. The non-handling pilot took action on his own initiative and shut down an engine. Unfortunately, it was the one engine that was supplying power. The helicopter crashed and all on board were killed. With most emergencies there is plenty of time to establish what is wrong before the instruction to take action is given by the handling pilot. There is a clear need in any emergency to always "Think deliberately and act precisely." As the captain, I feel the weight of responsibility.

Rumours about the sale of the company are rife, as are rumours about the renewal of the contract in November. Luckily for me, I am on a short-term contract, so I can cope if my flying ends for any reason. I sit down with management one day to discuss my future employment; it transpires that the client will stop using the S61N in mid-October and concentrate on using the Sikorsky S76. It is agreed that I will stop flying on 18th October, hand in my flight kit, complete my logbook and return to Scotland. I have been thinking of retirement for some time; working away from home on short term contracts has been difficult for everyone. Ann is able to come by train from Aberdeen from time to time to have a look at Norfolk. Perhaps it is time to retire from flying and move to the south of England, where it is a little warmer and there is more sunshine. All I need to do in the next few weeks is to fly safely, legally, and efficiently. On the 18th October 1995 I complete my last landing, make my last entry in a technical log, draw a line across my flying logbook, and hand in my survival suit, my aide memoir full of useful information, and my I/D tag. A brief handshake, then back to the house to plan the drive back north with Ann, who has made it down for a last look at the area. A few days later Ann and I set off for Scotland with the car loaded with kit.

A few weeks later I get a call. The company has been sold, the contract will finish shortly, and there will be redundancies. It is good not to be there; I have seen enough of redundancy programs during my flying career. With retirement starting, there will be new challenges ahead; I need to keep my body active and my mind busy on useful work. There will be a time to record events and to reflect on the big changes happening in the helicopter world.

However, I have completed 30 years of flying helicopters, of which 5,000 hours has been on the Sikorsky S61N – in my view, the Queen of the Skies. No bones broken, not a bump, bruise or burn, not even a scratch, but perhaps now a little deaf. Was all that safe flying the result of arduous training, frequent flying checks, hard work, a Guardian Angel, or just luck?

POSTSCRIPT: Total flying 11,608 hours, total S61N 5,345 hours, Belvedere 835 hours. A lot has happened since I finished flying helicopters in 1995.

As this book is being prepared for publication, it is interesting to see how much has changed during my lifetime, particularly in helicopter operations.

I was lucky in that coming to Scotland in 1981 to fly out of Aberdeen, Ann and I were able to buy a lovely bungalow in the town of Banchory on the River Dee. For our son Christopher, it was just a five-minute walk to Banchory Academy, one of the best state schools in Scotland. Arriving at age 10, he spent the first two years at the junior school, then moved on to the Academy for the next six years. He won the Dux prize for best all-round performance, both in the junior school and the senior section of the Academy. He was presented with this honour by the local MP, the Rt. Hon. Alec Buchanan Smith, who was appointed Energy Minister in Mrs Thatcher's Government. Christopher liked going to school and being involved in various activities in the town. These included scouts, golf, tennis, skiing at Glenshee, and helping out in a local ice cream shop. With fellow school pupils he formed a group, playing the guitar and the drums. For his 17th birthday some driving lessons were arranged, his best present ever, and he passed the driving test at the first attempt, driving round Aberdeen. At 18 he was on his way to Newcastle University studying Politics, gaining a First Class Degree three years later. He went on to Durham University to get his Masters, coming back to Newcastle to get his PhD. He so likes Newcastle that he now lives there with his wife Hazell and daughter Loretta.

Being a helicopter pilot supporting the offshore oil industry, my working life was anything but 9 to 5, five days a week, weekends off. For the first time in our married life, we were able to put down roots, and Ann became involved with the Episcopalian Church and became Secretary and then President of the Wives Club. She joined the tennis club and played matches both summer and winter and was membership Secretary. She also played badminton for a few years and, with a good partner, won the doubles one year. We both played golf and were able to join the golf club after five years on the waiting list. Ann was able to play regularly and even won the Captain's Prize one year. We were both involved in raising money for new all-weather tennis courts at Burnett Park. We both enjoyed exploring the local area, including the Dee valley and the Grampian Mountains, finding some lovely walks.

*Ann receives a "Goodbye" present from
the Banchory Tennis Club on moving to the South*

With my flying career finished in 1995, Ann and I had the opportunity to move south on retirement to somewhere a little
warmer, and with access to good rambling, tennis, golf, and
near the coast. So, after 15 years based in Banchory, we have
settled in the town of West Moors, Dorset, close to the New
Forest and seven miles from Bournemouth. We took up rambling
in a big way, using Ordnance Survey maps to explore Dorset,
Wiltshire, and the New Forest. By leading all ranges of walks
with our local rambling club, we have clocked up over 20,000
miles in the 25 years we have been here. 100 walks of various
lengths have been recorded in detail and are now available on
the internet. The beneficial effects of walking in company in
the countryside are well known. We will continue to do this
while we are able.

With a settled life we have been able to take long holidays overseas, visiting New Zealand, the US, Canada, and Europe. After

9/11, no more visits to the cockpits of the airliners for the family, don't even ask. But when visiting the Grand Canyon, the three of us took a trip in a helicopter; producing my flying licence secured me a front seat. After reassuring the US Marine pilot that I was not an authority figure he flew close to the caves near the Rim, which First Peoples had occupied for centuries. The Grand Canyon is impressive, and we have made two visits there so far. Bryce Canyon and Zion Canyon are also impressive if you appreciate geology on a big scale.

On the Search and Rescue scene, the responsibility for the whole of the UK now lies with the Maritime and Coastguard Agency. There are 10 new helicopter bases, one in the Shetland Islands, one in the Western Islands, and two on mainland Scotland. There are two bases in Wales and four bases in England. The helicopters involved are the Sikorsky S92 and the Augusta Westland AW 189. The S92 has a radius of action of 250 nautical miles and the AW 189 has a radius of action of 200 miles. They can all operate by day and by night in all weathers and are on call 24/7. The crews and engineering support are provided by Bristow Helicopters, and many are ex-military.

The RAF maintains a Search & Rescue Training Unit in Anglesey, providing training for military crews in mountain flying and winching over the sea and deck-winching with various-sized vessels.

As regards the offshore oil industry in the North Sea, the boom days are over. Several production platforms are now decommissioned and are being removed to sites where they are scrapped. The revenues accruing to various governments have been spent in different ways. The UK Government used the revenues generated as part of annual Government spending, thus reducing taxes. However, the pound became a petrocurrency, becoming overvalued. The result was a sharp increase in imports of manufactured goods, leading to industrial closures, and three million unemployed in the early 80s. The Oil Bonanza paid for the unemployment benefit. By contrast, Norway saved its oil revenues, putting money into various long-term investments as part of a Sovereign Wealth Fund, thus benefiting its population for many generations to come. Currently, each Norwegian citizen has a stake worth around US $200,000. New offshore oil fields are still being considered around the Shetland Islands, and with its small population it, too, has benefitted a lot from many years of oil related activity.

The new boom industry offshore is wind farms. All around the UK coast wind farms are being commissioned, some in sight from the coast, some out of sight over the horizon. With so many wind turbines being produced the unit price has come down, making the cost of generating electricity one of the lowest. The drive to produce electricity from renewable sources continues apace. Even our own roof-mounted solar panels on our house provide, on average, all the electricity we use. Most impressive.

My first helicopter tour with the RAF was on the tandem rotor Bristol Belvedere, operating in the Far East from a base in Singapore. I spent over three years in the area, seeing the helicopter out when it was scrapped in 1969. In all I flew 935 hours, a record I believe, serving in both Borneo and the Malay Peninsula. The last Belvedere I flew, XG 474, is now an exhibit in the RAF Museum at Hendon, North London. There is another example, XG 452, in the Helicopter Museum, Weston-super-Mare.

As regards the tandem rotor Chinook helicopter, it is currently the main transport helicopter in RAF service. Around the world, it is in use with many armed services, and after 40 years and 1,200 machines built, it continues to be improved and continues in production. I can look back to 1968 and volunteering with many others to go on the first six-week conversion course in Philadelphia. A few months later, the first order for RAF Chinooks was cancelled and my career was channelled into RAF Search and Rescue, one of the best helicopter jobs in the world. In all, I spent seven years involved in Search and Rescue. My first tour was in Yorkshire, and later an extended tour based in Anglesey, close to Snowdonia. The flying took me around the coast of the UK and into the mountains, searching for missing people in all weathers, day and night. I now envy today's rescue helicopter crews for the array of sophisticated equipment now available to them to do the task. The latest rescue helicopters are powerful, reliable, have long range and can operate in all weathers. When out walking, it is heartening seeing these helicopters carrying out training missions at low level, both onshore and offshore. Sometimes on the evening news we hear about their rescue missions taking place around our coasts when there has been an emergency situation and they have been scrambled to assist.

It is a long time since the Falklands War in 1982 and there have been striking developments there. After an extended campaign, all the land mines placed in the ground during the war have now been found and destroyed. At long last the splendid beaches are open for all to enjoy. A new all-weather airport, Mount Pleasant, is in operation for international flights. A small airport near Port Stanley handles flights within the Islands, mainly carried out by the Falkland Islands Government Air Service.

Since the war, the economy has grown more than tenfold, enriching the Islanders and the government. The average Islander is one third richer than the average UK citizen. Some entrepreneurs are millionaires. Car ownership is high and 4x4s are very popular. House building continues at a rapid rate, including the most expensive.

Much money has come from selling fishing licences to foreign countries wishing to fish for squid in its territorial waters. In 1982, rearing sheep was the only industry. Across the islands there are now over half a million sheep, reared for wool and to provide meat, especially lamb. Much of this produce is exported. A new development, tourism, brings in many thousands of short-term tourists every year, stopping off on their cruises to Antarctica. The Islands' population is growing and becoming richer; the government has surplus funds but makes no contribution towards the cost of keeping UK troops on the Islands. There has been considerable investment in wind turbines, and there are plans for a battery storage system as well as renewable energy projects for the more isolated islands. The currency, the Falklands pound, is on par with the UK pound, and notes and coins are issued as required. Postage stamps, especially the popular commemorative stamps, are issued by the government.

Croatia, too, has moved on a lot since the end of the Civil War, during which the country was divided into factions, two-thirds Croatian control, one-third Serbian control. Croatia eventually became one country under Croat control in 1995, following the Dayton Accords and subsequent Peace Agreement, ending the Civil War, which had lasted three and a half years. Since then, it has joined the European Union in 2013, following Slovenia in 2007, Croatia still has the Kuna as its currency but is considering joining the Euro. It joined NATO in 2009. Since the war ended, Ann and I have had three holidays there. Every time we went, we saw new roads, bridges, and hotels. The war-damaged buildings were being repaired, the shipyards reopening, and the yacht marinas filling up with visiting sailors. Along the coast the beaches were crammed with young holidaymakers, and the coastal cruise boats were doing brisk business. It is heartening to see such excellent progress, with people making good use of the new opportunities now that things are peaceful.

Our first 25 years of retirement have been very busy and productive. It afforded an opportunity for me to complete an Honours Degree Course with the Open University, catching up with Ann and Christopher. Learning new information, retaining it, and producing it for the written exams was hard work. The six-year course on Earth Sciences covered subjects such as Geology,

Oceanography, Evolution, Ecology, Oil-related Sedimentary Rock Basins and How the Earth Works (earthquakes, volcanos and plate tectonics). The one-week summer camps at Durham University, meeting students who had full time jobs and were doing their degree courses in their spare time, were inspiring. On the Geology course I enjoyed seeing exposures of rock strata in working quarries, and deciding whether the rock layers were laid down under the sea or in a desert, sand dune on top of sand dune, millions of years ago. The study of old fossils is fascinating; thousands of species have come and gone, while others have continued to the present day, clearly adapting to changes in the environment around them. In the last million years the Earth has experienced Ice Ages and Interglacial Warm Periods at regular intervals. The Milankovitch Cycles, a theory which takes into consideration regular changes in the Earth's orbit around the Sun and regular changes in the Earth's tilt, currently 23 degrees, provides an interesting explanation. Running the cycle forward would suggest it will be a very long time before the onset of the next Ice Age. Global warming, with consequent sea level rise and climate change, is set to continue.

*Graduated at last from the Open University,
the ceremony being held at Portsmouth Guild Hall*

Settling in West Moors, Ann and I joined the Recreation Association and brought out an annual magazine about the activities in the village. Both of us were on the Verwood Rambling Club Committee, where I was Secretary for five years. We became walks leaders soon after arrival in the area, encouraging us to explore for new walks and record them for future use by new leaders. We also supported the East Dorset Heritage Trust (EDHT), going on numerous visits to local big houses and occasionally to London to see the sights in the capital. As the years have rolled by, we have become more passive, joining the Ferndown Camera Club, the Royal Aeronautical Society and two horticultural societies. We have been encouraged to participate in the annual shows, for myself exhibiting cacti and alpine plants, and Ann with flowers from our garden. Friends and family play a large part in our lives, and we have never regretted moving here.

It is amazing to realise that we have retired close to where I was born in 1941, in Wimborne, Dorset, where my family at the time lived in the nearby Holt village as evacuees during the war. Aviation has taken me around the world, both on duty and as a holidaymaker. I have travelled a full circle, full of experiences, challenges and being well rewarded for my efforts. With my flying boots tidied away, my flight suits hung up, and my flying logbooks on a bookshelf, it is now truly Mission Completed.

The author

Born in Wimborne, Dorset in 1941, David Lanigan developed a love for flying at an early age.
This love led to a career with the Royal Air Force,
followed by many years with flying with private
companies. David and his wife Ann have one son,
Christopher, and they have now retired to Dorset enjoying membership of the local rambling
club and supporting the Dorset and Somerset Air
Ambulance.

The publisher

*He who stops
getting better
stops being good.*

This is the motto of novum publishing, and our focus
is on finding new manuscripts, publishing them and
offering long-term support to the authors.
Our publishing house was founded in 1997, and since
then it has become THE expert for new authors and
has won numerous awards.

**Our editorial team will peruse each manuscript
within a few weeks free of charge and without
obligation.**

You will find more information about
novum publishing and our books on the internet:

www . n o v u m - p u b l i s h i n g . c o . u k